Stories of the Celtic Soul Friends

Their Meaning for Today

EDWARD C. SELLNER

PAULIST PRESS
New York/Mahwah, N.J.

All scripture quotations are taken from The New Jerusalem Bible, copyright © 1985 by Darton, Longman & Todd, Ltd., and Doubleday, a division of Random House, Inc. Reprinted by permission. Excerpt from *Lives of the Irish Saints*, Vol. II, translated by Charles Plummer, Oxford: Oxford University Press. Copyright 1985 by Sandpiper Books Ltd. Reprinted by permission. Excerpt from *Studies in Early Celtic Nature Poetry*, by Kenneth Jackson, Cambridge: Cambridge University Press. Copyright 1935 by Cambridge University Press. Reprinted by permission. Excerpt from *The Patrician Texts in the Book of Armagh*, edited by Ludwig Bieler, Dublin: Dublin Institute for Advanced Studies. Copyright 1979 by the Governing Board of the School of Celtic Studies of the Dublin Institute for Advanced Studies.

Cover design by Diego Linares
Cover art by Cynthia R. Matyi
Book design by Lynn Else

Library of Congress Cataloging-in-Publication Data

Sellner, Edward Cletus.
Stories of the Celtic soul friends : their meaning for today / Edward C. Sellner.
    p. cm.
Includes bibliographical references.
ISBN 0-8091-4111-6 (alk. paper)
1. Celtic Church—History. 2. Celtic Church—Biography. 3. Christian saints, Celtic—Biography. I. Title.
BR737 .C4 S43 2004
274′.0089′916—dc21

2003007018

Published by Paulist Press
997 Macarthur Boulevard
Mahwah, New Jersey 07430

www.paulistpress.com

Printed and bound in the United States of America

Table of Contents

108915

For mentors and friends,

Diarmuid O'Laoghaire

Noel Dermot O'Donoghue

Ronan Drury

and

Gretchen Berg

Between Patrick and Brigit, pillars of the Irish,

there existed so great a friendship that they were

of one heart and one mind.

Liber Angeli from the *Book of Armagh*

But what happiness, what security, what joy to

have someone to whom you dare to speak on

terms of equality as to another self; one to whom

you can unblushingly make known what progress

you have made in the spiritual life; one to whom

you can entrust all the secrets of your heart....

Aelred of Rievaulx

Preface

I am grateful for all those who made it possible for me to write this book on soul friendship, especially my wife, JoAnne, and our sons, John and Daniel, as well as relatives and friends. I'd like to dedicate it to four significant mentors who have taught me much about soul friendship: Diarmuid O'Laoghaire, S.J., teacher and spiritual writer, who was the first, years ago, to welcome me to Dublin and to show me, a wandering scholar, the numerous bookstores where I might find resources for my research; Noel Dermot O'Donoghue, O.D.C., theologian and writer, who encouraged me to write about the *anamchara,* and who opened his apartment to me one summer in Glasgow; Ronan Drury, professor of pastoral theology and editor of *The Furrow* at St. Patrick's College in Maynooth, who gave me a place to study and write, and remains an inspiration for all the work that he does for the contemporary church; and last, but definitely not least, Gretchen Berg, O.S.F. who, as my spiritual director, has guided me through the maze of conflicts, confusions, and dreams that have colored my life over the last decade. As the desert elder St. Antony learned from his own spiritual mentors, I too took away something from each of them that continues to guide me in my work, my writing, and most importantly, my life.

Introduction

My great-great-grandfather, Martin Foy, was a storyteller. Born in County Mayo, Ireland, in 1838, he fled, along with his family, to Canada at the age of ten or twelve to escape the Great Famine. In a literary work that has survived in our family for generations, he describes his journey from Canada where his family had initially settled to a farmstead in southern Minnesota. In what he called his "jottings," later published as *Trials and Experience of Frontier Life on the Western Prairie*, he tells of traveling to Minnesota by railroad and steamboat, of facing "terrible blizzards" in winter and wild prairie fires in summer, of meeting "good" Indians (in contradiction of those who say "there is no good Indian, except a dead one"), of seeing a lake for the first time "shining brightly in the light of the moon," and of dancing to Gaelic fiddler music every Sunday night in a lumber camp where he worked for awhile. In all of his adventures, my ancestor states his belief of being led by a guardian angel, and adds: "We were something like the Israelites on their journey to the Promised Land." At home in Springfield, Minnesota, after his retirement, he invites old friends to visit him and says, "I don't propose to do much else in the future than to write stories." "Every person," he concludes, "has a story to tell, many of them much like my own." He asks his readers to "please excuse mistakes in both spelling and grammar. I have no pretentions to either; it was only a heart overflowing with emotion that prompted me to undertake this at all."

Clearly, Martin Foy appreciated storytelling, and knew from firsthand experience that as much as the body needs food and drink, so our souls need stories for sustenance and survival. I share with him that conviction. As long as I can remember, I have been fascinated with stories: the ones that my grandparents and parents told that shed light on my own inheritance and identity, the ones told to me by others that gave me a greater understanding of their outer world and inner life—as well as my own. As a former chemical dependency counselor, I know of the healing and transformative power stories can have. I also have come to see, as a theologian, teacher, and spiritual writer, that all the great spiritual traditions—including Judaism, Islam, Buddhism, Hinduism, and Christianity—relate their understanding of God and the destiny of humankind through the stories they tell of their founders, their heroes, their saints.

Nations, races, and tribes have particular stories which shape their members' identity, customs, and beliefs. While the stories vary, the motivations of these storytellers frequently include the desire to teach and to pass on a spiritual legacy. Another motivation, not to be excluded, is for the pure enjoyment and wonderment that is experienced by those who are telling and listening to these stories. Storytelling arises from the primal urge to give expression to what we see, hear, and experience that has evoked questions, wonder, awe. The earliest stories were probably told around a fire at night, with the beating of drums and the light from a fire exaggerating the facial expressions of the storyteller. All of this created a sense of camaraderie in which fellowship and community were formed that—along with the music, the fire, and the stories—dispelled the encroaching darkness. The origins of all spiritual and religious traditions include these myths, legends, and rituals that express a basic affirmation that the universe—and our own lives—have meaning, if we can but discern and accept the depth and amazing contours of its mystery. Stories can help us in that discernment process; they form the basis of any guidance or direction we might receive or give. Very often they provide intimations that, despite painful questions and conflicts, our lives are created fundamentally good, as the first book of the Hebrew and Christian scriptures suggests.

The ancient Celtic race had a profound appreciation of storytelling, both in verbal and written forms. They knew that sometimes, as Robin Flower states in his classic, *The Irish Tradition*, "a tale is better than food."[1] As a result, they had many types of storytellers—from the *seanchai*, the humblest teller of tales around the hearth in the home; to the *fili*, the learned bard at the courts of the Irish kings; to the monastic scribe seated with his quill pen in a scriptorium transcribing on vellum the stories of the saints. The responsibility of all of these storytellers was to remember and narrate the great sagas of their tribal and spiritual ancestors whom they considered, even if long dead, intimate members of their families. Perhaps the earliest personification of the storyteller in Celtic mythology is Cernunnos, the god of eros, fertility, and nature—the Lord of the Animals. His name means "horned one." He is often artistically depicted as seated cross-legged, with large and majestic antlers extending out and upwards from his forehead that symbolize his potency as a storyteller, seer, visionary, and healer of the tribe. The legends described by this variety of Celtic storytellers were frequently about both secular and religious heroes, immortal and mortal beings, who had strange visions, made voyages to other worlds, endured great hardships for tribe and gospel, and traveled frequently in companies of friends. Whenever and wherever they were told, the stories of their heroes are perhaps the clearest expression of the ancient Celts' religious beliefs, values, and spirituality.

One of the most interesting stories from the Early Celtic Church in Ireland tells of St. Brigit of Kildare and a young cleric, her protégé. It attests to the importance in one's life of an intimate friend, a person called by the Irish or Scots an *anamchara,* or by the Welsh a *periglour* or *beriglour,* terms that mean "friend of the soul" or, quite simply, "soul friend." Such a person acted in a number of roles, including those of teacher, mentor, confidant, confessor, or spiritual guide. Although this type of ministry was eventually equated by Western church authorities only with the ordained male priest in the sacrament of penance,[2] such relationships in the earliest days of Celtic Christianity were open to lay people and ordained, women and men alike. In this particular story about St. Brigit, printed in the early ninth-century *Martyrology of Oengus the Culdee,* we find a popular saying from the Middle Ages confirming the belief that everyone should have a soul friend:

> A young cleric of the community of Ferns, a foster-son of Brigit's, used to come to her with dainties. He was often with her in the refectory [dining-room] to partake of food. Once after going to communion she strikes a clapper. "Well, young cleric there," says Brigit, "do you have a soul friend?" "I have," replied the young man." "Let us sing his requiem," says Brigit.

"Why so?" asks the young cleric. "For he has died," says Brigit. "When you had finished half your ration I saw that he was dead." "How did you know that?" "Easy to say," Brigit replies: "from the time that your soul friend was dead, I saw that your food was put directly in the trunk of your body, since you were without any head. Go forth and eat nothing until you get a soul friend, for anyone without a soul friend is like a body without a head; is like the water of a polluted lake, neither good for drinking nor for washing. That is the person without a soul friend."[3]

This story, set in the context of a meal, with references to death, food, and water, has symbolic, sacramental connotations which most Christians of any age would easily recognize. It strongly suggests that Christian Celts believed that soul friends were crucial to human growth and spiritual development, and that such mentoring relationships were ultimately related to friendship with God, and thus to the salvation of one's soul. The history of the Christian Celts is filled with numerous examples of soul friend relationships, manifesting their importance in the Early Celtic Church. All the Celtic saints seem to have been changed profoundly by soul friendships—whether the soul friends themselves were female or male, or whether they offered a compassionate ear or a challenging word.

The Irish word for *history* is *senchas,* which means "old tales," traditions about the past.[4] This book is about the meaning and dimensions of soul friendships as they emerge in the ancient stories and legends of certain saintly Celtic heroes, male and female, who were spiritual leaders in the Early Celtic Church. My purpose in writing it is to introduce readers to that rich spiritual tradition, and to explain what that tradition can teach many people today—*professionally* (if they are spiritual directors, mentors, teachers, sponsors, pastoral ministers, confessors, counselors, hospice workers, or therapists), and *personally* (in their own friendships and intimate relationships).

Chapter one explores the historical origins of the stories that are found in surviving manuscripts from those Celtic churches which grew to prominence in the lands we now call Ireland, England, Scotland, Wales, Brittany, and the Isle of Man. Chapters two, three, four, and five, move directly to the stories of Ireland's "holy trinity" of Celtic saints—Patrick, Brigit, and Columcille—as well as those of the less-known saint, Colman of Land Ela. The legends and stories of each of these saints can provide insights into contemporary forms of soul friendship: how one is initiated into this form of ministry and relationship; what inner resources are available to those who act as soul friends; what virtues need to be developed in order to become an effective *anamchara*. The conclusion brings these insights together, and explains various steps or movements in listening effectively to another's unfolding story.

In examining the meaning and significance of the stories in this book, I presuppose, as does the writer Clarissa Pinkola Estes, that "in dealing with stories, we are handling archetypal energy," energy that can heal and change us powerfully. "Therefore," she says, "the handing down of story is a very big responsibility. In the best tellers I know, the stories grow out of their lives like roots grow out of trees."[5] I also agree with the psychologist James Hillman that by studying extraordinary lives, as expressed in heroic stories, they act as mirrors, reflecting back to us hidden dimensions of our own leadership and potentialities. As Hillman says, "These personifications of heightened imagination burn right into the soul and are its teachers."[6] Scripture scholar Marcus Borg rightly points out how the Bible itself had its origins in stories and storytelling, and how the primary stories from the Bible (what he calls the "macrostories") shaped—and continue to shape—the religious imagination and life of Jews and Christians alike.

To approach the study of theology and of spirituality with this deep respect for stories is to gain a new appreciation of their value and significance. These stories can teach us a great deal, as well as provide us with intimations into the meaning of both the human and divine. They can inspire us to reach beyond ourselves. They can also simply, yet profoundly, reaffirm our own faith. Borg says that the word *believe* did not originally mean believing in a set of abstract doctrines or teachings promulgated by a religious institution to maintain standards of orthodoxy or of unquestioning loyalty; rather, its roots in both Greek and Latin mean "to give one's heart to." This is, I believe, what the study of these lives of the saints makes clear.

Beyond the insights into soul friendship which these stories provide, they tell us how the holiness of the saints is not that of living perfectly or having a life without conflicts, struggles, and self-destructive behaviors we call "sins." Rather holiness (theirs *and ours*) is found in total dependency upon God, in the giving over of our hearts to this higher power. The saints truly gave their hearts over to God in trust, and their lives over to others in service and love. This is what makes their lives exemplary, what made each of them a "spirit person"—someone, according to Borg, who experiences the sacred frequently and vividly and becomes, in turn, a mediator of the sacred for others, "a person to whom the sacred is an experiential reality." What all spirit persons have in common, Borg says, "is that they become funnels or conduits for the power or wisdom of God to enter this world. Anthropologically speaking, they are delegates of the tribe to another layer of reality, mediators who connect their communities to the Spirit."[7] Various Gaelic words, in fact, attest to this understanding. The Irish words *niab* (which means vivacity, energy), and *noeb* (meaning holy), as well as the Welsh *nwyf* (meaning excitement), are all closely related. They express the idea that holiness is an active force, and that a spiritual leader is truly a vivacious person who, for the sake of the tribe or community, overflows with energy, life, and love.

Let us turn now to the stories of those spiritual leaders and the soul friendship associated with them. Considering that in Latin the word *historia* is the same root for both *history* and *story*, and in old Welsh, the word for *story* means "instruction" and "direction," we will begin to see how much guidance those stories from history provide. As I hope to make clear, the past is not something dead and gone, but a living reality in which we are connected intimately with our ancestors—and they with us. Nor is "tradition" itself some set of truths that need to be secured tightly in a box, but rather a gift from one generation to another, as the Latin word *traditio* implies: "a handing over," "a delivering," "a surrender." Tradition is the handing on of stories and the integration of the meaning of those stories into our daily lives. Above all, like the burning coals of a hearth fire, tradition is a powerful, passionate flame. In one of the earliest stories of St. Patrick, as we shall see, the great missionary bishop is portrayed as pulling up his sleeve, stretching out his hand, and, as his five fingers become a torch, lighting up the night. That is what tradition can be: a living presence, a flaming torch in the darkness.

While the story of Brigit and her friendship with a young cleric affirms the human need everyone has for a soul friend, my hope is that you, the reader, through these stories, will begin to name and affirm the importance of your own, as my great-great-grandfather Martin Foy encouraged us to do. To reflect upon the sacred and mysterious dimensions of your life-story in light of the stories of Jesus, Mary, and the saints, you will not only find sustenance for your spiritual journey, but you will be doing theology in its most basic sense as faith seeking understanding. I also hope that you will come to recognize the significant contribution soul friends have made and can make in your life, as well as the contribution you can make as a soul friend. The poetry of an unknown twentieth-century Irish writer describes the transformation that can happen with the help of a soul friend:

Anam-Chara
When rocks had torn the seams of my proud
    crests to spume
And peace was brief as pause between
    the ebb and flow
Beneath my studied calm, the undertow
Was sandwash wearing marrow from the soul

He plucked my shell words gently from the tide
And heard the echo of the pain inside
Then walked with blessed feet on my spent wake
Delighted by the patterns I could make.

CHAPTER 1

Celtic Stories
and Storytellers

*I am a storyteller. Warriors and young boys creep away
from the hearths of wine-halls to hear me....I give them
what is more precious than gold: treasure unlocked from
my heart....*

The Legend of Tuan mac Carell

The Celtic spiritual tradition is one of the most ancient
in Europe, with its origins going back to a people who
lived nearly 3000 years ago. They were the Celts, a
branch of the Indo-European family from which most of present-
day European, Middle Eastern, and Indian races are descended.
For almost a thousand years these Celts dominated the center of
Europe from the Black Sea to Iberia and from the Mediterranean to the North Sea and Ireland. Due to conflicts with
other tribes and their own desire to be near bodies of water, they
eventually settled in those places we now call Ireland, Scotland,
Wales, northern England, Cornwall, the Isle of Man, Brittany,
and Galicia in Spain. The precise origins of the Celtic race is
unclear. Some scholars suggest the area near India, pointing to

the similarity between Celtic and Indian music, art, mythology, numbers, language, and attitudes toward sexuality.[1] Others say that Celtic civilization emerged around 700 B.C.E. in the Hallein region of Austria where the so-called Hallstatt Culture was born. Another location, discovered by archaeologists at La Tene on Lake Neuchatel in Switzerland, points to the presence of Celts there around the early fifth century B.C.E.[2]

Whatever their actual geographical beginnings, the ancient Celts engaged in a great variety of occupations as warriors, farmers, adventurers, and traders. They were also a nomadic people, given to travel and migration. These pagan Celts were frequently identified by others as roving bands of shaggy-haired, mustachioed horsemen who would run or ride naked into battle, terrifying their enemies with their painted or tattooed bodies, starched hair, and wild screams. The Celts' enemies, the Greeks and Romans, regarded them as barbarians, and accused them of promiscuous sexual behavior. Plato states that the Celts also had a reputation for drunkenness, while Aristotle mentions their reckless indifference to danger. Many of their neighbors saw them as quarrelsome, impetuous, headstrong, and, as Caesar once said, "too much given to faction." These same commentators accused them of other barbarous acts, including head-hunting, and their spiritual leaders, the druids and druidesses, of human sacrifice. How many of these references are accurate or fictional, we cannot tell with certainty. Still, considering the native writings about the Celtic heroes, there is probably a great deal of truth to their descriptions.

The Celts themselves, before the coming of Christianity, believed that the divine pervaded every aspect of life. Spirits could be found everywhere—on mountaintops and high places, in rivers, streams, and holy wells, among ancient trees and oak groves. The earth was regarded as the source of all fertility, and the great forces of nature (moon, ocean, sun, and wind) were worshipped as manifestations of the divine. (It is no wonder the later Celtic Christians came to call God "Lord of the Elements.") Bards in Ireland described the land itself as female, and Ireland's landscape was identified with various parts of a woman's body. In many ways, women themselves were considered equal to men. Besides bearing children, they shared, as warriors and druidesses, some of the same leadership roles as men. Under the Brehon Laws, women also had specific legal rights that allowed them to divorce their husbands as well as protect, when necessary, their dowries.[3] The early stories of the Celtic bards reveal an appreciation for women, especially their beauty and leadership.

Wherever they went, the Celts brought with them a certain *Celtic* perception of the world: a belief in the spiritual dimension of all creation, a sense of kinship with the earth, a strong intuition which they called "second sight," a loyalty to family and tribe, and a valuing of friendship ties. Another of their main qualities was their appreciation of good stories. These characteristics persisted with the coming of Christianity to Celtic lands, and were reflected in the stories of their saints who were considered soul friends.

In this chapter we will briefly explore the historical origins of the Celtic soul friend by first of all considering the ancient Celts, their druidic leadership and stories, and then the rise of Christianity in desert and Celtic lands. In the latter case, as we will see, it was the monastic storytellers who made the lives of the saints and soul friendship so popular.

Pagan Celts and Their Spiritual Leaders

The ancient Celts, scattered as they were across the Continent of Europe, Britain, and Ireland, consisted of various classes. In Ireland, where the purest forms of Celtic culture survived, the social system consisted of three main classes or categories. The first was the land-owning aristocracy who were the tribal kings and their retinues of warriors, families, and relatives. Their emphasis on valor and vengeance in battle gave rise to the stories about brave knights that eventually became the basis of the later medieval Arthurian myths. The second class were the serfs, some of whom were free while others were slaves taken in battle or, like the youthful St. Patrick, kidnapped from foreign shores. This class was made up primarily of cattle-farmers or shepherds living under the protection of the kings. The third main class, small in number but socially very important, were the scholars and artists called the *aes dana*, Gaelic for "people of learning" or "people of poetry." This latter category included historians, experts in genealogy, lawyers, physicians, skilled craftsmen, and the poets and storytellers of the tribes—the bards. Many of these *aes dana* were also druids and druidesses, advisers to the kings and teachers of the tribes. All of these *aes dana* in Ireland were held in high esteem and had the privilege, as did the aristocracy, of traveling anywhere without permission.

Diodorus Siculus, one of the early Greek historians who wrote about the Celts, alludes to specific members of the learned class, the *aes dana*. Writing in the first century B.C.E., he says:

Among them are also to be found lyric poets whom they call Bards. These men sing to the accompaniment of instruments which are like lyres, and their songs may be either of praise or of obloquy. Philosophers, as we may call them, and men learned in religious affairs are unusually honored among them and are called by them Druids....Nor is it only in the exigencies of peace, but in their wars as well, that they obey, before all others, these men and their chanting poets, and such obedience is observed not only by their friends but also by their enemies; many times, for instance, when two armies approach each other in battle with swords drawn and spears thrust forward, these men step forth between them and cause them to cease, as though having cast a spell over certain kinds of wild beasts.[4]

Another commentator, a Roman, Julius Caesar (100–44 B.C.E.) furnishes one of the most insightful descriptions of the Celts, especially concerning the druids. He gives a comprehensive view of the Celts in his book, *Gallic War*, written about 52 B.C.E., in which he alludes to the customs, culture, and fighting habits of the Celts in Gaul and Britain. He also refers to the *aes dana*, seeming to equate the druids with the poets and bards. "Druids," he writes, "officiate at the worship of the gods, regulate public and private sacrifices, and give rulings on all religious questions. Large numbers of young men flock to them for instruction, and they are held in great honor by the people....Some of them continue their studies for twenty years."

This regulation and celebration of religious practices and rituals, and the consultation given on religious issues will be taken over by many of the saintly soul friends of the Early Celtic Church, as well as the formation and education of the young.

Like Diodorus, Caesar describes the druids as reconcilers between individuals and tribes, something the Christian *anamcharas* would become known for in the Early Celtic Church when they advise individuals, including kings, of proper actions and penalties for sins: "They act as judges in practically all disputes, whether between tribes or between individuals; when any crime is committed, or a murder takes place, or a dispute arises about an inheritance or a boundary, it is they who adjudicate the matter and appoint the compensation to be paid and received by the parties concerned."[5] The early Celtic saints, including women such as St. Ita of Ireland, are frequently portrayed in the stories about them as hearing confessions and giving out penances to not only members of their own religious communities, but to the laity as well. The Penitential Books that originated in Ireland in the sixth century and were written to guide soul friends in their role as confessors in the assignment of penances find their origins in the druidic practice, as Caesar says, of appointing the suitable compensation to be paid.[6]

Thus, we can see that the druids and druidesses, whose ranks included the poets and bards, were powerful spiritual leaders. They frequently taught their spirituality to the Celtic tribes, according to classical accounts, in oak groves. Like Native American shamans, they definitely functioned as mediators between the tribes and the spiritual realm: the world of tribal gods, goddesses, and spirits. For the ancient Celts and their pagan teachers, the natural and supernatural realms were inherently connected, and the spirit world was as close as the physical with only a thin divide between them. This strong awareness of the spiritual realm would eventually evolve into the Christian Celts' belief in the existence of guardian angels and of saints who acted as soul friends. Guides in the spiritual realm, the Celtic druids and druidesses were also reconcilers in the day-to-day life of the tribes. When conflicts arose between the tribes, they were the ones responsible to somehow mediate the differences. When certain grievances and outright crimes threatened to divide families and tribes, they were the ones who helped discern what responses might make amends for injuries and injustices. They also acted as "leeches," that is, physicians and healers, who diagnosed illnesses, physical and spiritual, and recommended medicines for both types. As teachers, poets, and bards, these Celtic shamans, many of whom were married, memorized the genealogies, legends, and spiritual traditions of the tribes, and passed them on to their students and their own children through the stories they told.

As Caesar suggests, becoming a druid or druidess seems to have involved a formation program of some twenty years, certainly a long and probably rigorous apprenticeship with those who were already shamans. These mentoring relationships were sources of education not only for those studying to be druids, but for all members of Celtic society. The druids and druidesses handed on to their students what they had memorized, as well as what they had learned from their own experiences. They also shaved the front part of their heads bare, and wore their hair long at the back. Later in the Early Celtic Church the tonsure of the Christian priests, which the Roman clergy and their followers opposed so vehemently, was one which left the hair shoulder-length with a high forehead, as can be seen by pilgrims today on the statue of St. Aidan on Lindisfarne, off the coast of northern England. Very likely this tonsure too was a carry-over from the druids of the pagan Celts. Above all, the love of learning found in the druidic schools, and the mentoring which the druids and druidesses did, became the foundation of the educational system which came into being in the Celtic monasteries when Christianity arose.

Ancient Stories

What we know from their own legends and myths, primarily those of Ireland and Wales, is that the Celts were a people drawn to beauty in whatever form it was expressed: beauty of landscape, of friendship, of the human body, of the soul. Their early works, eventually written down by Christian Celtic monks and based upon centuries of oral transmission (what one old manuscript describes as "the tradition of one ear to another"),[7] are filled with allusions to those significant aspects of human life. The transcribing of this native literature began in Ireland in the sixth century C.E., with fairly extensive narrative texts begun in the seventh, reaching in the eighth and ninth centuries what one scholar calls "periods *par excellence* of saga expansion and interpolation."[8] In Wales this written composition began considerably later, although, like the Irish tales, the Welsh stories go back to ancient times.[9] Both Irish and Welsh stories contain common themes concerning heroes, strange animals, shapeshifting, magical cauldrons, the number three, and the world after death called by the Irish *Tir na Nog*, and by the Welsh *Annwn*. The scribes who wrote these oral stories down for the first time were educated monks, knowledgeable of the great myths of Greece and Rome, of the Bible, and of their native folklore. They sometimes integrated aspects of these influences into their own storytelling, and, since the same scribes were writing about both secular and saintly heroes, some of the content seems at times to overlap. Still, these scribes, when they recorded the ancient stories, were probably very true to the original content of what the bards, druids, and druidesses had memorized.

The Irish sagas come as close to the ancient Celtic world as we can get, and the monks themselves, despite some of their inhibitions, seem to have faithfully reported the stories in all their sometimes quite explicit eroticism.[10] John McNeill refers to the monastic scribes' loyalty to their native culture and their friendship with bards as factors in themselves, being agents of the preservation of the national literature.[11] Kathleen Hughes notes other factors as to why Irish scribes included material that monks on the European continent, with their more restrictive views—especially concerning sexuality—might have excluded: that besides the close association between monastic scribes and the bards in Ireland, there was also the fact that the stories of secular and saintly heroes were written primarily for the laity, and that some of the clergy themselves in the monasteries were married.[12] For whatever the reasons, two facts are somewhat amazing: how quickly the Irish Celts seem to have accepted the new Christian faith with enthusiasm, and how much the Irish Church fostered and preserved the native culture and learning.

All the ancient stories of Celtic heroes, both men and women, are filled with bright colors, vibrant images, and poetic sensitivity to detail. They display a rich imagination, a deep appreciation of life's mystery, and a love of the natural world. Tuan, the ancient Irish storyteller whose own life was characterized by many transformations, summarizes the major themes of these ancient stories, themes that are also found in the early literature of Brittany: "Beauty, death, and dreams are the substance of my myth."[13] Of all these stories, the earliest ones that have survived are those from Ireland.[14] Some of these in particular influenced the depiction of the Celtic saints and soul friends.

Tuan's Stories of the Tuatha De Danaan

One category of Irish stories, called by scholars the Mythological Cycle, is concerned with the *Tuatha De Danaan,* tribes of the goddess Danu, a divine or semi-divine race which invaded Ireland before the coming of the Celts, and from whom many of the Celtic gods and goddesses took their name. These early peoples were said to have been skilled in magic and in druidic lore. Whatever their actual nature, as a heroic people they share many of the experiences of humankind, for the stories show them obsessed with beauty, wasting away with longing, tormented by jealousy, overcome with rage, grieving their losses, ashamed of their betrayals, and hoping for an afterlife, a Land of Eternal Youth, that would wipe away every tear from their eyes. These primal passions and expectations fill their days and at night disturb their sleep. At the same time, the stories tell of heroic accomplishments, perhaps precisely because they were so conflicted.

There are a number of unforgettable characters in the stories from the Mythological Cycle, many described by Tuan, chief of the first people to dwell in Ireland before the arrival of the Tuatha De Danann. This Tuan was a friend of St. Finnen, an Irish abbot of the sixth century C.E., who asked Tuan to tell him and his monks the origins of Ireland. Tuan proceeds to do so, bringing that history alive through his stories: "I am a storyteller. Warriors and young boys creep away from the hearths of winehalls to hear me. Greedy for tales of honor and history they watch my lips with bright eyes for I give them what is more precious than gold: treasure unlocked from my heart...." Tuan tells his audience that he has lived numerous lives and undergone many transformations: into Cernunnos, then into a wild boar, and, finally, into a great sea-eagle. This shapeshifting, so common among the Celtic heroes, is also an attribute of St. Patrick and other saints of the Early Celtic Church.

The King of the Tuatha De Danann, according to Tuan, was Nuada, a "flame-haired giant," who invaded Ireland with his people. They brought with them four holy objects: *Lia Fail,* the Stone of Destiny, which cried out at the touch of the rightful king; *Cliamh Solais,* the Sword of Light, from which no one escaped; *Slea Bua,* the Spear of Victory, which guaranteed success in battle; and the magical Cauldron of the Dagda, from which no one departed unsatisfied. Some of these objects represent the values of a warrior society; some are associated with the making of their kings; at least two appear in later Arthurian literature and lore, the sword transformed in medieval times into

Excalibur, the sword of King Arthur, and the cauldron into the "Holy Grail." St. Brigit too is said to have had a marvelous cauldron or "lake" of ale that fed the poor, the crippled, the outcasts.

Besides Nuada, other characters emerge in these early stories. There is Breas the Beautiful who, though renowned for his physical beauty, is "unforgiving of spirit and arrogant in manner." Dagda, "the Good Father," also appears here and represents, along with Cernunnos, the ancient Celts' devotion to fertility cults. Dagda's appetites for food and sex, in these stories, seem inexhaustible. Another divine figure, a son of Dagda, is Diancecht. He is one of the Tuatha De Danann who is described as a physician or "leech" with the ability of casting slain or mortally-wounded warriors into a healing well in which they are restored to full health. This story of the healing well is similar to the one about Dagda's magical cauldron. It also resembles the description found in the collection of Welsh stories entitled *The Mabinogion* which is full of stories linking Wales, Ireland, Cornwall, and Brittany. In the story of Branwen, daughter of Llyr, there is an Irish "cauldron of rebirth" in which "corpses were thrown in until it was full, and next morning the warriors sprang forth as fierce as ever."[15] The famous Gunderstrup cauldron, probably created in the second or first century B.C.E., shows an amazingly similar scene on one of its panels in which soldiers are being placed in a cauldron and coming forth reborn. It is another testimony to the Celts' respect for the healing arts represented by Dianchect, and eventually associated with Christian soul friends.

As in other aspects of Celtic mythology, we find in these stories goddesses depicted in triads. As the goddess Brigit, the patroness of bards and poets, was said to have two sisters who protected healers and craftsmen, in this mythological cycle appear three goddesses—Macha, Neman, and Morrigan—who as a triad are called "the Badb." The latter goddess, referred to as "a bearer of dreams that tangled in the darkness of her hair," combines beauty with fearsome, destructive power. Like Tuan and other Celtic heroes in the legends, Morrigan has the ability to shapeshift. She appears as an eel and a she-wolf in her battles with the Irish hero, CuChulainn, and most often as a raven, a symbol of death—an appropriate symbol considering the countless deaths of warriors that are found in these stories."[16]

Then there is Lugh whose name means "Shining One" and whose shield and sword seemed to burn with fire. With the help of Nuada and his warriors, this Lugh overcomes the Fomorians, a semi-demonic race who lived on the islands scattered around Ireland. This same Lugh, though he serves in the forces of Nuada, is the grandson of Balor of the Evil Eye, the chief of the Fomorians whose glance meant instant death to an enemy. It is Lugh who must kill him, and indeed succeeds in doing so by casting a slingshot into his grandfather's eye.[17] A pattern frequently found in Celtic mythology is of a major struggle between a hero and a lord of the Underworld, or the forces of darkness, in which the hero triumphs. In the stories of Lugh we find such a hero. The mythological figures, Lugh versus Balor, express the fight between the forces of light and darkness, of good versus evil. The same conflictual dynamics are portrayed in the earliest stories of St. Patrick when he lights an Easter fire on the Hill of Slane, an act which immediately antagonizes the druids of a pagan king. Lugh, in these pagan stories, is identified as a sun god of the

Irish whose feast, Lughnasa, celebrated on August 1, is one of the four major pagan Celtic feasts. The Irish, in particular, had a tremendous devotion to this god of the sun. With the coming of Christianity, their love of the sun-god is transferred to St. Michael the Archangel, a Christian warrior-figure of great power and luminosity who is identified with mountaintops and high places throughout England, Ireland, and Brittany. Worship of the sun is also reflected in the design of the high crosses that contain the symbolism of a circle holding the cross-beams. In early Irish poetry and prayers, Christ himself is sometimes addressed as the sun.

According to these early legends, the forces of Nuada and Lugh, the Tuatha De Danann, were eventually conquered when the Milesians, a tribe from northern Spain, and their neighbors, the Gaels, arrived in Ireland. The Tuatha De Danann themselves, however, continue to live in a realm beneath the earth, part of the fairy world called "the Side" which some Irish up to our own day believe has great influence, for good and for ill, on those who live in the upperworld.[18] Many of these mythological figures became identified as the gods and goddesses of the pagan Celts.

The Great Irish Hero, CuChulainn

Another category of Irish myths, the Ulster Cycle, takes its name from the Ulaid, a people of northeastern Ireland. Their king at the time the events are supposed to have occurred was Conchobar, who lived near Armagh. The central figure of the cycle is CuChulainn, nicknamed the Hound of Ulster, and son of Deichtine, his mother, and Lugh, the sun-god. Like the Welsh Pryderi, CuChulainn is extremely handsome and accomplished, from childhood on. He is given the choice between a long or short life, and chooses a short life that will give him fame rather than a long life with little distinction. CuChulainn is consistently able to perform extraordinary feats of valor in combat, and his head, like Moses' on Mount Sinai, Christ's on Mount Tabor, and the saints with their haloes, is depicted as encircled during battle by rays of light, symbolic of his physical and spiritual powers.

CuChulainn is the ideal male Celtic hero. He appears in a number of legends, most extensively in the longest and most important heroic saga of the Ulster Cycle, the *Tain Bo Cualnge*, translated as *The Cattle-Raid of Cooley*. This epic tells of an expedition made by Queen Medb (also called Maeve) of Connacht into the territory of the Ulaid in order to steal a famous bull from the district of Cualnge (present-day Cooley, Co. Louth). The saga itself may have been first recorded in the middle of the seventh century C.E.,[19] about the same time that the earliest surviving Lives of Sts. Brigit and Patrick were being written. The stories in this saga confirm many of the characteristics associated with the Celts in Gaul and Britain by the classical writers: the warrior society's valuing of physical prowess and male friendships; the leadership of strong women and goddesses who are decisive in their opinions and judgments; the heroes' ability to shapeshift and their practices of head-hunting; the heavy drinking; their pride in fine attire, the implements of war, and distinctive styles of hair; their strong erotic passions;

and, not least, the special place of the druids and druidesses as spiritual advisors of the tribes.

According to the *Tain*, CuChulainn's greatness is predicted by a druid, as happens in some Lives of the Celtic saints. Also, as in the saints' Lives, he is depicted as a man of numerous attributes, possessing "the gift of beauty, the gift of form, the gift of build, the gift of swimming, the gift of horsemanship,... the gift of battle, the gift of fighting, the gift of conflict, the gift of sight, the gift of speech, the gift of counsel...."[20] As in the earliest stories of St. Patrick which portray him bringing Christianity to Ireland, as well as cursing and destroying his enemies, CuChulainn too has both a light and dark side.

A man of many passions, CuChulainn's dark side is reflected in the stories about his anger and rage. From his youth, he is portrayed as having an angry temperament in his games with other boys, a characteristic that does not change when he becomes a young warrior. The numerous scenes in the *Tain* of his rampaging about the country, killing and taking the heads of his enemies confirms that this quality remained uncontrolled. He definitely is one of the most driven of all the warriors, reflected in the contortions of his entire body and face when preparing to do battle against his foes. This type of battle-frenzied state is known as *riastradh,* which the later Vikings equated with a specific type of fierce warrior whom they called a "berserker" (from which the phrase "going berserk" derives): "His haunches shook about him like a tree in a current or a bulrush against a stream...Then his face became a red hollow. He sucked one of his eyes into his head so that a wild crane could hardly have reached it to pluck it out from the back of his skull onto the middle of his cheek. The other eye sprang out onto his cheek."[21] This reference to one of his eye's springing onto his cheek is similar to a story of St. Brigit in which she is said to have plucked out one of her eyes, leaving it to rest on her cheek, so that her family would agree that she could remain a virgin rather than marry.[22] CuChulainn himself, in order to "quench the ardor of his wrath," is portrayed as being immersed in not one, but three vats of cold water at night[23]—just as we find Sts. Patrick, Kevin, David, Cuthbert, Gildas, and even Brigit doing in their life-stories.

CuChulainn also has another side, expressed ironically in references to his gentleness. One passage relates this attribute, as well as his own remorse for the behavior in which he had engaged the night before: "CuChulainn came on the morrow to survey the host and to display his gentle, beautiful appearance to women and girls and maidens, to poets and men of art, for he held not as honor or dignity the dark form of wizardy in which he had appeared to them the previous night...."[24] Another attribute, besides gentleness, was CuChulainn's capacity for deep and intimate friendships with both women and men. In psychological terms, he may have had what Carl Jung describes as "a finely differentiated Eros," a spiritual energy that gives a man "a great capacity for friendship, which often creates ties of astonishing tenderness between men and may even rescue friendship between the sexes from the limbo of the impossible."[25]

Judging from the stories about him, CuChulainn definitely had the capacity for physical, emotional, and sexual relations with both genders, reflected, first, in his love for his wife, Emer, and two other women: Princess Aifa, a fierce warrior, and Fand, a fairy-woman from the Otherworld. CuChulainn's strong eros can also be seen in his male friendships, especially with Fer Diad, who was "his friend, companion, and foster-brother." Theirs is a friendship, like David's and Jonathan's in the Old Testament, with strong and enduring bonds. CuChulainn describes Fer Diad as "my loved comrade, my kin and kindred. Never found I one dearer…We were loving friends. We were comrades in the wood. We were men who shared a bed." CuChulainn acknowledges the physical aspect of his spiritual love when he says to Fer Diad, "Dear to me is your splendid blush, dear your perfect and fair form, dear your bright clear eye, dear your bearing and your speech…I have never met such as you until now."[26]

As in other societies, ancient and modern, in which males are isolated from women for long periods, Celtic men evidently were not reticent in expressing themselves sexually with one another. Diodorus Siculus, quoted above, commented with disgust upon the sexual behavior between Celtic men: "Despite the fact that their wives are beautiful, the Celts…abandon themselves to a passion for other men. They usually sleep on the ground on skins of wild animals and tumble about with a bedfellow on either side."[27] Other Greek and Roman historians are also explicit on this subject. Strabo, who died about 26 C.E., wrote about "the young men in Gaul who are shamelessly generous with their boyish charms," and Atheneaus, two centuries later, repeats the statement of Diodorus about the Celts' male "bed-partners."[28]

The great love between CuChulainn and Fer Diad is echoed in the later Christian stories about soul friend relationships: in the expressions of warmth and love between male saints, such as Enda of the Aran Islands and Ciaran of Clonmacnoise,

Maedoc of Ferns and Molaise of Devenish Island, Finnian of Clonard and his students Columcille and Ciaran. It also finds resonance in the humorous scene on the bottom panel, north face, of Muiredach's Cross at Monasterboice, Co. Louth, in which two men, wide-eyed and seemingly in earnest, are pulling each other's long beards.[29]

Treasure from the Heart

Legends of the Celts (and there are many more than those briefly alluded to here) are, as Tuan the ancient Irish storyteller says, "more precious than gold," and a "treasure unlocked from the heart." This valuable treasure describes the numerous Celtic heroes who were beautiful in their physical appearance, passionate by nature, and accomplished in their deeds. Among the heroes, both men and women, there were gods and goddesses, warrior chiefs and queens, healers, hunters, druids, and poets. All these Celtic heroes seem part human, part divine, even part animal if we consider the animal names frequently associated with them, as well as their ability to shapeshift. And of course in these stories, there are allusions to the druids and druidesses who predicted the greatness of heroes, acted as mentors and friends, and perhaps most of all, taught wisdom. This wisdom had much to do with the ancient Celts' theology and spirituality, their understanding of the sacred and their celebration of it.

In these stories, there are no clear boundaries nor sharp divisions between male and female, body and soul, intellect and imagination, past, present, future, this world and the Otherworld, the living and the dead. The heroes with their shapeshifting transcend categories that Western culture and religion have come to define as separate realities, frequently in opposition to each other. Based upon their experiences, the ancient druidic teachers believed that the universe, the earth, is ONE, and so also all that dwell upon it. In the world of Celtic mythology, as in the world of our dreams, each human person contains elements of the "other" and of the so-called "opposite," and all men, women, gods, goddesses, animals, fish, and birds, as well as the environment, are interconnected, with their forms sometimes interchangeable. Everything, they believed, is in a process of transformation. What the druids and druidesses taught was to open oneself up to the mystery of this process, of this creation, to suspend judgments or preconceived notions of reality, and to enter another realm: the realm of the imagination, of vivid images, of the unconscious, of the soul. There one may find wisdom: the stance of embracing the universe and ourselves with love and with a child-like sense of wonder. This awareness of unity with all that exists is depicted artistically in the later Christian creation of the Book of Kells, with its interweaving of plants, animals, humans, angels, and saints in new combinations of originality and depth.

These Celtic stories also reflect not only this spiritual awareness, but characteristics of a spirituality in which soul friendships grew: a mystical, intuitive sense of the unseen world as not empty, but filled with spiritual presences—from the fairy-folk of the Side to one's dead ancestors who are never far from the living; a belief in the immortality of the soul, and that death is not the end of life but the beginning of another journey; a love of learning that had as one of its prime presuppositions that wisdom is more important than anything else, and comes as a result of both human effort and unexpected grace, a gift from the divine; and, of course, an appreciation for storytelling as an art that enriches and changes the listeners profoundly.

These themes of spiritual unity, of transformation, of wisdom will reemerge in the stories of the Celtic saints who, in turn, will be depicted as facilitators of those realities. Being a soul friend, as we will see, has aspects of all of these. Let us turn now to the coming of Christianity to the ancient Celts, and the rise of their own expression of telling stories of their heroes.

The Early Celtic Church

The precise origins of Christianity in Ireland and the other Celtic lands is unknown. We do have evidence, however, that British bishops were present at the Council of Arles in Gaul in 314 C.E., while the traditional date of St. Patrick's arrival in Ireland as a missionary is 432. The Early Celtic Church which emerged in Ireland, England, Scotland, Wales, and Brittany continued to exist quite independently of Rome from the fifth through the twelfth centuries with its own native leadership. It was never united administratively, but its monastic lifestyle, kinship with nature, respect for women's leadership, common stories and spirituality provided ecclesial unity in a fundamental way. What made it unique was its embracing of so many of the values and beliefs of the Celtic pagan culture which had preceded the arrival of Christianity on its shores.

Due to the rural environment as well as the tribal system of the ancient Celts, this Celtic Church developed its own structures and forms of leadership. The sixth century especially saw the rise of the great monasteries in Ireland and the Celtic parts of the British Isles and the European continent. These monasteries were headed by powerful abbesses or abbots, such as Brigit of Kildare, Columcille of Iona, Finnian of Clonard, Ita of Killeedy, Brendan of Clonfert, Kevin of Glendalough, Ciaran of Clonmacnois, David of Wales, Samson of Dol, Petroc of Cornwall. While other Western churches adopted the social structures of the declining Roman Empire as their own, dividing church territory into dioceses, headed by bishops who lived primarily in urban areas, the Early Celtic Church emphasized monastic leadership and communities that were originally quite small. Monastic leaders in the Celtic Church eventually were more powerful in the day-to-day administration of their monasteries than the bishops who lived in their midst. Many of the male leaders of the monasteries were married, as celibacy was not generally mandated until late medieval times, but even when leadership was limited to celibates or to the ordained, the monasteries themselves had many lay people (known as *manaigh*) attached to them.

From earliest times the Celtic Christians emphasized continuity with their pagan ancestors. Their passion for living, appreciation of sexuality, and love of wisdom and of beauty was passed on to the Celtic Christians, and expressed in the illuminated manuscripts, high crosses, and finely-designed croziers and chalices that can be seen today in Dublin's National Museum. The belief of the pagan Celts in the soul and their respect for the dead were also embraced by the Christian Celts. They came to consider the saints as family members, and even baptized the pagan feast of Samhain, which was celebrated at the beginning of the Celtic New Year, into the the Feast of All Saints, celebrated by the entire church on November 1. The earliest Celtic saints themselves were also seen as successors of the druids and druidesses. In the Lives or hagiographies of the saints that began to be written in the mid-seventh century C.E., the Celtic saints are often pictured as engaged in some of the same druidic exercises. They frequently seem to share the same powers of prophecy, healing, and second sight. According to these Lives of the saints, their births were often foretold by druids, while some of the greatest saints, including Brigit, Patrick, and Columcille (the "holy trinity" of Celtic saints) were educated by druid mentors. Though the early Christian legends pit the druids against the saints, the latter in many ways are portrayed as druids and druidesses who settle where the pagan spiritual leaders had once lived. Some historians suggest that St. Brigit's double monastery at Kildare was the home of druidesses before the saint's time who, like the vestal virgins in Rome, kept a perpetual fire burning. Whether true or not, Kildare means "the Church of the Oak," certainly a name with druidic connotations. Columcille himself referred in his prayers to Jesus as "my druid," and founded monasteries at Derry, Durrow, and Iona that were associated with oak groves.

As in ancient Celtic society, women continued to hold important ministerial positions in the Early Celtic Church. Some of the greatest and most well-known of spiritual leaders in the Early Irish Church were women, such as Brigit of Kildare, Ita of Killeedy, Samthann of Clonbroney, and Moninna (or Darerca) of Killeevy. In northern England, Hild of Whitby was a powerful Anglo-Saxon abbess whose spiritual formation had been provided by Aidan, an Irish monk. While the other Christian churches, influenced by Roman culture, increasingly isolated women from positions of authority and relationships of friendship with males, the Celtic Church encouraged their leadership. Contrary to the prevailing dualistic tendencies found among desert Christians and the inhabitants of countries bordering the Mediterranean, the early founders of the Celtic Church "did not reject," according to an early ninth-century manuscript—the *Catalogue of the Saints in Ireland*—"the service and society of women."[30] Women were valued and not ignored, judging from one of the earliest Irish martyrologies, that of Gorman, which lists over 200 female saints. Some of the earliest hagiographies of Irish women saints which have survived show Brigit actively engaged in preaching, Ita giving penances after hearing the confessions of laypeople, and Samthann in possession of a crozier, the symbol of a bishop, which worked miracles. One Life of St. Brigit has her ordained a bishop through the power of the Holy Spirit.[31]

Perhaps the greatest legacy that the Early Celtic Church passed on to the universal church was its gift of the tradition of the soul friend. Because of the earlier leadership of the druids and druidesses, Celtic Christians valued anyone who acted as a teacher, mentor, confessor, counselor, or spiritual guide. Everyone, from bishop to priest and nun to lay person, was expected to have an *anamchara*, as the famous saying of the time suggests: "Anyone without a soul friend is like a body without a head." The stories of the Celtic saints are filled with numerous examples of soul friend relationships between women and men,

men and men, and women and women. All of them seem to have been changed profoundly by those relationships. A pattern that emerges in the stories of these saints is that after a person has received help from an *anamchara*, he or she, in turn, goes on to become for others a soul friend: someone with whom we can share our greatest joys and deepest fears, discern our hidden gifts and confess our worst and most persistent faults. Such relationships, the early Celts believed, did not end with death, for the spiritual ties between soul friends transcended space and time.

Celtic Hagiographies

One of the main sources for gaining an understanding of the Celtic Church's tradition of soul friendship are the hagiographies or Lives of the early Celtic saints. In the history of Christian spirituality, hagiography is the genre of writing that developed in the early church which is specifically concerned with the lives and holiness of these spiritual leaders. The term comes from two Greek words: *graphe*, which means "writing," and *hagoi*, "about saints." Hundreds of these Lives were composed by hagiographers from the seventh to the thirteenth centuries C.E. in the Celtic monasteries.[32] The flowering of Celtic monasticism which began with the "golden age" or "heroic age" of the early Celtic saints in the sixth and seventh centuries was followed in the late seventh, eighth, and ninth centuries with the writing of these Lives. The Christian storytellers who first wrote down the legends of the saints drew upon the rich oral tradition of storytelling about the saints which had been kept alive, sometimes for centuries preceding any writing. This earlier stratum of stories had been passed on by pagan and Christian druids, poets, and bards, and by communities and "witnesses" who knew the saints firsthand.

The Life of St. Samson, the Welsh bishop who emigrated to Brittany where he founded a monastery at Dol, is the oldest extant hagiography of a Celtic saint. This Life was probably written in the early 600s at one of the monasteries of the Early Celtic Church.[33] A few years later, about 640 C.E., Jonas, a monk from Bobbio, Italy, wrote his famous Life on the great Irish missionary, Columbanus.[34] In Ireland, the first hagiographer known by name is Cogitosus, a Leinsterman who was asked by the community of Kildare in the latter half of the seventh century to write a Life of their foundress, Brigit. Soon after, two other writers, Muirchu, a resident of Armagh and a protégé of Cogitosus, and Tirechan, a native of County Mayo, wrote a Life of St. Patrick. On the isle of Iona off the western coast of Scotland in the late 680s, less than a hundred years after St. Columcille's death, his successor, the abbot Adomnan, wrote a famous Life about that important missionary.

The seventh century, then, was the beginning of Celtic hagiographies which later generations of storytellers would rely upon for their new or expanded versions of saints' Lives. After the seventh century, the eighth and ninth centuries in particular saw the creation of more hagiographies, a number of them influenced by the Celi De, a reform movement within the Celtic churches which emphasized liturgical renewal, devotion to the saints, and soul friendship.[35] Although the Lives of the Celtic saints which have survived were primarily compiled in the high medieval period (thirteenth to sixteenth centuries), many were written during this earlier period, and almost all contain primitive material that takes us back to the earliest days of the Celtic Church, providing insight into the everyday life of Celtic Christians and the type of spiritual leadership they encouraged.

During the early medieval period federations of monasteries known as *paruchiae* came to dominate the ecclesiastical landscape. In Ireland, by the seventh century, three monasteries in particular, those of Armagh, Kildare, and Iona, made claims to widespread jurisdiction and property over smaller monasteries and churches. It is interesting to note that the three earliest Irish Lives to survive are those written by scribes at Armagh promoting St. Patrick, at Kildare describing the wonder of St. Brigit and her double monastery, and at Iona lauding the accomplishments of St. Columcille. Other monasteries imitated their example, so that in the following centuries the country was dotted with a great variety of federations and monastic alliances.

Almost all of these Lives were written anonymously. Although there is no evidence that any of the hagiographers were women (no woman left her name on any surviving documents), some may have been, since women's communities, no less than men's, were places of learning and of scholarship. St. Brigit's double monastery at Kildare with its increasing wealth and scriptorium would have been one of the most likely places for female scribes to thrive.[36] The saints' Lives suggest that a considerable number of Celtic women devoted themselves to monastic living in the Early Celtic Church, and litanies of the saints also refer to many holy women.[37] Most of the hagiographies, however, which have survived are Lives of male saints. This may be due to the fact that many of the women's communities were absorbed by their male counterparts after the death of their founder or were destroyed by rapacious Vikings who were especially effective in assaulting smaller religious houses. Some were also assimilated by the Normans who, following their invasion of Ireland in the twelfth century, established their own convents. Patriarchal attitudes which negated the value of women's lives and leadership came to dominate much of the Western Church, and this too contributed to the scarcity of stories about female saints.

When hagiographers sat down to write the Lives of the saints they did so with a variety of motives. At the time of an increased appreciation in the Western Church for early saints and martyrs and their relics, hagiographers of the Celtic saints wrote to explain the greatness of their own spiritual ancestors and to give credence to their relics. At a time when the larger and wealthier monasteries were vying for political recognition, they wrote to prove their own monasteries' distinctiveness, if not superiority, and probably to prove which smaller churches belonged to whom. At the time when large numbers of monastic members necessarily demanded larger revenues, they wrote to gain financial support from their neighbors and to attract the pilgrim trade to their shrines. However, besides these very human and at times self-serving motivations there were others as well.

If we look closely at the texts of the writers of the Celtic Lives, a major reason they composed their hagiographies was to present the individual saint as a model and an exemplar of holiness for others to emulate. This motivation is most frequently expressed in the prefaces of the hagiographies, from the earliest to the latest Celtic Lives. Adomnan, writing on Iona in the seventh century, states that he hopes "to place before my reader's eyes an image of his [Columcille's] holy life."[38] Bernard of Clairvaux, who composed his *Life of Saint Malachy* in Gaul during the closing days of the Celtic Church, clearly expresses his purpose for writing: "It was always considered praiseworthy to record the illustrious lives of the saints so that they could serve as a mirror and good example...."[39] Thus hagiographers primarily wrote the Lives because they believed that the saint whose life they were describing had something important to teach people about Christian holiness, prayer, service, and ultimately union with God. As exemplars, Celtic saints acted as *anamcharas* or soul friends. Monastic storytellers also wrote to reveal the Celtic saints as powerful spiritual mentors, capable of helping those who turn to them in prayer. They believed that the patron saint of their monastery was, although dead, very much alive, and that he or she had a spiritual power capable of transforming the lives of those who called upon the saint. For many hagiographers, this spiritual kinship with the saints was based upon the beliefs of their pagan and Christian ancestors and, most likely, their own experiences of prayers being answered by saintly soul friends.

Literary Influences: The Stories of the Desert Christians

In order to tell the stories of the saints and to express the mystery of their lives, a mystery that touched their own, the hagiographers of the Early Celtic Church necessarily turned to certain sources. When possible, they relied upon information from living friends and monastic colleagues of the saints them-selves. Writers such as Adomnan and Bede refer directly to these "learned and faithful ancients."[40] From these ancients or the oral tradition that they had passed on, hagiographers con-structed specific incidents connected with a particular saint that would enhance his or her reputation. Inspired by certain hagiographies in other lands, they also frequently borrowed con-tents directly from them or modeled their own writings upon other works. Those most popular at the time the first Celtic hagiographies were composed were Athanasius's *Life of Antony*, John Cassian's *Conferences,* and Jerome's Lives, especially the *Life of Paul*. Another hagiography, Sulpicius Severus's *Life of St. Martin* (of Tours), also influenced significantly a number of early Celtic Lives, including the hagiography of Columcille by Adomnan.[41] The source for all of these hagiographies, however, was the example and ascetic lifestyle of the early desert Christians who had their own tradition of spiritual mentoring, aspects of which became associated with the Celtic *anamchara*.

These desert Christians, pioneers of monasticism in both the Western and Eastern churches, were mostly laypeople who had left their homes and traveled into the desert regions of Egypt, Syria, and Palestine in the third, fourth, and fifth cen-turies C.E. Many of them, inspired by the examples of the desert elders such as Antony (251–356) and Pachomius (292–346), desired a more heroic lifestyle where "the air was purer, the heavens more open, and God nearer."[42] They began to live alone as hermits or together in communities and eventually became valued as teachers of prayer and as therapists, healing spiritual diseases which they called "sins." These desert "fathers" and "mothers," as they came to be respectfully and lovingly called, instructed those who came to them not only with words of advice, but more importantly through the spirituality they lived. A maxim of theirs was "Be an example, not a lawgiver."[43]

In the Lives or hagiographies of these spiritual leaders and in the wisdom Sayings, the *Apophthegmata Patrum et Matrum*, which survived, two seemingly contradictory characteristics consistently appear: their great appreciation of friendship and an equally strong love of solitude. There is much evidence in these written works of the warmth, love, respect, and genuine affection the early desert Christians felt for each other. They warmly embrace each other upon meeting and before they depart. They engage in friendly banter, and yet also seriously discuss the spiritual progress that each is attempting to make. They share their daily work and, at least once a week, celebrate Eucharist together. Most of all, they call each other friends and root that friendship in Jesus' name and memory. As one of them, Abba Theodore, says so poignantly, "Let us each give his heart to the other, carrying the Cross of Christ."[44] It is this capacity for deep friendships that attracted others to them, giving them the courage to open their hearts and confess their most secret sins. This capacity for friendship and ability to read other people's hearts became the basis of the desert elders' effectiveness as spiritual guides.

John Cassian (c. 360–435), an early visitor to the desert, highly recommended this practice of self-disclosure to a responsible elder in his later writings. As the desert elders modeled self-disclosure to their charges by openly acknowledging their sins and struggles, so the younger monks, Cassian learned, were expected to confess their own secrets, inclinations, and wound-edness. Throughout Cassian's writings are numerous references to the importance and healing effects of speaking directly from the heart to another person. This self-disclosure was a form of lay confession, since most of the elders and desert guides were not ordained. Before disclosing any sickness or sin to another person, however, Cassian advises that the monk engage in a personal inventory or general examination of his life. "All the corners of our heart," he writes, "must therefore be examined thoroughly and the marks of all that rise up into them must be investigated with the utmost wisdom." Only then will we manage "to destroy the lairs of the wild beasts within us and the hiding places of the venomous serpents."[45]

After this inventory, Cassian recommends that its results and everything arising in the heart be shared with an elder, for "an evil thought sheds its danger when it is brought into the open, and even before the verdict of discernment is proferred the most foul serpent which, so to speak, has been dragged out of its subterranean lair into the light by the fact of open avowal, retreats, disgraced and denounced. Its dangerous promptings hold sway in us as long as these are concealed in the heart." Such open and honest confession can help set a person free of all sorts of captivity, for it pulls "into the light from your shadowed heart" the "most loathsome serpent" hiding within. Through the power of such self-disclosure "the grip of this diabolic tyranny" is wiped out and "forever laid to rest." When one confesses to some spiritual person who is immersed in the all-powerful words of Scripture a cure can be found immediately for these "serpent bites." So also "the means of driving the fatal poison from the heart" can be discovered.[46] This healing and the knowledge of self that comes through self-revelation to another can help a person avoid the repetition of self-destructive patterns of behavior that previously characterized one's personality and life. As Alcoholics Anonymous discovered in the twentieth century,[47] Cassian was simply saying that a personal inventory and confession to a reliable guide on a regular basis is good for the body and for the soul. It was a conviction that the later Christian Celts made their own, and what they equated with the ministry of the soul friend.

What the stories about the desert Christians also reveal is that, despite their love of solitude, or perhaps precisely because of that love, friendship had a special meaning for them. In cultivating silence and some degree of solitude, they evidently had a greater capacity for and appreciation of friendship itself. What is also apparent from the stories is that their willingness to open their hearts to one another included a willingness to share their cells. Numerous examples are given that their cells were shared with companions, occasionally for only short visits, and sometimes for a lifetime. According to Nora Chadwick in her classic, *The Age of the Saints in the Early Celtic Church,* the *anamchara* was originally someone who, as a companion, shared another's cell and to whom one confessed, revealing confidential aspects of one's life. Thus, Chadwick says that the Celtic tradition of spiritual guidance was strongly influenced by the desert Christians, and that the rise of the *anamchara* in the Celtic churches was a natural development which may be related to the *syncellus,* "the one who shares a cell," in the Greek Orthodox Church.[48] Considering the cell's importance in desert spirituality as a place where one encounters God and learns everything, to share one's cell with a soul friend, then, is to share one's inmost self, one's life, one's mind and heart. Cassian in his writings compares friendship itself to those who by the union of character, "not of place," are joined together "in a common dwelling." This bond between friends, he says, is indissoluble: "This, I say, is what is broken by no chances, what no interval of time or space can sever or destroy, and what even death itself cannot part."[49]

The wisdom of the desert Christians, especially expressed in Cassian's writings, had a significant impact on the development of spirituality among the Celtic Christians and upon the evolution of soul friend ministry itself. This influence came primarily through the literature that was written about those desert guides which eventually reached the Celtic churches as monasticism spread from the East to the West. Knowledge of this form of spiritual mentoring may also have been brought in person by desert monks or hermits who, while fleeing the persecutions against them early in the fifth century, traveled to Ireland and Britain years before the missionary Patrick arrived.[50] The values of the desert Christians, including their attentiveness to spiritual diseases and the confession of sin, may also have been brought back by the numerous Celtic pilgrims in the early medieval period who visited the holy places where Jesus had lived and the nearby cells of the monks.[51]

In whatever way the Celtic Christians learned about the desert elders, their spirituality and their practice of offering support and guidance to others can be easily discerned in the later hagiographies of the Celtic saints. It is also reflected artistically on numerous stone high crosses scattered throughout Ireland and Britain, especially the scene of the desert hermits Paul and Antony breaking bread together in the Egyptian desert.[52] The early Celtic soul friends too embrace an ascetic lifestyle, frequently wearing the skins of animals rather than woolen clothing and eating the simplest of diets. They, like the desert elders, value solitude and, in the midst of many communal and familial responsibilities, seek out isolated places where they can find soul-space: room for developing in silence and in one's depths greater intimacy with God. They too appreciate the type of friendship in which what the desert guides called *exagoreusis*, the opening of one's heart to another, leads to *hesychia*, serenity and peace of heart.

Spiritual Kinship with Jesus

Besides the writings about the desert Christians and the Life of St. Martin of Tours, the ultimate literary source for all of the Celtic hagiographies was the Bible, primarily the New Testament. Some references are made to the Old Testament, but these tend to be more by way of briefly comparing a particular saint to some Jewish hero than actually full stories.[53] The Lives of the Celtic saints, however, are intrinsically linked with the stories of Jesus. Celtic hagiographers, immersed in those stories, portrayed each saint not only as an extraordinary person, but above all as an *imago Christi,* a living symbol or image of Christ. Believing, as they did, that Jesus was *the* revelation of both what it means to be divine and to be fully human, they showed the Celtic saints doing in their time what Jesus did in his: healing the sick, feeding the hungry, praying in solitude, having intimate friendships with both women and men, calming the sea, even raising the dead. Overall, when one considers the stories of the

Celtic saints which follow, we can discern how much they resonate with the life and ministry of Jesus. In effect, the saints' Lives reflect each one's spiritual kinship with him: how all of them, by uniting their hearts and minds with his, were changed profoundly by Jesus and his story. By implication, it suggested to the readers of those hagiographies how their own spirituality was meant to be shaped, as the saints' lives were, by the life of Jesus who was considered to be a primary soul friend.

In addition to this religious pattern which represents the saint's path to holiness and to spiritual wisdom, other sides of the saint's personality frequently appear in these early stories, as we will see. At times the saints seem to be living according to a different standard than that of the Sermon on the Mount. In some of the legends about St. Patrick, for example, we find him cursing his enemies, especially the druids, and in other ways attacking and punishing those who are opposed to him. Other monastic founders, voyagers, and missionaries sometimes employ similar means for maintaining their claims against each other or of vanquishing their foes. These stories in particular reveal the influence of the earlier pagan culture which had its own understanding of what constitutes a genuine hero. Here, in the tales with their sometimes humorous overtones, and in the stories of the saints' kinship with animals and even their potent cursing, we find intimations of how much the Christian hagiographers were often influenced by the ancient pagan bardic storytellers.

Whatever the saints' depiction or mood swings, the early hagiographers saw little demarcation between ordinary tales and religious ones, and there was often a blending of the two. This blending is clearly evident when we find how frequently hagiographers incorporated into the Lives of the saints certain folktales which were popular at the time they wrote.[54] Traces of these folktales appear in the stories of Brendan's voyage to the Promised Land, Brigit's talented fox at the court of an Irish king, David's marvelous horse which Findbarr rode across the Irish Sea, and Kevin's encounter with a fairy-witch. Celtic hagiography is full of these mythic components, the language of folktales, fairytales, visions, and dreams.

This "language," related so much to the transforming power of symbols, was not used to deceive or to mislead readers of the hagiographies, but to provide them with intimations of the saint's greatness and assurances that each saint and soul friend was especially loved, protected, and guided by God. Ancient people, including the writers of the Gospels, the fathers and mothers of the early church, and the Christian Celts themselves did not invent the great mysteries described in the saints' lives (i.e., birth, love, suffering, forgiveness, death, and rebirth). They experienced them first, and then used symbolic language in an attempt to express their awesome mystery to their readers.

This was especially true of the four soul friends whose stories unfold in the next chapters of this book: Patrick, Brigit, and Columcille, who make up the "holy trinity" of Celtic saints, and Colman of Land Ela. Each of their hagiographies is a classic, disclosing what their authors considered to be authentic experiences of the sacred. As a wisdom document from the past, each can also bring us into contact with what is of enduring value for our contemporary world. By examining their Lives in more detail, they might act as a mirror, as Bernard of Clairvaux states, reflecting experiences of soul friendship for us today.

CHAPTER 2

Patrick of Armagh
Shaman and Spiritual Guide

One night I saw the vision of a man called Victor, who
appeared to have come from Ireland with an unlimited
number of letters. He gave me one of them and I read
the opening words which were, "The voice of the Irish."

St. Patrick, *Confessio*

O f all the Celtic saints, Patrick is the best known and
most popular, a man whose Latin name, Patricius,
means "one who frees hostages"—surely a most
appropriate designation since, as a former slave himself, he is the
first on record in Late Antiquity to speak out forcefully against
slavery and most remarkably (considering Roman culture),
against women being taken and held as slaves. His impassioned
stance, many long centuries before slavery was even discussed by
Christians as unethical and only much later abolished in the
West, surely stands as one of his greatest achievements. What
many people fail to acknowledge or do not know about this spiritual leader whose feastday, March 17, is celebrated worldwide
with so much indulgence,[1] is that Patrick himself was not a

native of Ireland. Although controversy over his origins and when he actually lived continues, he most likely was born about 390 C.E. near the west coast of England or Wales, and died in northern Ireland, near Armagh, in 461.[2]

As is the case of many of the earliest saints who later became identified as soul friends, we do not have a great deal of accurate information about him because of the social turmoil of the early fourth and fifth centuries. Still, two autobiographical writings of Patrick's did survive: a *Confessio,* written in his mature years as a missionary bishop, telling the story of his life and defending himself against detractors at home who were questioning his integrity, and a *Letter to Coroticus* in which he protested the captivity and martyrdom of some of his Irish converts by a Welsh chieftain with that name. Both documents provide insights into Patrick's great love of the Irish whom he adopted as his own sons and daughters in the Christian faith, as well as his innate mysticism, reflected in his visions, prayer experiences, and intense connection with the natural landscape.[3]

Patrick's *Confessio,* included in the *Book of Armagh,* is the earliest recorded Irish literature. In it, Patrick tells us that he was born into a Christian family somewhere in Roman Britain, that his father, Calpornius, was a deacon in the early church and his grandfather, Potitus, a priest, and that at the age of sixteen he underwent a horrible crisis. At a time when the Roman Empire was withdrawing troops from Britain in order to protect Rome itself from barbarian attacks, Patrick was captured and taken from his home by slavetraders who had become increasingly more active in the power vacuum. Along with others, he was sold into slavery in Ireland, and possibly taken to the region of County Mayo. While tending sheep and feeling increasingly more isolated and alone, God "made me aware of my unbelief," Patrick says, "that I might at last…turn wholeheartedly to the Lord." A captive six years, he finally escaped from Ireland with the help of certain dreams in which a voice guided him to freedom. Then, a few years after his return to his family in Britain, he had what was to be one of his most significant dreams: "One night I saw the vision of a man called Victor, who appeared to have come from Ireland with an unlimited number of letters. He gave me one of them and I read the opening words which were, 'The voice of the Irish.' As I read the beginning of the letter I seemed at the same moment to hear the voice of those who were by the wood of Voclut which is near the Western Sea. They shouted with one voice: 'We ask you, boy, come and walk once more among us.' I was cut to the very heart and could read no more, and so I woke up."[4]

No one knows with any certainty the identity of Victor, although some scholars suggest that he may have been a disciple of St. Martin of Tours.[5] Whoever he was, Victor is obviously significant, considering that only two other figures are specifically named by Patrick in his *Confessio*: his father and grandfather. Patrick interpreted this dream, similar to the one of his hero, the missionary St. Paul (cf. Acts 16:9–10), as a genuine call from God revealing his own vocation. In the seventh century, a monk of Armagh by the name of Muirchu (pronounced "Murra-hoo"), identified Victor, Patrick's dream figure, in his hagiography on Patrick as an angel, a guardian spirit, who guided him throughout his life. By the end of the ninth century, at the time of the Celi

De reform movement, this angel is definitely called an *anam-chara*—not only of Patrick, but of the entire Celtic race: "Victor was Patrick's soul friend, and he is the common angel of the Celts. As Michael of the Jews, so is Victor of the Irish."[6]

The description of the saint's captivity, early dreams, and especially the appearance of Victor at a crucial time in his life reveals the similarity of Patrick's experience with that of the shaman: the wisdom figure, counselor, and spiritual guide of primitive and Native American peoples who advises individuals and tribes about ultimate realities. According to this spiritual tradition, such a person has personally undergone some intense form of crisis or ordeal, and as a result of it becomes a specialist of the human soul and of the spiritual realm. More specifically, the scholar Mircea Eliade describes the essential role of a shaman as that of defending the psychic integrity and spiritual wholeness of the community against death, diseases, "the world of darkness," and "the powers of evil." Eliade also makes clear that the shaman is a person who not only gives guidance to others, but receives it. His or her spiritual power and vocation of service to the tribe is usually linked with at least one "guardian" or "tutelary" spirit, revealed during an illness, an ecstatic experience, a vision quest in the wilderness, or in a dream. Such a helpful spirit, identified at times with some animal, bird, or ancestor, sometimes a grandparent, becomes an alter ego or another self, and is called simply a friend or companion of the shaman.[7] Victor, the dream-figure who became Patrick's soul friend, of course, fits this latter category.

In the very earliest hagiographies, the Celtic saints, including Patrick, are portrayed as descendents of the pagan druids and druidesses whom God gave miraculous powers to fight evil, corruption, poverty, and disease. Early Patrician storyteller, Tirechan, in fact says that Patrick was in the "service of druids" until he was twenty-two years old.[8] In these hagiographies, the Celtic saints' vocations are linked intimately with God and the entire spiritual realm, including angels who act as spiritual guides to them. This theme is common in all the saints' Lives: how angels are present to them, especially at crucial life transitions and turning points. In a saint's early childhood, for example, angels sometimes give him or her a name; in young adulthood, they may encourage the saint to pursue a religious vocation; in maturity, they guide him or her to where a monastery is to be built; in later years, they sometimes lead the saint to foreign shores; and finally, before death, they accompany the saint to his or her "Place of Resurrection." Even after the saint's death, they are frequently seen by those who survive as carrying the saint's soul to heaven.

In certain hagiographies of the Irish saints in particular, angels, disguised as clerics, baptize the child Brigit and name her; they help Finnian construct his church at Clonard; they guide Findbarr to Cork; they encourage Maedoc of Ferns when he is tired of his ministry, experiencing what we today might call burnout. Some angels even clean Patrick's hearth for him. As dream-figures, angels warn Ita about the extreme diet which threatens her health, and assure Brendan when he begins to wonder if he will ever reach the Land of Promise. Probably due to their pagan ancestors' belief in spirits and the spiritual realm being so closely intertwined with the physical, Christian Celts had a special respect for angels and considered them, in addition to human mentors, as important spiritual guides for everyone.

This portrayal of the Celtic saints as shamans who as spiritual guides are themselves guided by spiritual entities is particularly vivid in Patrician hagiographies. Because Muirchu wrote the earliest Life of Patrick which has survived,[9] his account will serve as our source for stories that shed light on Patrick's soul friend ministry. While his interpretation of Patrick's life relies initially upon Patrick's own writings, Muirchu changes the historical figure into the legendary—with the help of written and oral sources and, of course, his own vivid imagination. In Muirchu's storytelling, Patrick is transformed from a humble, dedicated missionary as revealed in the *Confessio* into a powerful shaman-evangelizer or larger-than-life Christian druid who, while mentoring others in the faith, is himself mentored by the angel Victor.

Muirchu's Life of St. Patrick[10]

Writing some 200 years after the historical St. Patrick, Muirchu begins what he calls his "sacred narrative" with an acknowledgment of his difficulties, of his own humble talents, and of his debt to Cogitosus, St. Brigit's hagiographer. He goes on to describe Patrick's origins, captivity in Ireland, gradual conversion, and escape. Here Muirchu is obviously relying upon biographical information alluded to in Patrick's *Confessio*, while adding specifics of his own:

> At the age of sixteen the boy, with others, was captured and brought to this island of barbarians and was

kept as a slave in the household of a certain cruel pagan king. He spent six years in captivity, in fear and trembling before God, in many vigils and prayers. He used to pray a hundred times a day and a hundred times a night, giving gladly to God what is due God....He began to respect God and to love the Lord Almighty, for up to that time he had no knowledge of the true God. Now the Spirit truly lived within him. After enduring many hardships there, including hunger and thirst, cold and nakedness; after pasturing flocks and being visited by Victor, an angel sent to him by God; after great miracles known to almost everyone, and divine prophecies as well, in the twenty-third year of his life Patrick left the earthly, pagan king and his works, and entrusted himself to the heavenly, eternal God. Together with strangers— aliens and pagans who worshipped many false gods— Patrick then sailed for Britain by God's command and was accompanied by the Holy Spirit in the ship which lay ready for him.

Muirchu, early in his account, thus establishes Patrick's spiritual credentials: that he is, above all, a holy man who has the Holy Spirit as an intimate companion to whom he listens attentively. In the terminology of Marcus Borg, Patrick is obviously a "spirit person": a person to whom the sacred is an experiential reality who in turn becomes a mediator of the sacred for others.

When Patrick happily arrives back in Britain after his long separation from loved ones, he is welcomed by his family who naturally insists that he never leave them again. Patrick, however, Muirchu says, did not fully consent to their desires, and continued to see "many visions." At this point in Muirchu's account, a pattern, other than the one described earlier, begins to emerge which is frequently found in the stories of heroes and those pursuing wisdom. This pattern, first delineated by Joseph Campbell, in his classic *The Hero With a Thousand Faces*, describes how all of us go through certain conflicts, trials, and rites of passage that can lead to the creation of a new personality, one more spiritually and psychologically mature. This journey to greater wholeness and holiness, Campbell says, is often revealed in the stories of religious and cultural heroes, male or female. As such, a "monomyth" is reflected in all heroic mythic accounts, consisting of three stages or movements: departure, initiation, and return.

In the first stage, which Campbell entitles the "call to adventure," the hero leaves home or that which is familiar to him or her—whether it's a certain routine, job, way of perceiving life (or of being perceived). This call of life to the soul can come at any time, and can happen in all sorts of subtle and sometimes dramatic ways. As an invitation to adventure, it can be announced at night in the recognition of certain failures, challenges, or false accusations; at dawn, in the phantoms or images of dreams; during the day, in experiences of boredom, unhappiness, sickness, grief, or guilt. Sometimes it comes more happily, through the discovery of a certain passion or when a person unexpectedly falls in love. However it comes, if the invitation to adventure is accepted, one is propelled into the next stage.

Campbell calls this second stage the "road of trials" when a person enters a painful liminal state filled with ambiguity and usually great anxiety. This stage is experienced as a time of "betwixt and between," precisely because one has left the familiar but has as yet not reached another state. In the stories of heroes, it is expressed symbolically in a great variety of ways: as a descent into hell (Dante's *The Divine Comedy*), being swallowed by a whale (Jonas), going into a wilderness (Moses and the Israelites), or facing crucifixion and death (Jesus). Whatever the description, this road of trials is experienced as a very lonely part of the journey in which certain tasks must be accomplished and temptations met. At the same time, Campbell assures, this second stage is precisely when help is given from human, angelic, or even animal mentors who become guides through the desert or wilderness. Benefiting from such help, a person finds "the treasure," receives a "blessing," becomes "master of two worlds": the earthly and heavenly realms. Ultimately wisdom is gained, and, as a result of the hero's adventure, he or she enters the last stage.

This final stage, the "return," is when a person who has not merely survived the road of trials, but prospered from it, returns to his or her homeland and becomes a spiritual mentor and guide to his or her own tribe, society, nation, or church. This involves the ministry of leadership or mentoring, of freely sharing what has been learned from one's experiences while encouraging others to do the same. It may result of course in another new adventure, wilderness sojourn, or some form of crucifixion, for what has been learned is not always well received by those people or institutions which have been left at home. Nonetheless, there is in this last stage a new experience of personal freedom, centeredness, and clarity of vision; of being united at a new level of integration with one's deeper self and God.[11]

Traces of the three stages that Campbell says characterize a hero's journey can be identified in Muirchu's stories of Patrick, as well as those of other Celtic saints. They are typically found in the life of the shaman, saint, or soul friend.

Patrick's Call to Adventure and Road of Trials

According to Muirchu, Patrick, against the objections of his kinsfolk and probably many hesitations of his own, leaves his homeland once more and sets out on a journey in search of wisdom. He does this when he is just reaching a transitional stage in adulthood, and significantly he does so, not because it is the "reasonable" thing to do, but because his heart tells him it is necessary. As others before him and since have experienced, Patrick is given help from both human and angelic mentors, visible and invisible guides, including St. Germanus (ca. 378–448 C.E.),[12] a bishop of Auxerre, and the angel Victor: "When Patrick had spent a considerable time there (some say forty years, others thirty), his most faithful friend of old, named Victor, who had foretold everything to him in a large number of dreams, told him that the time had come for Patrick to go and fish with the net of the Gospel for the wild, barbarian peoples whom God had sent him to teach." According to Muirchu, Patrick is ordained a bishop in Gaul, following the unsuccessful mission to Ireland of a previous missionary, Palladius, about whom historians know little. He returns to Britain for a short time, and then sails across the sea to Ireland with the help of a favorable wind. Now begins Patrick's "road of trials" in which he battles the powers of evil that Eliade associates with the shaman, while experiencing his own temptations and doubts.

Upon landing in Ireland, Patrick first travels to the northern parts of the island in order to visit Miliucc, the man who had once been his master when he, Patrick, was held captive as a youth. Although Muirchu at one point in his narrative has identified this former master as a "cruel, pagan king," he later identifies him as a druid whom Patrick served for seven years.[13] Their relationship must have been quite close considering what follows. According to Muirchu, Patrick's intention in seeking out Miliucc was not only to redeem himself by buying his own freedom from his former master, but to bring the news of salvation to Miliucc, thus freeing him from the slavery of sin. As sometimes happens in ministry, however, Miliucc evidently did not understand what Patrick hoped to accomplish or why he had come: "When Miliucc heard that his slave was about to come and see him, he became frightened that he might be subject to his slave and the latter might become his master. The devil put it into his mind to commit suicide with fire. He gathered all his wealth together in the castle where he had lived as king, and set himself on fire along with it. Holy Patrick, standing at the spot on the right flank of Sliab Miss, from which, on his return full of grace, he had first viewed the district where he had lived as a slave…saw immediately, right under his eyes, the king's pyre. Stunned by this sight, he stood there for two or three hours without uttering a word, sighing and mourning and weeping."

Patrick's anguish is profound and his disappointment deep. It is his first major crisis in ministry since his arrival back in Ireland: an experience of personal loss, as is apparent by his

grief, and also a time of self-questioning as he realizes that sometimes even the best of intentions can be misinterpreted. He may
even have wondered whether it might not have been better if he
had never returned to the land of his captivity, and that his former master might in fact have been better off without his "inter-
ference." Whatever Patrick's feelings, Muirchu intimates that
the crisis is somehow resolved in the saint's letting go:

> Finally Patrick spoke these words: "I know not, God
> knows, why this man and king chose to burn himself in
> fire rather than believe at the end of his life and serve
> the eternal God." Having said this, he prayed, armed
> himself with the sign of the cross, turned at once and
> went back to the territory from which he had come.

As a result of Patrick's increased missionary work, his
hagiographer says, "the faith began to spread." Here in his narrative, Muirchu explicitly refers to the spiritual help that Patrick
receives: "Let our account return to what was said earlier. An
angel used to come to Patrick regularly on the seventh day of
every week, and as one person talks to another so Patrick
enjoyed the angel's conversation. Even when, at the age of sixteen, Patrick had fallen into captivity and spent six years in servi-
tude, the angel came thirty times to meet him, and he enjoyed
the angel's counsels and their conversations before he left
Ireland [as a young man]...." This passage reveals the great intimacy Patrick enjoys with his spiritual guide. Still, despite the
angel's help, Patrick's ministry, developing as it was, is not without further difficulties and challenges.

As Easter approaches, we find Patrick setting out on foot with his companions across a great plain near Tara, the holy place of the pagan Celts. There he confronts the unconverted King Loiguire and his druids in a match that pits saintly shaman against pagan druid—a contest that stands at the heart of Muirchu's hagiography. Here Muirchu relates one of the most famous stories connected with the legendary Patrick. In his storytelling he uses various biblical allusions to show Patrick's spiritual heritage and kinship with Christ. He compares, for example, Patrick's confrontation with that of Moses and the Pharaoh's magicians in the Old Testament (cf. Exod 5) and with St. Peter's contest with Simon the Magician in the New Testament (Acts 8:9 ff). Muirchu also draws upon images of fire and light, especially popular because they were (and are) Christian symbols of faith and of God's presence. Fire was also a significant symbol of the pagan Celts, and in Muirchu's account we see how the lighting of it on the Hill of Slane, before the druids did on Tara, was considered a very grievous crime:

> So St. Patrick, as he celebrated holy Easter, kindled the divine fire with its bright light and blessed it. As it gleamed in the darkness it was seen by almost all the inhabitants of the flat plain. So it came about that it was also seen from Tara, and everyone wondered at the sight. King Loiguire called together the elders, councilors, and druids and said to them: "What is this? Who is it who has dared to commit this sacrilege in my kingdom? Let him be put to death." They all replied that they did not know who had done it, but

the druids answered: "O king, may you live forever! This fire which we see and which was lit this night before one was lit in your palace of Tara will never be put out unless it is put out this very night; what is more, it will surpass all the fires of our customs, and he who has kindled it and the kingdom which has been brought upon us by him who has kindled it on this night will overpower us all and you....It will spread over the whole country and will reign forever and ever."

The king is deeply disturbed at these words, and at dawn leaves Tara with numerous chariots. Patrick is not frightened by their approach, but goes out to meet them. Muirchu here describes the inevitable conflict with all the dramatic flourish of an excellent storyteller:

They then began to talk with one another, and one of the two druids, called Lochru, was insolent to the saint's face and had the effrontery to disparage the catholic faith in the most arrogant terms. St. Patrick glared fiercely at him as he spoke,...and then, with strange power, he shouted aloud and confidently addressed the Lord: "O Lord, who can do all things and in whose power all things lie, who sent me here, may this impious man who blasphemes Your name be now carried up out of here and die without delay." At these words the druid was carried up into the air and then dropped outside from above. He fell head-first, crashing his skull against a stone, and was smashed to pieces. As he died before their eyes, the pagans were afraid. The king with his followers was angry with Patrick at this, and determined to kill him....

At this point in the story, Muirchu is painting a picture of Patrick as a powerful leader whose actions seem more typical of a hero from the Irish sagas, such as the stories of the sun-god, Lugh, or of CuChulainn, than characteristic of a Christian saint. Muirchu consciously did this in order to enhance Patrick's status in the eyes of his Irish readers who expected that their heroes—no matter how saintly—would engage in such activities. He makes clear, however, that the saint has such powers only because of God's intervention *and Patrick's prayers.* Nevertheless, he shows Patrick cursing his enemies (an old and highly respected druidic custom), as well as transforming himself and his men into deer in order to escape the deadly plot of King Loiguire. This ancient practice of shape-changing was common among the druids as well as certain secular heroes, as we've seen. Muirchu emphasizes once again Patrick's spiritual prowess as a recognized *Christian* hero by comparing him to the resurrected Christ: "The following day, that is, Easter Day, as the kings and princes and druids were at table with Loiguire—for this was their most important feastday—they ate and drank wine in the palace of Tara. Some were talking while others were thinking about what had happened when St. Patrick, accompanied by only five companions, entered through the closed doors, as we read that Christ did, in order to vindicate and to preach the holy faith at Tara before all the nations."

Here the conflict between Patrick and the druids reaches its climax in an explosive contest of magical powers, a confrontation between the forces of good versus those of evil, epitomized by the saint and one of the surviving druid leaders:

The druid invoked demons and brought very thick darkness on the land as a sign; and they all muttered angrily. Patrick said: "Drive away the darkness." But the druid could not. The saint then gave a blessing in prayer, and suddenly the darkness was driven away and the sun shone. All the onlookers shouted aloud and gave thanks. After this contest between the druid and Patrick in the king's presence, the king said to them: "Throw your books into water, and we shall venerate the one whose books come out unscathed." Patrick answered: "I shall do so." But the druid said: "I refuse to undergo a trial by water with this man, for he considers water to be his god." (He had heard, no doubt, that Patrick baptized with water.) So the king replied: "Then agree to ordeal by fire." Patrick responded: "I am ready," but again the druid refused, saying: "This man worships in alternate years now water, now fire as his god." And the saint said: "That is not true. But you go yourself, and one of my students will go with you into a divided and closed house; while you shall wear my garment, my student will wear yours, and so you two together will be set on fire and be judged in the presence of the High God."

As is clear by now, Muirchu is portraying Patrick not only as a great Christian shaman figure, but someone who is definitely linked with fire and the earlier traditions of the Celts' worship of the sun and of the sun-god. The saint's hagiographer proceeds to tell us that Patrick's proposal was accepted, and a house was built, one half made of green wood and the other of dry wood. One of Patrick's students, a boy named Benignus, went into the dry part of the house, wearing the druid's cloak, while the druid, wearing Patrick's, went in the green half of the house. Within an hour, the druid was consumed by fire, and Benignus survived. With such wonders, the king is faced with a major decision. He tells his assembled court, "It is better for me to believe than to die." After taking counsel, on his followers' advice, he "believed that day and turned to the eternal Lord God, as did many others on that occasion."

Patrick's "Return" and His Spirituality

With the conversion of King Loiguire and his court, the saint enters the "return" stage of his spiritual journey. Patrick has overcome, through the help of Jesus and his own trust in God's power, the anguish and perhaps self-doubt that he had experienced at the death of his former master. He has triumphed over the wiles of his opponents at the court of Tara. He has vividly demonstrated his own shamanic powers. Now Patrick is ready, we can deduce from Muirchu's account, to begin his missionary work in earnest, and although he would encounter many other trials along the way, a definite turning point has been reached: "Holy Patrick, following the Lord Jesus' command, left Tara, and went forth to teach all peoples, baptizing them in the name of the Father and the Son and the Holy Spirit." As a result of his success, Patrick has now become, Muirchu tells us, "the bishop of all Ireland, if I may say so, and her illustrious teacher." Muirchu's intention as a hagiographer is not only to promote the fame of the saint, but also the reputation of Armagh, the monastery from which he writes and the city that Patrick is said to have founded. He thus goes on to give specific examples of Patrick's greatness, and, of course, by implication, the greatness of Armagh. He also reveals the saint's role as an effective evangelizer and spiritual guide when Patrick baptizes, despite the objections of her parents, a young woman named Monesan, confronts a man named Coroticus (who had appeared, as mentioned earlier, in a letter which survives) about his evil ways, and converts to Christianity a savage ruler, nicknamed "Cyclops." This latter story shows that in addition to Irish folk tales popular at the time he wrote, Muirchu was also familiar with Greek and native Irish mythology, for both Greece and Ireland had ancient myths concerning a horrible one-eyed monster who preyed upon the innocent.[14]

Muirchu is a theologian, as are all the hagiographers, giving his interpretation of Patrick's life and ministry in the context of the Christian faith. Aspects of Patrick's spirituality that can be found in Muirchu's stories are related to the hagiographer's own theological views and the values of the Early Celtic Church. The following story shows how Patrick is dedicated to prayer and especially devoted to the cross: "Concerning Patrick's constancy in prayer, we shall attempt to write down a few of many things we might tell. He used to recite daily all the psalms and hymns and the Revelation of John and all the spiritual canticles of the

Scriptures, whether he was staying in one place or traveling. He also signed himself with the victorious sign of the cross a hundred times at every hour of day and night, and wherever he saw a cross he would descend from his chariot and go out of his way to pray before it."

This practice of signing oneself in the form of a cross was an ancient Christian practice, performed for a variety of reasons: to sanctify every action of the day, to encourage oneself against temptation and conflicts, to strengthen and be reminded of one's baptismal vows, to protect oneself against the devil. That Muirchu has Patrick engaged in this devotion a hundred times "every hour of day and night" is surely an exaggeration. Patrick would not have gotten much sleep, nor would he have had much time to do anything else! Patrick's hagiographer is simply stating, through the use of hyperbole, that the saint had a deep devotion to the cross, a powerful symbol of Christ's crucifixion and triumph over death. This aspect of Patrick's spirituality was shared with his converts and fellow Celts, for the Irish landscape which had once seen only standing stones and giant prehistoric megaliths was soon dotted with tall crosses, located near almost every church. These early crosses were at first made out of wood, probably similar to the ones which are still visible at Gougane Barra marking the spot where Findbarr had his cell, on tiny "Cuthbert's Island" off the shore of Lindisfarne, or in front of Thomas Merton's hermitage today in the hills of Kentucky. Adomnan, the hagiographer of Columcille specifically refers to such a cross marking the spot on Iona where St. Columcille stopped to rest and was comforted by a white pack-horse, already mourning his approaching death. In Ireland, these simple wooden crosses were eventually replaced by the more highly detailed stone high crosses of Monasterboice, Clonmacnoise, and Kells. In Cornwall, where a visitor frequently sees stone posts with crosses carved into them, the original simplicity is maintained—in stark contrast to the large and elaborate stone calvaries found in Brittany.

Muirchu alludes to another practice associated with Patrick's spirituality in a story concerning the young boy, Benignus, who was mentored by Patrick before becoming his successor. The ascetic practice he describes was common among both Celtic saints and warriors (as we saw with CuChulainn) attempting to rid themselves of bodily lusts and anger. Perhaps what is most intriguing in the story is not so much Patrick's immersion at night in a river's cold water in order to pray, but that during his prayer he gazed up at "the wonders of heaven": the stars, constellations, and the moon's passage across the open sky—all of which, Muirchu says, "were familiar to him." Considering his own *Confessio,* as well as the depiction of him in other hagiographies, Patrick seems to have been well acquainted with nature's marvels, and highly appreciative of them:

> I will briefly relate another miracle of the holy and apostolic Patrick. At one time when he was in his usual place of prayer during the night, he beheld the wonders of heaven which were familiar to him. Wishing to test his beloved and faithful student, Patrick said to him: "Please, tell me my son, whether you experience what I experience." Then the small boy, named Benignus, said without hesitation: "I know

already what you are experiencing. For I see heaven open and behold the Son of God and His angels." Then Patrick said: "I see now that you are worthy to be my successor." At once they walked at a quick pace to his usual place of prayer. As they were praying in the middle of the river bed the boy said to Patrick: "I can stand the cold water no longer."

Muirchu seems to imply in the passage above that, although Patrick eventually had a worthy successor, Benignus did not have the same stamina (nor stature) as his spiritual mentor. The only ones with whom Patrick can readily be compared, his hagiographer implies, are earlier heroes of Judeo-Christianity.

Another story reveals not only the travel habits of Patrick and his compassion towards those in need: Muirchu's portrayal of him as a guide with amazing torch-like fingers shows his affinity to both Moses and Jesus whose bodies, like Patrick's, were physically transformed on Mount Sinai and Mount Tabor (cf. Exod 34:29 and Matt 17) as a result of their intimacy with God:

Patrick had a habit of not traveling from the evening of the Lord's night [Saturday night] until Monday morning. Once on a Sunday, when he was spending the night in a field in honor of the holy day, heavy rain and storm set in....Patrick's charioteer came to him and told him he had lost his horses and grieved for them as he would grieve for dear friends, unable as he was to search for them because he could not see in the dark. This aroused the charity of the kind father,

Patrick, and he said to the weeping charioteer: "God, a ready helper in all trials, will send help at once, and you will find the horses for which you lament." Then Patrick pulled up his sleeve, stretched out his hand, and raised it. His five fingers, like lights, lit up the surroundings, and in the light of his outstretched hand the charioteer found the horses he had lost, and ceased his weeping.

Besides reference to great heroic figures whose lives were touched by fire, this story of Patrick's amazing fingers may have had its origin among the desert Christians, when Abba Joseph, for example, after being asked by a fellow monk what more he should do to be saved, "stretched out his hands to heaven, and his fingers became like ten lamps of fire. He said: 'Why not be totally changed into fire?'"[15]

Following a story about Daire, the man who reluctantly gave Patrick land called Willow Ridge for his monastery at Armagh, the hagiographer turns to the saint's last days. In Muirchu's presentation, Patrick once again receives guidance from his angel, Victor, who suddenly appears to him in a burning bush. This allusion to the burning bush of Moses reemphasizes the Irish saint's spiritual kinship with the patriarch from the Old Testament,[16] and Patrick's own heroic stature. What we also find in the following passage is the affirmation of how much Patrick loved Armagh:

After so many miracles which have been written down elsewhere and which the world celebrates, the

day of Patrick's death was approaching. An angel
came to him about his death. He therefore sent word
to Armagh, the place he loved more than any other,
with orders that a number of men should come for
him and bring him to the place where he wished to
go. Then, with his companions, he began to make his
way towards Armagh, his beloved place, as he had
wished. Beside the road, however, a bush was ablaze,
but it did not burn down, as had happened to Moses
before. In the bush was the angel Victor, who often
used to visit Patrick, and this Victor sent another
angel to Patrick to stop him from going where he
wanted to go. He said to him: "Why do you go on a
journey without Victor's guidance? Victor calls you;
change your route and go to him." So Patrick changed
his route as he had been told and asked what he
should do. And the angel answered,: "Return to the
place from which you came (that is, to Saul)."

At Saul, located outside of the town now called Downpatrick in
northern Ireland, Patrick received, according to Muirchu, two
special requests: that Armagh would be preeminent in the Irish
Church, and that all the Irish people would be judged by Patrick
himself at the end of time. With these assurances given to him
on the seventeenth day of March [the day on which Patrick is
said to have died], Muirchu's account is concluded with mention, once more, of the angel Victor, Patrick's soul friend, and,
appropriately, the image of fire:

When the hour of his death was approaching he received the sacrament from the hands of bishop Tassach for his journey to a blessed life, as the angel Victor had told him....And the angel said to Patrick: "So that your relics will not be removed from the ground, one cubit of earth will be placed on your body." That this was done at the command of God has been shown recently, because, when a church was being built above the body, the men who dug up the ground saw fire burst forth from his tomb and retreated in fear of the flames of fire.

Patrick's Soul Friendship

Though the term *anamchara* does not explicitly appear in Muirchu's *Life of the St. Patrick,* it is found in the eighth-century *Riagail Padraic*, or *Rule of Patrick.* In it, one of the primary duties of a bishop is to be a soul friend to his people—"...a spiritual adviser to the ordained" as well as to the laity, "princes and chieftains" alike. Patrick certainly functioned in that capacity. He was Ireland's first Christian soul friend not only to individuals whom he mentored but, through his inspiration, to all those who have Celtic roots. The same Rule states that "each person who does not trust to a pious soul friend forsakes his proper guise" (i.e., his or her baptismal identity). The document implies that any holy Christian, ordained or lay, could act as a spiritual guide, confessor, or soul friend.[17]

In Muirchu's storytelling, as we have seen, Patrick's ministry of soul friendship is closely linked to the role of being a shaman or spiritual guide. He is depicted as a powerful Christian druid with the ability to transform winter into spring, darkness into light, himself and his men into deer. As a shaman, Patrick follows the "hero journey" outlined by Campbell: He leaves the security of family and friends to visit foreign shores; he faces his inner demons of discouragement and despair when his former master commits suicide; he courageously challenges King Loeguire and his druids at Tara; he goes on to minister to those who thirst for faith, meaning, hope. Patrick fulfills what Eliade describes as the shaman's essential role: fostering the spiritual growth of a community and defending its psychic integrity, its soul. This is explicitly manifest in all the years of Patrick's missionary activity, and most dramatically in his confrontation with the king and his druids. As the latter action demonstrates, Patrick's soul friendship was concerned not only with one-to-one conversions, but with broader social and political changes as well. He knew that if individuals are to grow in their Christian faith, they must have a climate, a culture which could and would nourish those values. That is why Patrick went directly to the source of political and religious power: the court where king and druids ruled. This willingness to enter the political and religious realms of pagan Ireland in order to bring about positive change certainly required a great deal of courage on Patrick's part.

The term *courage* derives from the Latin word *cor,* or heart. Courage is fearlessness of heart: a freedom from fear that gives a person the ability to act despite danger, controversy, or pain; a capacity to face challenges and conflicts rather than run from them. If we look closely at both Patrick's *Confessio* and

Muirchu's hagiography of the saint, we can see that the courage Patrick brought to his spiritual leadership had its origins long before Patrick landed on Irish shores as a missionary. It was first acquired when he, as a teenager, was abducted against his will, and taken to Ireland as a captive and eventual slave. As is typical of shamans, this experience of isolation, far from family and friends, became, for Patrick, a form of initiation into his ministry of being a spiritual guide. If "all true wisdom is only to be learned far from the dwellings of men, out in the great solitudes," as a native shaman once said, and if it is "only to be attained through suffering,"[18] it is clear that Patrick, in the solitude and loneliness of shepherding, was initiated into the mystery with which shamans discover their vocation: an experience of death and resurrection. Patrick, in effect, acknowledges this in his *Confessio*. When he arrived in Ireland, he says, "I did not know the true God," but, as he tended herds of sheep each day, "more and more my love of God and reverence for him began to increase." And he continues: "My faith grew stronger and my zeal so intense that in the course of a single day I would say as many as a hundred prayers, and almost as many in the night. This I did even when I was in the woods and on the mountains. Even in times of snow or frost or rain I would rise before dawn to pray."[19]

Reflecting back upon what would be for anyone a very painful crisis, especially for an adolescent, Patrick shows in his *Confessio* that he did not consider those years as lost time. They had taught him personally a great deal about the reality of God, and about himself. Because of them, he was able to identify the legacy of his Christian parents and ancestors as his own; to realize *for himself* the importance of Christian faith, hope, and love.

They had also taught him firsthand the hardships of being a captive, and contributed to his desire, as a missionary, to free all those held captive by even worse forms of slavery: the slaveries of ignorance, of superstition, of sin. No wonder he came to be called by others, and to call himself, "Patricius." Surely it was also during those years that Patrick learned from his apprenticeship with druid teachers not only those things that he would later use against other druids at Tara, but those aspects of Celtic spirituality and culture that could be integrated into Christianity. Whatever he brought back with him when he returned later to Ireland as a free man, Patrick seems to have realized in the depth of his being that his first time away—with all its hardships and uncertainties—had been worthwhile.

Thus Patrick's story follows that of other shamans: people who allow their own struggles and woundedness to teach them a wisdom that can eventually be used for the tribe. In the most basic sense, in fact, shamans are wounded healers, that is, those who recognize that the call to ministry often begins in unexpected places and often, it seems, in the hurts, wounds, and crises that are neither chosen nor foreseen. In no way, however, did Patrick interpret that painful chapter of his life when he was a captive as something to be buried and forgotten, and put safely away behind closed doors. This openness to learning from the wounds and crises of his life is alluded to in Muirchu's account when he describes how Patrick's family, after his escape from Ireland, insisted that he never leave them again; and how Patrick, Muirchu says, "did not consent." Patrick perhaps had already perceived, even before the significant dream of Victor calling him back, that Ireland was not done with him yet, and that his original sojourn there held intimations of his own life-work—that of helping others discover for themselves the God of true freedom, the God of love. Perhaps he knew, even before he could articulate it to himself, that the past carried gifts for him that could be used in his later ministries. In his soul he might have been aware that true freedom is found, not by avoiding past anguish and painful memories, but by bringing them to consciousness, acknowledging them, and finally, with God's help, letting go of them and moving on.

Becoming a Soul Friend

By implication, the stories describing Patrick's life and ministry reveal that the task of any soul friend, whether a person is living now or once lived in the earliest days of the Celtic Church, is that of acting as a shaman and spiritual guide, someone who facilitates transformation both for individuals and for the society and churches in which they live. A person's initiation into this vocation can begin with experiences of crisis, loss, suffering, illness, powerlessness, and yes, of wonder, too—the wonder, sometimes, like Patrick's, of discovering God's presence in the beauty of nature or in the occurrence of unexpected dreams.[20] These experiences can teach us knowledge of ourselves that includes both a realistic assessment of personal strengths as well as of human limitations. They can also open us up to the mysterious reality of God and to the entire spiritual realm that surrounds us and which touches our daily lives. The vocation of becoming a shamanic soul friend, in fact, is ultimately related to one primary experience: that of being loved by

God. As John the Evangelist writes, "Let us love, then, because he first loved us" (1 John 4:19).

With the help of God and of that larger spiritual realm which God's love encompasses, we can become mediators for others, soul friends who put people in touch with that spiritual reality as we attempt to stay intimate with it ourselves. Standing on the threshold of what for many people is invisible, we can act as doors that provide at times perhaps only a glimpse, but at least a glimpse of that reality. Like the shaman, a person in such a ministry values highly the two resources upon which Patrick relied: (1) our own life experiences, especially those which have initially opened us up to the presence of God and of our own humanity; and (2) that greater spiritual reality with its community of spiritual helpers. How can we incorporate these two resources into our spirituality and work? Patrick's life shows us ways.

First, we can begin to be more respectful of our sacred journeys and of our own "school of suffering." Since the focus of spiritual guidance is experience, and since much of that experience is touched by human suffering, soul friends must be attentive to their own experiences and pain if they are to understand and accept what others bring them. As wounded healers, we are respectful of those dark times and dark places in which our first inclination may be to run away. We are respectful of those human limitations which we may at first want to completely hide from others and perhaps, most of all, from ourselves. As shamans and spiritual guides we have come to realize, after maybe years of denial, that the broken places in our lives and personalities are where transformation happens, where intimations of God's love and compassion are found. We may, at last, come to see that our wounded nature gives us the freedom not to have to fix every problem, not to have to have all the answers, not to have to play God. To learn from suffering when it comes (as it will) can create bonds between people. It allows others to see us, not as removed from the pain of living, but deeply immersed in it; not somehow "above" their pain, but companions with them on their life journeys.

Making one's own wounds a source of healing, of course, calls for a great deal of patience and courage, a constant willingness to see our own pain as rising from the depth of the human condition which all people share. It presupposes that the human condition is such that we are all mortal and in some ways broken, and that the task of a shamanic guide is not that of taking away all pain, but encouraging it to be shared. As Henri Nouwen says in his spiritual classic on the wounded healer, "Community arises where the sharing of pain takes place."[21] A shaman or spiritual guide uses his or her knowledge of healing for others, and for confronting and challenging institutions and practices that cause unnecessary hardship and pain. Such a person realizes that any reform or changes begin with oneself.

A specific method for coming to appreciate what our human experiences, especially our wounds, might teach us is found in the practice of writing out the story of our lives. This practice has been recommended, from the ancient Greek philosophers who advised their students to keep a journal, writing in it each day and night,[22] to the modern self-help movement, Alcoholics Anonymous, which recommends writing out a Fourth Step, a "searching and fearless" inventory of one's life.[23] In some ways, St. Patrick's *Confessio* was such an inventory, a document written because of his own wounds of feeling falsely accused, and of being betrayed by an early soul friend, a man whom he describes as "my dearest friend" to whom "I had confided my very soul."[24] Writing an account of his life, for Patrick, was good for his soul. It allowed him, once those wounds were acknowledged, to accept his past, as well as affirm it gratefully for what it had taught him. Writing about our own lives can do the same. It seems to be intrinsic to the experience of being human, that we cannot change anything unless we acknowledge and accept it first.

Once we have written down our story, it is helpful to share it with someone else, preferably a trusted friend. If self-knowledge is the foundation of any spiritual mentoring or guidance we do, some degree of it can be found by this reflection on our lives, what the ancients spoke of as an "examination of conscience." This self-examination can contribute tremendously to peace with self and God, to our own soul-making. Through such storytelling, a person can begin to avoid the repetition of self-destructive patterns of behavior that may previously have characterized his or her life and work. It can also lead, as is evident in Patrick's *Confessio* and the more famous *Confessions* of St. Augustine, to a new appreciation of the mysterious ways God works in our lives. Gratitude, after all, is the virtue out of which all truly effective ministry flows—not out of guilt or shame, but out of love and, as mentioned, the experience of being loved. Patrick's ministry flowed out of this primary experience: not only his love for the Irish, and their love for him, but his belief that he was being guided by a loving power greater than himself.

The second way we can begin to incorporate the spiritual resources available to us is for us to name our helping spirits and communicate with them. We recall that Patrick frequently received guidance from angels, especially Victor who in Muirchu's account is described as "his most faithful friend of old," a spiritual guide who "foretold everything to him in a large number of dreams." Victor, as we recall, originally appeared in Patrick's *Confessio* as a dream figure, a man carrying letters from the Irish who requested that Patrick "come and walk once more among us." In Muirchu's later writings this dream figure, Victor, is transformed into an angel to whom the saint prays "a hundred times during the day, and a hundred times during the night." The two of them evidently had an intimate relationship, for as Muirchu says, "As one person talks to another, so Patrick enjoyed the angel's conversation."

A primary message, then, of Patrick's hagiographer is that it was the saint's sensitivity to the spiritual realm and his reliance upon it that eventually made him such an effective shaman and spiritual guide. Contemporary soul friends, especially those just beginning this form of ministry, need to incorporate this wisdom. Soul friends who have been acting in that capacity for years need to be reminded of it. To be a competent or gifted spiritual guide, a person does not rely upon his or her own powers alone. As a specialist in the human soul, a soul friend needs to know one's helping spirits as well as one's dark side. Such helping spirits may include those inner gifts which are uniquely ours, as well as those spirits found outside ourselves—although, in the spiritual realm, as Celts know, divisions between "inner" and "outer" lose their significance.

Some people today consider the concept of angels or other spiritual beings as superstitious and absurd. Still, there is a long tradition in humankind about guides that remain invisible to human eyes (at least, much of the time!). Tribal peoples recognize the help of spirit-guides. Ancient Greeks and Romans also believed that every person has a genius, daemon, or "heavenly twin" which provides personal care and guidance. Such "intimate friendship with that protector," the scholar Peter Brown says, "verged on the merging of their identities."[25] Other religious peoples, including the Jews, desert Christians, Moslems, and Eastern Orthodox refer to such spiritual guides and protectors as "guardian angels" to whom one should pray.

Today, despite the lingering influence of the eighteenth-century Enlightenment with its emphasis on reason and the rational for defining reality, more professional counselors and spiritual directors are beginning to acknowledge the presence of what have been termed "invisible guests," and to advocate imaginal dialogue with them.[26] Carl Jung, in his autobiography, tells of the significant help given to him not only by human mentors but by "ghostly gurus," one of whom, like Patrick's Victor, first appeared in his dreams and became an important inner guide to his understanding of the psyche or soul.[27]

Whether asleep or awake, great numbers of us have had memorable experiences of being protected or of being saved, perhaps from some sudden accident or near-fatal illness.[28] Others of us have had keen experiences of being led to the right places or the right person at the right time by some spiritual power. May Sarton, a writer famous for her journals, names that experience of synchronical "angels," and implies these spiritual beings manifest themselves at unexpected times when we most need them for our spiritual and mental health.[29] (This was certainly true of

Patrick's Victor.) Psychological evidence also shows influences at work in our sleep and in our dreams which extend far beyond the reach of ordinary conscious life. Dreams can act as doors into the unconscious; symbolic letters, like those sent from the Irish to Patrick in his dreams, demanding attention and follow-through. Jungian psychologists, among others, advocate our attempting to integrate these unconscious elements with our conscious life if we are to achieve greater maturity and some degree of serenity.

To be initially besieged by dreams that are not immediately understood is one of the signs of a shamanic vocation. As a master of thresholds, a soul friend needs consistently to attempt to understand and integrate his or her conscious and unconscious life. Dreams and the figures which they contain can provide us with resources for that integration. If we are to get to know some of those potential spiritual mentors, it is important for us to be attentive to our dreams, as Patrick was, especially those that are repetitive or filled with vivid colors, loud sounds, or memorable contents. The medieval church-man, Thomas Aquinas, equated dreams with the ministry of angels. He posited that they are one way that God communicates with us, providing enlightenment and practical direction.[30] We can receive that guidance by recording our dreams on a regular basis, and by naming certain figures in them that may be particularly intriguing or mysterious. Following Patrick's example with Victor, we could become more familiar with our dream figures, spending time with them on a daily basis. We might choose to carry on imaginative conversations with them in a journal, listening for what they have to tell us. We might draw or paint them, attempting to remember the details our dreams provide. We might simply pray to them, not only during our waking hours, but especially before falling asleep at night. Celtic Christians through the centuries approached their sleep with a variety of prayers to God, angels, and the whole communion of saints.[31] They believed that help was always available and frequently received—*spiritual* help from the *spiritual* realm. The lesson of the early Celtic soul friends and of Patrick in particular is that God's care for us is made manifest in many diverse ways, including through our angelic dream figures.

Courage and the Cross

As has by now become apparent, soul friendship is initiated by two movements that are frequently intertwined: the movement toward valuing our life experiences as revelatory, and the movement of relying more on powers other than our own. It presupposes that spiritual resources are readily available to us, especially those found in our wounds and in our dreams. It takes for granted, as other shamanic traditions do, that this ministry is not done for self-aggrandizement or personal glory, but for the well-being of a person's tribe or community. Taking this into account, a contemporary soul friend would obviously not engage in some of the more dramatic mythic aspects of the Patrician legends, such as attempting to control the weather or, as Patrick does in Muirchu's account, killing one's opponents. Control, or violence of any kind, are of course to be excluded from any form of Christian ministry that we do. While violence is usually more easily identifiable, it is "control" that is frequently more subtle in its manifestations—but sometimes even more violent in its outcome than any physical act. The psychologist, Alfred Adler, spoke of a will-to-power in all of us, while the pastoral writer, Paul Tournier, identifies and describes it as it applies to those in the helping professions. Tournier posits that counselors, psychologists, teachers, and spiritual guides, in particular, may have such a "shadow side" in which they often unconsciously are tempted to exercise power over those whom they serve.[32] While consciously we may tell ourselves that we want the best for the other, and that our motives are altruistic, the urge to exercise power, if unrecognized and thus unresisted, can lead to the unconscious practice of violence on the psyches of others, or outright physical or sexual abuse.

Controlling someone else's life is not an aim of soul friends, for it keeps those who seek our guidance from maturing; it keeps them too much dependent upon us and not enough on their relationship with God, their primary soul friend. No matter how altruistic our motives may seem, in attempting to control we fall too easily into the role of playing God—a characteristic severely condemned by the desert elders that they associated with sins of pride. Other, more recent sources would see those attempts as simply rooted in lack of trust and lack of love. "Where love reigns," Jung says, "there is no will to power; and where the will to power is paramount, love is lacking."[33] Letting go and letting God work is our primary task as a soul friend for others.

This type of ministry calls for the kind of courage which Patrick consistently demonstrated in his own work: the courage in which one seeks to liberate others from false attachments and false loves, as one liberates oneself. It is a ministry that seeks positive change for individuals and for communities. It recognizes the need to confront and challenge those people, systems, and institutional practices that are forces of darkness and injustice, including those found within our churches, towards which we may at times feel, justifiably, a great deal of anger. Such courage is not easily found. It is not a commodity that can be purchased, nor is it based upon an isolated act of the will. Courage is a quality that develops slowly, over years, along with one's character. It grows, like a plant turning toward the sun for nourishment, as a person increasingly relies on spiritual resources that are available, especially from God, the source of true freedom and light. For the Christian, examples of this courage are found not only in the lives of certain favorite saints, like Patrick, but in Jesus' life, first of all. For soul friends, the call to their vocation that begins with their own experiences of death and resurrection is visually symbolized in the cross of Christ, a symbol that is used in all our sacraments—from the first signing at our baptism to the final blessing before we are laid to rest. It can be a powerful reminder to us of how human suffering, when handed over to God, can change lives dramatically and leave a living legacy that triumphs even over death.

If we recall from our analysis of Patrick, one of the major characteristics of his spirituality was his devotion to the cross. As his hagiographer tells us, "wherever and whenever Patrick saw a cross he would descend from his chariot and go out of his way to pray before it." For Patrick, a shaman who always carried in him the wounds of his captivity, it was not simply a pious object but a genuine symbol of hope, reassuring him that God was with him, and always had been, in his pain. Patrick's courage was rooted in his spirituality of the cross. It gave him the strength to return to the land where he had been physically held hostage; it allowed him, after his former master committed suicide, to move on; it made him the great hero that he was to become. Remember how stunned Patrick was when his former master committed suicide, but how, as Muirchu says, he was given the strength to keep going, having "armed himself with the sign of the cross." When armed or strengthened by the sign of the cross, a soul friend, like Patrick, is given the courage and freedom to confront not only his or her own demons and dark side, but the greater darkness and larger demons of the society and churches in which we live.

Apostle of Ireland

The historical St. Patrick died in relative obscurity, but as time passed he and his accomplishments grew in popular imagination. Beginnings of a cult can be seen in the seventh century when, around 632 C.E., Cummian, probably an abbot of Durrow, refers to Patrick as *papa noster* (our father).[34] By 670, about the time Tirechan and Muirchu were getting started on their hagiographical writings, St. Patrick was also known in Gaul. From there, devotion to him was carried by Irish missionaries and pilgrims to the rest of continental Europe. Muirchu's *Life of Saint Patrick*, with its fascinating stories and fiery conclusion, became the basis for later Patrician hagiographies and an important reference for hagiographers writing other saints' Lives. Primarily because of the earlier writings, as well as the increasing political influence of the secular and religious leaders of Armagh, Patrick was eventually identified not only with the territory around Armagh itself, but all of Ireland. Much of Patrick's emergence as the "apostle of Ireland" was due to the art of storytelling but, as is evident from his autobiographical works that have survived, much also had to do with the genuine holiness of the man, and the Irish people's love of him. In Ireland, besides St. Patrick's Day, he is remembered in a special way each year in the pilgrimage thousands of people make up the steep slopes of Croagh Patrick, a mountain in County Mayo where he is said to have fasted and prayed. His cult is universally recognized, and a larger-than-life statue of him looks down from the heights above the high altar of St. Peter's in Rome. No one knows for sure where his body lies, though there is a huge boulder in Downpatrick, northern Ireland, with his name inscribed upon it, supposedly marking his grave. More likely, his remains are in the crypt of the Church of Ireland nearby. Armagh, however, is traditionally said to be the place that he loved the most, described by him in a later ninth-century hagiography as "a deep thorpe, a dear hill, a fortress which my soul haunts."[35] Its windswept landscape perhaps reminded him of the movement of the Spirit in his life and, when he looked back over a lifetime of ministry, of reasons for gratitude: "The Lord, indeed, gave much to me, his poor slave, more than as a young man I ever hoped for or even considered."[36] Considering the significant influence of his dream-figure, it seems fitting that the Roman Catholic cathedral in Armagh today has, in addition to numerous statues of angels, a ceiling portrait of the angel Victor who acted as Patrick's own spiritual guide and soul friend.

CHAPTER 3

Brigit of Kildare
Pastor and Pioneer

When Brigit was in a certain church and was sitting beside the door of the place, she saw a man walking in the valley by the bank of a river bent under a load. She felt pity for him and said to her nuns, "Let us go to the man and carry his load with him on our way."

Vita Prima Sanctae Brigitae

The founders of the early Celtic monastic communities were, first of all, father and mother to their members. Their very names of "abbot" and "abbess" have their origin in the terms *abba* and *amma* of the desert Christians. In many diverse pastoral roles, they attempted to take care of their community's physical and spiritual needs by performing duties appropriate to heads of large families. They were responsible for protecting the well-being of the community and the rights of individuals. They made sure that all monastic members had clothes on their backs and food in their stomachs. They directed the workers, both lay and ordained, and disciplined the recalcitrant and lazy. As the Lives show, they also welcomed guests and pilgrims with a warm embrace and water for washing their visitors' tired feet. In the midst of all these activities, their primary role was that of attending to the spiritual needs of their people, and ultimately helping each of them—no matter what their age or talent—reach heaven. For women leaders, this pastoral care was expressed in the titles their communities gave them, such as *mater spiritualis* (spiritual mother), or, simply "mother," as Hild of Whitby was affectionately called by those who knew her.[1]

Among all the founders of the early Celtic monasteries, St. Brigit is the best known, a woman whose pioneer work and pastoral leadership touched many lives. The oldest Lives speak of her natural beauty, physical and spiritual, a quality that was equated with Celtic heroes. Stories about her in the various hagiographies also portray her as someone who was frequently consulted not only by lay people, but by other spiritual leaders as well, such as Finnian of Clonard, Brendan of Clonfert, and Kevin of Glendalough. Like the desert father Pachomius,[2] she too, while being actively engaged in all sorts of pastoral duties, is found preparing food for her community, waiting at table, and caring for the sick, poor, and marginalized. While she was the patroness of learning (depicted in an ancient statue of her with a book in one hand and a quill pen in the other that is found in a little chapel near Pontivy, Brittany), it is clear that Brigit's generosity was one of the qualities that most endeared her to the people of her time. This quality is expressed in an ancient poem attributed to her that is filled with evocative images of the ancient Celts' heavenly Tir na Nog; the cauldron of their god, Dagda; and the mystical Holy Grail of later Arthurian myth:

Brigit of Kildare

I should like a great lake of ale
For the King of Kings.
I should like the angels of Heaven
To be drinking it through time eternal...
I should like the men of Heaven at my house;
I should like barrels of peace at their disposal;
I should like vessels of charity for distribution;
I should like for them cellars of mercy.
I should like cheerfulness to be in their drinking.
I should like Jesus to be there among them.
I should like the three Marys...to be with us.
I should like the people of Heaven, the poor, to be
     gathered around us from all parts.[3]

Although historical knowledge of St. Brigit is extremely elusive, since her life is so interwoven with pagan myth and Irish folklore, the *Annals of Ulster* tell us that she lived from about 452–524 C.E. As founder of Kildare and spiritual guide of both women and men at her monastery, she was considered such an important female wisdom figure to the Irish that she was named "the Mary of the Gael." She is described in an ancient Christian Celtic hymn as "ever excellent woman, golden sparkling flame."[4] This imagery of fire, a symbol of transformation and regeneration in many spiritual traditions, appears in a number of Celtic hagiographies including, as we've seen, Muirchu's account of St. Patrick. As in the stories of the medieval mystic, Hildegard of Bingen,[5] hagiographers also portray the presence of fire at crucial turning points of Brigit's life and ministry. Nuns at her monastery kept an eternal flame burning—one that was still lit, according to the pilgrim-writer, Gerald of Wales, when he visited Kildare in the 1180s, over 600 years after Brigit's death.[6] It remained lit until the Reformation, and only in 1993 was it rekindled by the Brigidine Sisters of Dara Park in Kildare.[7]

Historians, as mentioned earlier, believe that this custom of keeping a fire burning in honor of the saint may have originated with female druids residing at Kildare long before the saint arrived. Their leader supposedly was a high priestess who bore the name of the goddess Brigit or Brighid ("the exalted one"), since she was regarded as the goddess's incarnation.[8] Some also believe that St. Brigit herself was a *ban-drui,* a female druid, before her conversion to Christianity.[9] Besides linking the site of Kildare with the pagan goddess, there are other references that show how the cult of Brigit, the saint, overlapped with the earlier one. The feastday of the goddess Brighid, for example, was celebrated every February 1 on *Imbolc,* one of the Celts' four most important feasts. This was the festival of spring when the sun emerges from its winter sleep and the goats and sheep begin to produce milk for their young. After Christianity arrived in Ireland, St. Brigit's feastday came to be celebrated on the same day, while she herself was prayed to as the guardian of farm animals, of healers, and of childbirth, including midwifery. One of her legends says she was present as midwife at Christ's birth. Clearly St. Brigit's life stands on the boundary between pagan mythology and Christian spirituality.

Early hagiographies depict St. Brigit as quite different than many of the male saints whose Lives present asceticism and living in solitude as the ideal of holiness. St. Antony goes into the desert to be alone and to fight with demons; St. Martin maintains his anchoritic lifestyle even after becoming bishop of Tours; St. Benedict lives his early adult life in a cave and rolls in nettles and thorns to fight the temptations of the flesh; even St. Patrick to some degree, as is described in his *Confessio*, spends his adolescence alone shepherding on a mountaintop in Ireland. Brigit's life is not like that. From the beginning hers is associated with ministry: deeds of hospitality and generosity, of kindness and compassion. Also, unlike the legends of some of the male monastic founders, such as St. Kevin of Glendalough, she is not at all a "reluctant" spiritual mentor, but a woman who constantly draws people together because that is what she wants to do—out of love for them, not because it is her duty. One other aspect of her hagiography is quite unique. While on the continent, most early medieval hagiographies of both women and men portray female saints as models of suffering and male saints as models of action, Brigit—along with other Irish women—does not follow that pattern. She is certainly as active and effective in her ministry, if not more so, than any male saint. Like earlier stories in which pagan goddesses travel throughout Ireland in chariots,[10] Brigit's preaching and evangelizing in a chariot testifies to her own significant leadership and perception as a great Irish hero.

The earliest surviving hagiography of Brigit was written by Cogitosus (ca. 620–680 C.E.), a monk of Kildare, within 150 years or so of her death. His *Life of Brigit* contains numerous folklore stories, many of which were probably told originally about the goddess Brigit. Still, there is important historical information found in it, including one of the clearest descriptions of an early Irish monastery and church. It also provides a full discussion of Brigit's various ministries and, as we will see, of her close friendship with animals and birds. Although it provides more of a fascinating glimpse into the life of her monastery during Cogitosus's time than much historical information on St. Brigit herself, intimations can be found in his account of those saintly qualities which she brought to her work—as well as implications for contemporary soul friends.

Cogitosus's Life of St. Brigit[11]

Cogitosus begins his hagiography by acknowledging his sources and the overall purpose of his work: "I have decided to reveal without the least cloud of ambiguity a few of the many stories handed down to us by our older and more experienced brethren. From these words I hope that the greatness and holiness of this virgin of so many noble virtues will be recognized by all." Another of Cogitosus's reasons for writing, of course, was to link the legendary St. Brigit with the monastery of Kildare where he resided, expressing not only her greatness, but Kildare's. Then Cogitosus turns directly to Brigit's pastoral concerns, describing how the nun sent for "a distinguished man" to act as bishop in the community, "wishing," as she did, "to provide wisely and properly for the souls of her people." "Going herself to meet him," Cogitosus writes, "she brought him back into her company so that he might govern the church with her in his episcopal rank, and so that none of the ordained would be missing in her churches. Afterwards, he was anointed head and chief of all the bishops, and she, the most blessed abbess of all the

women. By their holy partnership and with the helping aid of all
the virtues, she built her principal church at Kildare. Because of
the talents of them both, her episcopal cathedral and monastery
spread—like a fruitful vine with branches growing in all directions—throughout the entire island of Ireland." As is apparent in
these early references, Brigit's monastery at Kildare, like numerous other monasteries in Britain and Gaul,[12] must have been a
"double monastery" consisting of members of both genders.

Having set the stage, as it were, with these preliminary
remarks in his "prologue" about Brigit's leadership, and Kildare,
Cogitosus moves to the narration of the saint's ancestry and certain of her character traits, including the pursuit of wisdom:
"Saint Brigit, whom God predestined beforehand and created in
his own image, was born in Ireland of very noble Christian parents who descended from a good and very wise race, the Etech.
Her father was Dubthach and her mother Broicsech, and from
childhood she pursued wisdom....No one can fully tell the good
deeds which she performed even at this early age, but we will
record just a few of her countless miracles and set them down
as examples."

Brigit's Many Miracles and Her Compassion

Most of Cogitosus's hagiography is concerned with miracles
associated directly with Brigit. These miracle stories do not seem
to follow any chronological order. At this stage of hagiographical
writings, such chronology was not considered all that important.
In fact, the early hagiographers, including Muirchu and
Cogitosus, consciously sought to portray the saints' personalities

as static and, for the most part, unaffected by events. These writers were not "process-oriented," as we are today, nor did they presuppose psychological "development." Rather, they valued the monastic virtue of *constantia*, and believed that the saints, as heroes and reflections of a supposedly unchanging God, should also appear unchanging.[13] Cogitosus is intent upon showing how Brigit, as another Christ, does many of the same things we find Jesus doing in the gospels. He also, at least implicitly, is calling the reader's attention to Brigit as a wisdom figure whose miraculous powers, like those of any leader with integrity, are used for service to the tribe or community.

What is interesting to note regarding traces of the "hero pattern" which can be discerned in Cogitosus's Life of Brigit is that Brigit's "road of trials," by comparison with Patrick's, begins not when she leaves home (which may be more characteristic of male heroes in the past), but precisely while she is still living there. What is also intriguing from a psychological perspective is how Brigit's first "time of testing," according to Cogitosus, occurs in the context of her relationship with her mother and not, as later hagiographies show, with her father:

> When Brigit had grown to be a young woman, she was assigned by her mother to the work of curdling (that is, making butter from the churned milk of cows) so that she might demonstrate the same competence as other women her age. With them during this quiet time she was to return as much as possible of the cows' milk and the customary quantity of butter. Brigit, however,…gave away her milk and distrib-

uted her butter to the poor and to strangers. The time came for all, including Brigit, to return the milk of the cows. When Brigit's co-workers were showing their products, Brigit also was asked to do the same. Unable to postpone the reckoning and trembling in fear of her mother because she did not have any butter to show since she had given it all to the poor, she confidently turned to God and prayed, afire with the inextinguishable flame of faith. There was no delay, for out of the goodness of his divine mercy, the Lord heard the prayers of the young woman. Just as God is a helper in unfavorable times, so he was present then, and, in response to Brigit's trust in him, supplied her with an abundant amount of butter.

In this story, Cogitosus, as theologian, is making a point that will recur throughout his hagiography that the foundation of Brigit's ministry and the source of her miraculous powers is her profound faith in God. The example she gives as a spiritual guide is rooted in the saying of Jesus which keeps appearing throughout the Life: "Everything is possible for one who has faith" (Mark 9:24). The underlying lesson of Cogitosus's stories, then, is that although Brigit is a great saint and exemplar, what she was able to accomplish can be accomplished by anyone who believes as she did, with so much trust.

Now the hagiography moves to one of the major turning points in Brigit's adult life: the time when Brigit surrenders her life to God and receives the clothing of a nun and, Cogitosus implies, of a bishop. The symbolic language found in this story confirms Brigit's leadership abilities, and affirms, through the image of the blossoming wood, her own generativity:

> Sometime later, her parents, as was to be expected, wanted to have her married. Inspired by God and yearning to devote her life to Christ in perpetual chastity, Brigit set out to find the holy bishop MacCaille of blessed memory. This bishop, divinely inspired, recognized Brigit's desire for holiness and her passionate love of chastity, and placed a white veil on her venerable head and on her shoulders a shining pallium [a bishop's garment]. Genuflecting before God and the bishop, she knelt humbly in front of the altar and dedicated her virginity to God Almighty, touching as she did so the wooden base which was the altar's foundation. This wood, in response to her outstanding virtue, turned green, and continues to grow up to the present day—as if, instead of being cut and fashioned, it still has roots. To this very day, it heals faithful people of their sicknesses and diseases.

Turning from the properties of wood which reflect Brigit's own strength and healing abilities, Cogitosus relates a series of miracle stories that are intimately connected to the saint's compassion: "I think that I also must record the strength and virtue with which this most illustrious woman is said to have served God and which is still associated with her ministry. One time when Brigit had cooked some bacon in a large cauldron for some guests who were coming to dinner, she felt compassion for a hungry dog which was begging her for food and gave it to him instead. Later, however, when the bacon had been taken from the cauldron and divided among her guests, there was more than enough to go around—as if none had been given away." Brigit's compassion, Cogitosus suggests in other stories, is not limited to hungry dogs, but includes the workers at her monastery whom she protects from a downpour of rain, and bishops whom she fed: "Once certain bishops came to her home and were her guests, although she did not have enough food for them. Generously aided by God's power (as was customary when she needed help), Brigit milked her one cow three times on the same day, contrary to her usual routine. The result was truly miraculous, for her one cow produced as much as three of the best cows might ordinarily yield."

The theological lesson that Cogitosus emphasizes with his stories of the hungry dog and thirsty bishops is that when a person is generous good things happen unexpectedly. One discovers, not that less is available when goods are shared, but that more is found precisely when they are given away. This is one of the great paradoxes of Christian faith and of human living, taught by Jesus himself when a few loaves and fish were mysteriously multiplied to feed a multitude (cf. Mark 6:30).

Cogitosus continues his narrative with one of the most famous early Brigitine stories. In the telling, he discloses an aspect of Brigit's work in which she seems frequently engaged— that of shepherding: "Once when she was feeding her flocks, as shepherds do, in a grassy meadow which was wet from the abundant rainfall, she returned home with her soaked garments. Since the sunlight was entering the house through the windows, she was temporarily blinded by the light. Thinking that a sun-beam was a wooden crossbeam, standing firmly, she hung her cloak on it, and, indeed, as if it were made from a stately tree, the cloak actually hung on the flimsy ray of sun. The neighbors of the house were amazed by this extraordinary miracle, and highly praised this exceptional woman." Although this charming story about the sunbeam may have been a quite popular motif in hagiographies on the Continent of Europe at the time Cogitosus was writing,[14] it does reveal St. Brigit's power over nature as well as her association with symbols of fire and light that earlier myths had identified with the goddess Brighid. Whatever its origins, it is a simple story that once again portrays Brigit the saint as a woman with miraculous abilities. Cogitosus states that her fame spread as the result of these miracles.

At the same time as the hagiographer tells the reader of her spiritual powers, he links them closely to Brigit's concern for the most avoided and dreaded of early medieval people: lepers. Numerous stories appear in Cogitosus's and other Brigitine hagiographies concerning Brigit's compassion toward those who suffered from an incurable disease which tragically affected many in her time: "On another occasion, certain lepers asked the venerable Brigit for beer. Although she had none, Brigit saw water that had been drawn for her bath, blessed it with the power of faith, and changed it into beer of the highest quality. She then drew it and generously gave it to the thirsty." As an Irish woman, it seems only appropriate that Brigit's miracle would be changing water into beer rather than, as Jesus had done, water into wine!

Brigit's Self-Discipline, Love for the Poor, and Friendship with Animals

By now it is clear that the heroic pattern taking shape in Cogitosus's hagiography of Brigit is different from that which is found in Patrick's. Brigit is a woman whose "road of trials," as we've seen, begins at home, not on a journey far away. As is also becoming apparent, Brigit's ministry is not battling druids and the forces of darkness as it is being available to those in need. Brigit responds compassionately to all sorts of people, even when she probably doesn't always *feel* that way. This is surely a heroic stance, and one that involves great self-discipline—even more than standing in cold water for the night, as Patrick and other male saints did. Cogitosus implicitly refers to this self-discipline when he discusses Brigit's love of the poor and her availability to them: "As the numbers of her miracles increased daily, so many that they can hardly be counted, she expressed a great amount of compassion and holiness toward the poor who begged her for alms at both opportune and inopportune times...." At this point in Cogitosus's narrative, we can see that Brigit is living out what Campbell refers to as the "return" stage of the hero's journey: when all that one has learned on life's roads (and seeming detours) is made available for others.

This theme of making herself and her wisdom available to those too often ignored by others is expressed in many of Cogitosus's stories. Brigit's deep love of the poor and of lepers (a love that must have been reciprocated) evidently included exceptional patience and generosity. Cogitosus, in fact, compares her to Job, the long-suffering figure from the Old Testament, and relates how she even gave away the fine vestments of a bishop to those who needed them more: "Brigit once donated to the poor the vestments of Bishop Conleath which he usually wore at the altars when he offered the sacred mysteries on the solemn feasts of the Lord and on the vigils of the apostles. These vestments were of exquisite beauty and had been imported from abroad. At the time a solemn feast arrived, when the most high priest of the people would customarily have donned the donated vestments, St. Brigit (who had given the original vestments of the bishop to Christ who had assumed the form of the poor) handed over in their place other vestments, similar in all respects, both in texture and in color. These substitute vestments were conveyed in a two-wheeled chariot at that very hour by Christ, disguised as a poor man, whom she clothed. Because she had willingly presented the original vestments to the poor, she received the second set to replace them just in the nick of time."

The idea for this particular narrative in which Christ appears as a poor man most likely originated in an earlier story found in the *Life of St. Martin* by Sulpicius Severus.[15] Both stories are teaching a lesson that Jesus wanted his followers to know well: "In truth I tell you, in so far as you did this to one of the least of these brothers of mine, you did it to me" (Matt 25:40–41). As this story of Brigit giving away sacred vestments shows (and other stories imply), hers is a spirituality which reflects the belief that in a special way Christ lives among the poor and among lepers, perhaps the most rejected, desperate, and filled with self-loathing of all. Like the Old Testament prophets, Brigit's actions remind Cogitosus's readers that worship of God and social justice are intertwined, and that authentic

Christian spirituality includes outreach to the poor, the forgotten, the abused, the marginalized. That no fewer than twenty-three of the thirty-two chapters in Cogitosus's hagiography have to do with her concern for the marginalized or her guests (friends and strangers alike) attests to this as a major theme in the Life.

The description of Brigit in Cogitosus's storytelling is that of a powerful founder, yet gentle pastoral woman whose time and energy are heavily invested in people's lives. There is another dimension to her personality to which certain stories allude. She, like Patrick, seems to have a strong meditative side that includes an intensely ecstatic, if not outright mystical prayer-life. She prays, however, not when removed from her active life, but while deeply immersed in her work. One story puts Brigit in the kitchen, and though it focuses on her control over a certain pet, it speaks more about the reflective side of her personality: "While Brigit was lost in meditation on heavenly things, raising, as she always did, her conversation from earthly to divine concerns, she dropped a large piece of bacon, along with some other meat, on the floor. After a month had passed, a search was begun, and the piece of meat was discovered, whole and untouched, precisely where her dog was usually found."

In addition to this story about the dog, Cogitosus supplies his readers with a number of fascinating stories which tell of Brigit's close relationship with animals. One is about her taming a wild boar, an animal which today is still being hunted in the forests of Brittany: "Once a wild and giant boar who lived in the forest became frightened and fled from its natural habitat. Driven in headlong flight, it came to a herd of Brigit's best pigs.

When Brigit spotted the boar among her animals, she blessed it, and from then on the boar, fearless and friendly, remained with her pigs. You see, brothers and sisters, both dumb animals and wild beasts could not resist Brigit's words nor her wishes, but were tamed and, obeying her, became friends."

Another story of Brigit, this time about a fox, was evidently a popular one, for not only is it is found in other Brigitine hagiographies, but the fox itself, compared to other animals in Celtic folktales, is the most frequent character that appears in them.[16] The theological point of his story, of course, is familiar: the importance of compassion in the life of every Christian. But Cogitosus knew his audience, and rather than lecture them about this truth, he clothes it in the type of story which would most appeal to his seventh-century Irish readers:

> On another occasion, when a foolish man saw a fox walking toward the castle of the king, he thought it was a wild animal. Dimwitted as he was, he was ignorant of the fact that the fox was tame, a frequent visitor to the king's court, trained in various skills, and of agile body and subtle instincts; in short, a grand and distinguished mascot of the king and his nobles. While a huge crowd watched, the poor fool killed the fox. At once, the man was denounced by those who had witnessed the deed, put in irons, and dragged before the king. When the king learned what had happened, he was enraged. He ordered the man to be killed, unless a fox, as clever as his own, were given to him in recompense. The king also ordered the man's

wife, his children, and all that he had to be reduced to slavery.

When holy and venerable Brigit learned what had happened, she felt great compassion for the miserable fool and ordered her chariot to be prepared. Grieving in her innermost heart for the poor unfortunate who was unjustly condemned, she rode along the road which led to the castle of the king, pouring out prayers to God as she passed over the flat plain. There was no delay, for the Lord heard Brigit as she continued to pray so fervently. He commanded one of his wild foxes to go to her. When the fox approached the speeding chariot of holy Brigit, it leaped up lightly and landed inside. Then nestling up under the fold of Brigit's garment, it sat tamely in the chariot with her.

When Brigit arrived at the king's castle, she began to beg that the poor fool who was being held be freed of his bonds and let go. The king was unwilling to listen to her pleas, swearing that he would not free the man unless he were recompensed with a fox as gentle and as clever as his had been. At this point Brigit brought forth her fox into the midst of the court. The fox played before the eyes of everyone in exactly the same way as the other fox had done, acting before the king and all those gathered there with the same gestures, cleverness, and docility as the first. When the king saw this, he was satisfied and, acknowledging the resounding approval of the multitude who were in admiration of this wondrous event, he ordered the man who had earlier been charged with a crime to be released and set free.

Cogitosus ends his animal stories with one about wild ducks, and then summarizes how Brigit's holiness drew both people and wild animals to her and, through her, to the God who made them all. "On another day when St. Brigit saw some large ducks swimming in the water and at times flying through the air, she commanded them to come to her. A huge flock of them, in winged formation, and apparently without fear and with great enthusiasm to obey, flew to her as if they were used to human commands. She petted them, held them in her arms for a short time, and then let them fly off through the air, returning to their place of origin....From all these miracles we can easily conclude that all kinds of wild animals, flocks, and birds listened to her commands."

Brigit's Ongoing Help

Before concluding his narrative, Cogitosus reassures his readers, as most hagiographers do, that the miraculous power of Brigit did not cease with her death. As he explicitly says: "Not only did Brigit in her earthly life, before she put off the burden of flesh, work numerous miracles, but the grace of God continued to work miracles in her monastery where her venerable body rests. We ourselves have not only heard of those miracles, but we have also seen them with our own eyes." In reference to one of those miracles, he gives us a fascinating glimpse of the church at Kildare and the liturgical life of a double monastery. His description of it reveals a finer and much wealthier monastery than the more primitive one which Brigit probably had founded over a hundred years before he wrote. (The reference to crowns suspended over the tombs was a custom that originated in the East that was also found in Gaul, including at the shrine of St. Martin of Tours):[17]

> I must also mention the miracle which occurred at the time when the church of Kildare was restored. At that time the bodies of the two saints, Archbishop Conled and the noble virgin Brigit, lay in their sarcophagi, his to the right and hers to the left of a beautifully adorned altar. These sarcophagi are richly decorated with gold, silver, jewels, and precious stones. They also have pictorial representations in relief and in colors, with crowns of gold and silver hanging suspended above them. Due to the increased numbers of the faithful of both sexes, the original church has been enlarged. Its groundplan is large, and its roof rises to a dizzy height. Its interior contains three large oratories, divided from one another by walls of timber, but all under the same roof of the larger church. One wall, covered with linen curtains and decorated with paintings, traverses the eastern part of the church from one side to the other. Two doors stand in either side of this wall: through the door on the right the bishop, with his clerics and those assigned to celebrate the holy rites, proceeds to the sanctuary and to the altar to offer the divine sacrifice

to the Lord; through the door on the left the abbess enters with her virgins and with pious widows in order to participate in the Supper of Jesus Christ, which is His flesh and blood. The remainder of the building is divided lengthwise into two equal parts by another wall, which runs from the western side to the transverse wall. The church has many windows. Priests and lay people of the male gender enter by an ornamented door on the righthand side; matrons and virgins enter by another door on the left. In this way the one basilica is sufficient for a huge crowd, separated by walls according to order, station, and gender, but united in the Spirit, all praying to Almighty God.

Brigit's hagiographer concludes his narrative with a paean to the monastic city of Kildare. Filled with enthusiasm and obviously wanting to portray Kildare in the best possible light, Cogitosus seems to compare it to the heavenly Jerusalem itself. In passing, he also refers to numerous pilgrims and crowds of people who came there to celebrate Brigit's feastday on the first of February, the day on which she died, and *dies natalis*, the true day of birth for those who have spent their lives and energies for others.

Brigit's Inner Strengths and Our Own

Celtic people's love for Brigit, the saint (combined on some unconscious level with their pagan ancestors' affection and respect for the pagan goddess), only increased the years following her death. By the Middle Ages, she was known throughout Ireland as the patron saint of travelers and pilgrims. From our vantage point she might also be considered the patron saint of soul friends, since it is with her in particular that the ancient tradition of soul friendship itself is very much identified. As her cult spread, hundreds of churches and holy wells were named after her, not only in the Celtic lands, especially Ireland, Brittany, and Cornwall, but also in such countries as Portugal, Italy, Switzerland, Belgium, Germany, and Austria. She was definitely one of the earliest female saints to provide leadership to the emerging Celtic churches and monasteries, and thus holds a special place in the history of the Irish Church. That she was the topic of the first hagiographies written in Ireland (at least, of those which have survived), and that it is a *woman's* life which was recorded says a great deal about the openness of the Christians in Ireland to women's leadership gifts, and of course her own stature. What they especially respected, Cogitosus implies, was Brigit's hospitality and generosity, creativity and endurance, all qualities especially helpful in her work as a pioneer and a pastor. By returning to some of the stories about her, other attributes that contributed to her effectiveness as a soul friend can also be discerned. If (as is true) the ancients equated the word *virtue* with inner strength, we will see that some of Brigit's primary resources were the qualities which she nurtured in herself, and which every contemporary soul friend might do.

Like Patrick, one of the first qualities of Brigit's that can be identified in the hagiography by Cogitosus is that of courage. Her name, *Brigit,* means courage or strength, and as is apparent in the stories about her, courage is, in fact, one of her greatest strengths. We see this courage manifest in a number of episodes. In an age when children and young people had no rights or identity, except what their parents gave them, Brigit overcomes her initial fears of her mother's expectations of her and gives away milk and butter to the poor. At a time when women were expected to marry, raise children, and stay home, she courageously goes in search of someone who will understand and bless the vocation which she has discerned as hers. In a society where lepers were avoided and outright ostracized, she puts one in her own chariot "so that the sick man…would not be worn out by the long trip." In a church which was increasingly coming to value fine liturgies, religious articles, and holy relics, she courageously donates Bishop Conleath's sacred vestments to the poor. Cogitosus clearly depicts Brigit as a pioneer who was not afraid to take risks that might offend long-established standards, expectations, and roles. As such, she shows women and men today that, despite the misunderstandings some people might have about their work, it is possible, even necessary, to act on one's convictions and to defend one's views.

Another strength, besides courage, which aided Brigit in her pioneer work was her commitment to collaboration. That particular quality is especially distinguished in Brigit's life and work. Intimations of it appear from the beginning of Cogitosus's hagiography (when he mentions Brigit's initiating the search for a bishop) to the end of his narrative (when he describes her church where clergy, vowed religious, and laity worshipped together "as one"). Brigit's genuine desire for collaboration is expressed explicitly when Cogitosus describes Brigit as "going herself to meet him," the new bishop, showing no reticence in making him feel welcome in his new environment, and working with him "in holy partnership." Brigit's willingness to collaborate can also be discerned in her care for her community, her availability to hungry bishops, and her presence at the court of the angry king who had lost his favorite fox. Collaboration, for the abbess of Kildare, seems to have been based upon her keen awareness of the pastoral needs of her people, and her willingness to do what must be done for their well-being. It was also based upon the belief that more can be accomplished by working together with others than attempting to do everything by oneself.

When we consider all the stories about Brigit, however, perhaps her greatest resource was her compassion—a spiritual strength that Cogitosus and other Brigitine hagiographers consistently link with her. This compassion, intimately related to the solidarity she felt with the people most neglected (the poor), the rejected (the lepers) of her times, and those without any rights at all (the slaves), surely was something she had learned as a young woman whose mother, a later hagiographer said, was a slave and whose father had banished her and her mother from his home at an early age.[18] Raised by a druid, Brigit's concern and sensitivity for the marginalized was precisely the result of her own marginalization, her own upbringing that made her keenly aware of the feelings of all outcasts. This compassion of Brigit's, however, was not just a sentimental feeling for the downtrodden—romanticizing them as heroic sufferers while doing nothing herself to help alleviate their pain. Nor was it a type of compassion that takes so much personal responsibility for other people's lives that it leaves those most affected by poverty and unjust structures out of the decision-making and real work that needs to be done to change the status quo. Rather, the kind of compassion reflected in Brigit's ministry is that of acknowledging life's suffering and injustices on this earth as *ours* —not just *theirs*—and working *together* to bring about individual and social changes.

Dimensions of this type of compassion can be found in a revealing story about St. Brigit which, although brief, contains much wisdom: "When Brigit was in a certain church and was sitting beside the door of the place, she saw a man walking in the valley by the bank of a river bent under a load. She felt pity for him and said to her nuns, 'Let us go to the man and carry his load with him on our way.'"[19] The key phrases, "his load" and "our way," of course refer to the transformation that happens when we truly respect another's burden, and rather than taking it from him or her, we help carry it "on *our* way." Again, it is clear that Brigit's compassion presupposes collaboration in which people help each other help themselves, and in that reciprocal process discover that the weight of our own burdens is mysteriously lightened as we help someone else carry his or her load. This is one of the basic principles behind the success of Alcoholics Anonymous, an organization that teaches how alcoholics and chemically-dependent people help maintain their own sobriety and spiritual health by helping others maintain theirs, especially through being a sponsor.[20]

Judging from the numerous stories about Brigit's compassion, that attribute especially seems to be the basis of her spiritual power and, along with courage and dedication to collaboration, reasons for her effectiveness as a soul friend. No wonder that a later hagiography tells the story of how, when she was asked during a ceremony to choose a particular beatitude to live by, she chose "the beatitude of mercy."[21] Despite the elusiveness of verifiable historical facts about her, in the frequency and consistency of the stories regarding these attributes we can find traces of the original historical Brigit, the saint. Other aspects of Brigit's personality found in the symbolic language of hagiography can also teach us more concerning her effectiveness, as well as about soul-friendship today.

Befriending Our Instincts

As we recall from Muirchu's account of Patrick, one of Patrick's primary resources in his work was the help he received from angels, especially Victor. In Brigit's stories, Cogitosus focuses not so much on angels as he does on the saint's friendship with animals and birds, and the trust and affection they had for her. While this emphasis in Brigit's life seems to be quite unique in its consistency, one of the most common themes that appears in the hagiographies of many of the early saints, male and female, is how intimate they are with animals and birds. In almost every saint's Life some mention is made of animals who assist the saints and whom the saints befriend or protect: Patrick defends a fawn at Armagh when his companions want to kill it; Kevin of Glendalough shelters a blackbird in her nest; Maedoc of Ferns saves a stag from pursuing hounds; and, Columcille's white horse sheds great tears at his master's approaching death on Iona.

In these hagiographies, animals are portrayed as fellow creatures of the earth who, when once befriended, become helpers to the saints, sometimes even assisting them in building their monasteries or acting as spiritual guides.[22] This familiarity of the saints with animals was possibly due to the early Celtic Christians living so close to nature in a rural environment filled with creatures like the fox, badger, boar, stag, and wolf, as well as many birds. It is certainly an aspect of their spirituality that is reflected in their writings. The *Annals of Innisfallen*, for example, note the events of 917 C.E. by saying regretfully: "...a mortality of cattle and birds such that the sound of a blackbird or a thrush was scarcely heard this year." Love of animals is also manifest in the colorful art found in the illuminated gospels, such as that of the Book of Kells where, amid the pages of whirls, spirals, and geometric circles, there are wrestling animals, writhing snakes, birds, cocks and hens, cats and fish, all painted in bright colors of wine-red, indigo yellow, emerald green, and deep ocean-blue. However it is expressed, this natural affinity of the saints with animals and birds is a quality that in the twelfth century came to be linked almost exclusively with St. Francis of Assisi whose legends were influenced by the Celtic spirituality already in Italy, brought there by the Irish missionaries, Columbanus, Gall, and others.[23]

Psychologically and spiritually astute, Cogitosus and the other hagiographers of the Celtic saints are making the point, at least implicitly, that it is wise for people, especially spiritual leaders and soul friends, to trust their natural instincts, represented by the animals and birds which appear so frequently in the early Lives. Instincts, although still not fully understood by scientists or psychologists, can be defined as predictable and relatively fixed patterns of behavior that serve and promote the survival of an animal or species. Instinctive behavior is inherited, and, for the human race, it may be an inheritance that is both physical and psychic. Among animals and birds, certain types of behavior are considered instinctive, such as food-seeking, sleep, self-defense, courtship, reproduction, and parental activities (i.e., nest-building and protecting the young). This list varies greatly from species to species. Though it is not known with certainty how many instinctive activities of animals and birds actually carry over into the human sphere, it is likely that the human race shares in many of them.[24] This should not seem surprising, especially when we take into account creation's inherent unity— manifest, for example, in the subliminal effect the passage of the moon has on the earth and the creatures which live upon it: in the movement of the tides of the oceans and our own "interior" tides, including the menstrual cycles of women and emotional cycles of men. Internally motivated in both animals and humans, instincts and instinctive behavior may be triggered by external conditions, such as the approach of an exceptionally severe winter that affects the early migration of birds and the frenzied activity of squirrels. In humans, it may be premonitions, a sense of danger or of approaching conflict that constellates the instinctive side.

Our earliest human ancestors were extremely close to the natural world physically and psychologically. Before the rise of human culture and individual consciousness, there existed what some have called a "participation mystique" in which an individual had little awareness of distinctions between oneself and one's group, or the group with its environment, especially the world of plants and animals. This physical and spiritual kinship of humankind with animals produced the phenomenon of "totemism" in which tribes identified themselves with certain animals, and believed themselves protected by them. Campbell says that these early tribes, living so close to nature, highly revered animals and birds as "tutors of humanity."[25] Eliade states that specific human qualities were identified with both wild and domestic animals and, for shamans, the majority of familiar and helping spirits are believed to take animal forms. Among Eskimos today, for example, Eliade says, "the fox, the owl, the bear, the dog, the shark, and all kinds of mountain spirits are powerful and effective helpers."[26]

With the rise of human consciousness came the creation of myths, symbols, and rituals that were used to explain the meaning of human existence and to express the mystery surrounding all of life. In the Judeo-Christian myth of origins we find Adam and Eve, before the Fall, represented as living in harmony with animals, birds, and each other. With the Fall, however, sin and separation enter the world, disrupting humanity's primary relationships to self, others, God—and the environment. Among other spiritual traditions, this disruption of humanity's intimacy with the natural world was increasingly depicted in the stories of male divinities and male heroes fighting animals and nature as forces to be conquered and overcome. This pattern also appears in the Book of Genesis (cf. 1:28), when the first man and woman are told by God to conquer the earth and "be masters of…all the living creatures." In the stories of female divinities, however, this opposition, hostility, or antagonism between man and beast is often missing. One of the most popular goddesses of the ancient world, "the Lady of the Beasts," was closer to what

118

Erich Neumann calls "the wild, early nature of man, i.e., to the savage instinct-governed being who lived with the beasts and the free-growing plants."[27] She was worshipped from India to the Mediterranean, a geographical area in which the Celtic race is said to have dominated at one time.

The goddess Brighid was a Celtic manifestation of this "Lady of the Beasts." Her feast of *Imbolc* was associated with cows, goats, and the lambing season, and besides healing and poetic inspiration, she was identified with animal husbandry and the moon—at which so many dogs, wolves, foxes, and coyotes howl. In Cogitosus's stories about Brigit, the saint, with her cows, sheep, dogs, foxes, boars, and ducks, we can see how much of the goddess Brighid and "Lady of the Beasts" reside in her. In fact all of the early Celtic saints, both female and male, are implicitly portrayed as heroes who are not in opposition to the natural world, but who, through their friendships with animals, have rediscovered the "lost world" of humanity's first ancestors: the original harmony and innocence of the Garden of Eden.

This is the underlying theological and psychological message of many of the stories of the Celtic saints and animals, especially in the stories of St. Brigit: humanity's need to recover a proper relationship with the natural world, as well as to discover harmony within by befriending the instinctive side. Those stories are also telling us today that during times of crisis or life-transition, it is especially important to pay attention to our instincts if we are not only to physically and emotionally survive, but to grow in holiness and wisdom. Relying upon our instincts is crucial to survival as a pioneer, for in positions of leadership which are being created (or rediscovered), there are not always road maps, accurate (or realistic) job descriptions, nor a great deal of encouragement from entrenched leaders who seek to defend the status quo. Whether one was a pioneer in the Early Celtic Church, like St. Brigit, or whether one is a pioneer today in our churches and society, it is frequently necessary to rely upon one's instincts. To befriend them or to allow them to befriend us is to be guided and transformed to new levels of awareness and of energy.

Listening to Our Bodies

If the animals in the Celtic stories symbolize certain helping instincts, as they did in primitive societies, which ones of Brigit's animals might be especially helpful to us and our work or ministries? How might we begin to recognize when we should be paying attention to them? Here, again, we must return to her stories and the mythological language of the Celtic hagiographies—a language of symbols and sacred numbers which was a direct inheritance from the pagan Celts. For them, like other ancient peoples who relied upon both wild and domestic animals for food, clothing, transportation, and warmth, certain animals and birds were equated with particular traits.

As we recall, early in Cogitosus's writings, Brigit is making butter for her mother from cows' milk. At other times, she is seen milking a favorite cow for unexpected guests, and later giving her best cows away to an ungrateful leper. Among the Celts, cows had great social value, and because of the necessity of milk for sustenance in early agricultural societies, including that of Ireland, a cow became a symbol of prosperity and nourishment.

For Christian Celts in the Early Irish Church, it also represented intimacy with God. In later hagiographies, for example, Brigit as a newborn child is washed in milk to show her special relationship with God, while in the Life of St. Ciaran of Clonmacnois, the hide of a white cow that had belonged to him at Clonard was said to have miraculous powers. What can be discerned in Cogitosus's stories of Brigit is that she listened to that instinctive side of herself which recognized the need to nourish others if she herself was not only to be a saint, but a whole person psychologically. This, of course, is expressed repeatedly throughout Cogitosus's account of her care and compassion for animals, birds, and for men and women alike.

What may be overlooked, however, is that Brigit also wisely understood that if she was to respond lovingly to what at times must have seemed like constant demands, she had to nourish and care for herself. This self-protective side of Brigit is expressed especially in the stories of her as being engaged in prayer and contemplation—often, it seems, when her life and schedule were filled to overflowing, as can be detected in the stories about her in the kitchen dropping meat while praying. Implied in these stories is that when we find ourselves dropping or mislaying things, when we are feeling pulled apart in all directions, when our heads ache or our stomachs are upset, it is precisely then that we should listen to our instincts of self-protection and self-defense. Disorientation, irritability, tiredness, and other physical pains can remind us that if we don't care for ourselves we will lose the ability to care adequately for others. Such symptoms of stress can reveal to us, if we listen, our need for prayer and relaxation—even though people (whether one works for church or corporation) might have exceptionally high and sometimes totally unrealistic expectations of us—or we ourselves may be operating under the illusion that we should be either perfect or indispensable.

The story of Brigit and the wild boar she befriends teaches something else. For the Celts, pork was a favorite food, and the boar in particular was especially valued and perceived as endowed with supernatural qualities. (Shape-shifting was often associated with pigs, and wild boars were believed to lead heroes to death and to the underworld.[28]) Because of its ferocity, the boar was adopted as an image of war, and was identified as a symbol of strength and power. In Cogitosus's story, we recall, Brigit discovers the frightened animal in the herd of her best pigs, and rather than attempting to expel or even kill it, "she blessed it." "From then on," Cogitosus adds, "the boar, fearless and friendly, remained...tamed." Brigit's hospitality and protection of this wild boar shows her respect for all of creation and perhaps the wildest elements in herself. It also reveals the need for us to acknowledge and listen to our own ferocity: the times when we are, perhaps without realizing it consciously, extremely angry or filled with rage. These feelings, when repressed, are frequently manifest in low-backaches, stiff necks, constipation, liver disorders, and ulcers which can literally cause us to spit blood. Such repressed feelings can lead to severe depression and, for women, can even adversely affect their reproductive organs.

If we take time to listen to the wisdom of the body, it may be that we will discover hidden, yet powerfully-destructive resentments demanding acknowledgment. It may be that we will find, if rage is not to dominate our lives, that certain things must change, perhaps ourselves. It may be that we discern that, underlying our anger, resentments, and rage, is some kind of fear—a fear perhaps of being perceived as incompetent, or a fear that our lives are meaningless, or that we are unloved. Perhaps it is that fear which forces us, like the boar in Brigit's story, from our "natural habitat"—that place of harmony in the world and of gratitude for being in it. Brigit's story teaches how an act of "blessing," of naming and accepting what the "wild boar" in us wants to tell us, can overcome all sorts of fears, and sometimes even lead to long-lasting bonds of friendship with those who were once the source of so much rage and unhappiness.

The stories about foxes and ducks which are found in Cogitosus's writings can also be interpreted in terms of instincts and the body. The story about the foxes (one which is killed by a man, and another which saves him) is a study in contrasts: between the "foolish," "dimwitted," and "ignorant" man who not only gets himself into trouble, but his entire family, and the "clever," "agile" foxes with their "subtle instincts." If the fox in legends, folklore, and fairytales is almost universally represented as a symbol of cleverness and ingenuity, Brigit's story is saying that it is precisely when we are feeling foolish, incompetent, or ignorant that we must rely upon our ingenuity (i.e., *outfoxing* those who would put us down, or our own feelings of inadequacy). This is especially true for pioneers who frequently find themselves in nerve-wracking places, uncharted waters, strange lands. Being in such situations can cause a great deal of insecurity and anxiousness, and can manifest itself physically in loose bowels, insomnia, panic attacks, and the sometimes-overwhelming desire to fill our feelings of anxiety and emptiness with food, alcohol, drugs, or promiscuous sex. We may want to flee; but we might also decide that we should stay, despite our feelings of insecurity, self-questioning, fear, or disgust. This is what the wild ducks do, in the second story, when they see Brigit and hear her invitation to remain where they are rather than flying away.

Ducks, like geese, ganders, and swans, have an ability to both walk on land and swim in water. As such, they are symbols of transformation. Those which remained with Brigit in Cogitosus's story reveal how freely choosing to stay might be, in fact, the way in which we experience personal, sometimes dramatic, change. As we recall, when the ducks did not leave, Brigit "petted them, held them in her arms for a short time, and then let them fly off through the air, returning to their place of origin." To discover the "place" where our originality and creativity are affirmed, we must learn to listen, as the ducks are said to have listened to Brigit, and then choose what it is we are to do. It is important to our self-esteem that if we choose to go to a different place or decide to take a different path in our life-journey, we do so for the right reasons.

In other words, though all instincts are inherently good, given by the Creator for a purpose, there must be some discernment of which ones to act upon and which ones not to follow. Folklore and fairytales make this point, as Bruno Bettelheim reminds us of how some animals, such as those that aided Cinderella and Snow White, can be especially helpful on one's "hero journey," and how some definitely are not. (Remember the wolf in the story of Little Red Riding Hood who—one might say—does not have her best interests at heart!) Even the birds in the story of Hansel and Gretel play seemingly contradictory roles: some of them make the children's life miserable by eating the crumbs which Hansel has strewn in the forest in order to find his way back; others actually function as guides to both of the children and help them return home.[29]

Implied in these stories is that although instincts can contribute a great deal to survival and transformation, some discernment must be made regarding our response to them. We should not blindly give ourselves over to the instinctual components in our body and soul but, rather, with the guidance of others (and our own reason and experience) decide what to rely on and what not to. Jung warns that while "loss of instinct is the source of endless error and confusion," we should not completely identify ourselves with our instincts (which appear frequently in our dreams as animals), nor should we run away from them.[30] One of the objects in therapy, according to Jung, is to make our animal instincts conscious. At the same time, he says, we should not give them boundless freedom but rather incorporate them in a purposeful whole. Unlike his mentor, Sigmund Freud, who assumed that the growth of the individual and culture consisted in a progressive subjugation of the animal in humankind, Jung insisted that a person (and society) "thrives only when spirit and instinct are in right harmony";[31] that is, when attention is paid to both soul and body, and vice versa.

When animals appear in legends or in our dreams, Jung says, discernment must also be made regarding what they might tell us about the Self: the larger personality maturing within us which is an expression of our soul.[32] In our dreams especially, the more primitive the animal, the closer it may be to the Self. Thus, it is always important to take seriously what sort of animals, birds, or even insects appear in our dreams, for they may be telling us of some critical aspect of our personality, work, vocation, or soul that is being overlooked. They may also be offering us creative possibilities we may never have *consciously* thought we had. Certainly the stories of both animals and angels leading the saints to the sites of their new monasteries or to their "Place of Resurrection" affirm the importance of paying attention to those realities in our lives, for they have an eternal dimension which we ignore at our own peril.

It is precisely in terms of the Self that Cogitosus's stories of Brigit feeding hungry dogs and shepherding sheep provide us with confirmation of her vocation as a pastor. As is apparent by now, Brigit in many ways was functioning in that capacity to the members of her community as well as to the laity and bishops whom she visited and who visited her—through her preaching, collaboration, and many acts of pastoral care.[33] This dimension of her work is only reaffirmed by the symbolic meaning of the dogs and sheep which appear in her stories. The dog, because of its domestic associations, often appears in Celtic legends and folklore (and at the feet of medieval knights and ladies on tombs) as a symbol of faithfulness. In Christian symbolism, it came to have another meaning as well, derived from the function of the sheepdog: that of guarding and guiding the flocks, "an allegory of the priest."[34]

In this pastoral context, the stories of Brigit caring for sheep are even more intriguing. The image of the sheep or ram was one of the favorite symbols of ancient civilizations, from Egypt to China to Greece and Rome—a sign of human survival and fertility. For the fathers of the early church, it represented Christ's spiritual generativity. The earliest pictures of Jesus, found in the Roman catacombs, show him as he is said to have described himself (cf. John 10:14), carrying sheep. Christians also believed that sheep as well as lambs stood for the human soul which, as Jesus said, was so worthwhile that he would leave the many to find just one which was lost (Luke 15:3–7). Since Christ's time, of course, shepherding has been consistently identified with the work of being a pastor—a person whose time and energy are given for the care and spiritual nourishment of others.[35] It is significant, then, that Brigit is depicted by Cogitosus as a young woman frequently engaged in shepherding, especially because this activity in the Old Testament was primarily associated with men, and among many ancient peoples was considered a task too harsh for women. Whether this was also true among the early Celts, we do not know. Still, whether Irish women cared for sheep or did not, Cogitosus is making the point with his portrayal of Brigit as a shepherd that she too, like Christ, the Good Shepherd, was engaged in pastoring. This care of souls—as humanity's long and ancient spiritual traditions and Brigit's own life remind us—is not limited by race, gender, or sexual orientation.[36]

Whether female or male, lay or ordained, all of us are in need of befriending our instincts, listening to our bodies. The problem, of course, in humankind's history is that the human body and the instincts, along with women in general, have been denigrated for so long and so severely. Brigit's stories, and those of the other Celtic saints, remind us of the need to reclaim the instincts and the body as sources of true knowledge and genuine spiritual wisdom. Women in our own times have been in the forefront of proclaiming the inherent wisdom of the body, but increasingly men are discovering the value of their "wild side" as well.[37] Great numbers of people have been raised by the principle of mind over matter, which intrinsically presupposes domination of the body by our intellect, our minds. Many of us have discovered that such attempted subjugation of the body can lead to dire consequences in terms of physical and spiritual health. Military formation programs, and other types of programs such as Outward Bound, however, have long recognized the value of teaching their recruits to trust their instincts, their bodies, their "guts," and so have shamanic traditions, ancient and contemporary.[38]

Integrating the Spiritual and Physical Realms

Although Brigit probably never met Patrick, since he died in 461 C.E. and she wasn't born until about 452 C.E., both leaders had a significant effect upon the growth of Christianity in Ireland. Both are also linked closely together in legend and popular affection. Through the stories of their hagiographers, both emerge as pioneers, pastors, and as the Celtic scholar Louis Gougaud says, "incomparable spiritual guides to souls."[39] In Muirchu's account, Patrick is depicted as a Christian druid and evangelizer who made a significant impact on the political and religious institutions of the pagan Celts. Brigit, Cogitosus reveals, was also a shamanic figure who not only could miraculously churn endless vats of butter and change water into beer, but more importantly could heal people of physical and deep psychological pain. Both saints undergo and survive their own "road of trials," and both seem to welcome the challenges they face as pioneers, neither stopping to complain nor engaging in a great deal of self-pity.

There are important differences, however, in the stories about them other than the shape of their own road of trials. While Patrick dramatically battles discouragement, death threats, and in Muirchu's account at least, the dark powers of the druids, Brigit spends her time engaged in the more ordinary routine of milking cows, shepherding, and cooking meals, in effect responding to the needs of all sorts of people at "opportune and inopportune times." While both preach extensively when it comes to their ministries of evangelization, Patrick appears to be less patient, more willing to curse or destroy his enemies than Brigit, who seems more willing to go the extra mile. Muirchu as a storyteller emphasizes Patrick's extraordinary powers in his confrontation at King Loeguire's court, representing what might be considered the political dimension of Christian ministry, while Cogitosus focuses upon Brigit's healing and compassionate acts, many of which were done one-to-one. Despite these differences in focus and ministerial approaches, both saints are concerned with the conversion of people, and in that context take seriously every person they meet. Both place their ultimate trust not in their own powers to transform institutions and human hearts, but in God's.

Although most of us today would reject any stereotyping in which men are equated solely with political-social activities and women exclusively with home and/or one-to-one ministries, what the mythic language of the stories is teaching is the need for each of us (no matter what our gender, or what work calls forth our energies) to accept fully both the spiritual and physical sides of our humanity, symbolically represented by the saints' close friendships with angels—the creatures of the heavens—and animals and birds—the creatures of the earth. Like Adam and Eve in the Garden of Eden, Brigit and Patrick had knowledge of both realms, and were intimate with each. This harmony with God, the earth, and themselves reveals how the vocation of the soul friend, as much as it might be linked with marvelous powers of transformation, is very much based first of all upon uniting one's life with God, while being in touch with both our angels and our instincts. As Patrick's stories encourage us to learn from and to integrate our experiences, Brigit's stories advise us to listen to our bodies and be attentive not only to our external surroundings, but to our interior tides.

Shining Lamp

St. Brigit's feastday, as mentioned earlier, is celebrated February 1. Except for a round tower, a restored medieval cathedral, and the foundations of its firehouse, little remains now at Kildare of that glorious monastic city of which Cogitosus wrote so enthusiastically. What does remain, as the recently rekindled fires there express, is the reputation of Brigit as a powerfully compassionate woman with many leadership traits. An authentic human being, she was above all a pastor and a pioneer, the kind of person who, according to Thomas Merton, has the capacity, while creating new institutions, of existing outside of them; someone who has within herself or himself the resources for affirming one's own identity *and freedom* in any situation, controversy, or conflict.[40] In that light, in the context of her freedom to create and to respond with compassion, Brigit continues to be, as a medieval hagiographer described her, "a shining lamp" to countless generations, especially our own.

The stories of Patrick and Brigit in the preceding chapters have provided us with examples of how shamanism, spiritual guidance, pastoring, and pioneer work can be effective expressions of soul-friend ministry. In the next chapter, Adomnan's *Life of Saint Columba* (or Columcille, as he is called in Ireland) will show how teaching and tutoring are also important *anamchara* roles.

CHAPTER 4

Columcille of Iona
Teacher and Tutor

Columba never could spend the space of even one hour without study, or prayer, or writing, or some other holy occupation....From his boyhood he had been brought up in Christian training in the study of wisdom.

Adomnan's *Life of St. Columba*

The great monasteries which Brigit and the other pioneer saints established in the Early Celtic Church were dedicated to the education of young leaders, women and men, in religious and secular life. The pagan Celts in Ireland and throughout Europe already had a highly-developed fosterage system in which children of the tribe were frequently brought up by another family or tribe. They believed that such exchanges strengthened alliances between them, as well as introduced each child to a wider world of learning. When Christianity arrived, it did not seem unusual for their children at an early age to enter the monastic schools to be educated—boys from about the age of seven to seventeen, and girls from seven to thirteen. Relationships created between fosterer and fostered, teacher and student were recognized as among the most sacred of bonds. According to their legal traditions, the teacher owed the pupil "instruction without reservation and correction without harshness"; in return, the pupil was obliged to help the teacher against being impoverished, and to support him or her, if necessary, in old age. At the monastic schools, lay people not only received an excellent education, but were important teachers in their own right, for according to J. M. Flood, "nearly all the poets, physicians, lawyers, artists and historians were laymen."[1] Through their skills and dedication, Christian Ireland in particular kept the classical heritage of the Greeks and Romans alive, as well as the ancient pagan Celtic heritage of legends and stories that had been preserved orally by the druids, bards, and poets.

In the writings of the hagiographers, the Celtic saints appear as creative teachers and talented tutors who took their vocation very seriously. Their first students came to them, as had those of the desert Christians, drawn by the saints' reputation for holiness and their own yearning for wisdom. The lessons they learned, of course, were not taught in fine buildings or large classrooms, but in the open air on the sides of mountains, near glistening lakes, along windswept seashores, or in the shadows of oak and pine trees. Inspired by their own druid mentors, and Christ himself, the saints as teachers believed that all study had a spiritual dimension, and that their students' learning did not end with the completion of a certain number of courses, but was part of a lifelong spiritual quest. As instruction became more formalized, teachers and students studied together in their tiny cells of stone or wood. The course of education they followed was divided into seven stages or, as they were called, "seven degrees of wisdom." A student who had passed through to the highest grade was known as an *Ollave*, or *Doctor*. Their subjects included the study of Scripture, music, astronomy, poetry, the classics of Greece and Rome, and the writings of the early church fathers, especially those of Cassian, Jerome, Ambrose, and Augustine.[2] As a result of these years of learning and the experiences they shared, some of the students became lifelong soul friends, not only with each other but with certain teachers whose affection and encouragement they remembered gratefully.

Study was highly valued in the Early Celtic Church, as an early monastic Rule makes clear: "The kingdom of heaven is granted to the person who directs study and to the one who studies and to the one who supports the pupil who is studying."[3] Education was seen as involving teachers, students, foster and natural parents in a community of learning that was, for all of them, ultimately related to the reign of God and salvation of their souls. Such a conviction surely contributed to the effectiveness of the teaching that was done in the monasteries and to the commitment of the teachers themselves. By the late seventh century, the Irish monasteries especially were known for their hospitality and generosity toward foreign students, many of whom traveled to Ireland from Gaul, Germany, and England to study. As the Venerable Bede explains, "The Irish welcomed them all gladly, gave them their daily food, and also provided them with books to read and with instruction, without asking for any payment."[4] Another Englishman, Aldhelm of Malmesbury, writing about 686–690 C.E., complains that his native land should publicize its own worthy teachers, especially since

"Ireland teems with lecturers, who are as numerous and bright as the stars in the sky."[5]

Numerous saints are shown to have had this dedication to study and writing, manifest in their great eagerness to write and to possess books. In one of the later Lives of Columcille, the dearest wish of his colleague, St. Cainnech, seems to have been a church filled with books. There are frequent references in other Celtic Lives to books that remain unharmed by water. Some of these books were believed to have healing properties; some, according to Gerald of Wales, were considered to be "the work, not of men, but of angels."[6] What is apparent in all the Lives of the saints, in and outside of Ireland, is their obvious passion for learning, and the intense feelings of spiritual kinship established between teachers and students which lasted a lifetime—and beyond. The hagiographers also reveal, above all, the integrity and commitment of the teachers themselves. The saints taught most often by the quiet example of their lives which made a far greater impact on their students than any proselytizing they might have done or tutorial methods they might have used. As Bede said of Aidan of Lindisfarne (ca. 600–651 C.E.), who brought Christianity from Iona to Northumbria: "The best recommendation of his teaching to all was that he taught them no other way of life than that which he himself practiced."[7]

Of all of Ireland's bright stars, Columcille was perhaps the most brilliant teacher and tutor, recognized for his intellectual and creative gifts. A protégé of Finnian of Clonard (d. 549 C.E.), Columcille, in particular, is described in an Old Irish hymn as "the tutor" who "used to sow the word of teaching," and who, as a scribe and scholar, wrote "three hundred bright, noble books."[8]

The earliest poem about him, the *Amra Choluim Chille* ("Eulogy to Columcille"), composed about 600 C.E., a few years after his death, describes him as "a perfect sage with faith in Christ." These are a few of the poem's more striking stanzas:

> He numbered the stars of Heaven,
> this teacher of all things,
> this Dove, this Columcille....
> Sages held him close to their hearts.
> He was our jewel....
> He was sweet to listen to.
> Being a priest was but one of his callings.[9]

Like Patrick and Brigit, Columcille appears in hagiographies as a powerful shamanic figure and pioneer. Educated by druids, he addressed Christ as "my Druid," founded monasteries located in the midst of oak trees, and eventually settled on the island of Iona, called the Isle of Druids and of Dreams.[10] Considered one of Ireland's greatest poets, writers, and storytellers, his life reflects a spirituality that deeply valued learning, while his personality brought many diverse talents to his work as a teacher, tutor, and soul friend.

Columcille of Iona

Columcille, or Columba, as he is called in Britain, was the founder and first abbot of the monastery on Iona, a tiny island located off the western coast of Scotland. He was born in Donegal, Ireland, December 7, 521 C.E., into a clan which traced its origins to Niall of the Nine Hostages, a king who ruled the island from 379 to 405. Because of this royal lineage, some biographers believe that Columcille could have become a High King of Ireland if he had not become a monk. He did not choose to pursue a secular political career, however, but a monastic vocation, receiving the name Columcille, which means "dove of the church." (*Columba* simply means *dove*.) Some say that his secular name was Criomhthann, the fox [11]—an intriguing possibility considering the traits with which that animal is associated, *and* the controversy concerning Columcille's later decision to leave Ireland at midlife. As a youth, he studied under a variety of ordained and lay mentors. His earliest teacher was a priest, Cruithnecan, who baptized him and whom Columcille's hagiographer describes as his *nutritor,* or "spiritual provider."

Gemman, a Christian bard in Leinster, is said to have been Columcille's tutor when he was studying as a deacon. The latter may have inspired the younger man to pursue his own gifts in the areas of poetry and storytelling. (In his maturity, Columcille was identified as patron and defender of all the bards in Ireland at a time when they were being attacked.) Finnian, the founder and abbot of Clonard, was an especially close mentor who taught Columcille before he was ordained a priest. A story about Finnian which appears in the *Book of Lismore* relates how Columcille's friend foresaw, as sensitive and intuitive teachers do, the future greatness of at least two of his students: "Once a vision appeared to Finnian in which two moons arose from Clonard, a golden moon and a silvery moon. The golden moon went into the north of the island, lighting Ireland and Scotland. The silvery moon went on until it reached the Shannon, lighting the center of

Ireland. The first, Finnian realized, foretold Columcille's wisdom and the grace of his noble family; the second had to do with Ciaran's monastery at Clonmacnoise, and his many virtues and good deeds."[12] This vision also foretold, of course, how Columcille would be claimed by both Irish and Scots as their special saint when he left Ireland for Iona at the age of forty-two.

Before his departure in 561 C.E., Columcille was very involved in pastoral ministry and evangelization in Ireland. After his ordination at Clonard, he moved about the island founding numerous monasteries of his own, the chief of which were Derry in northern Ireland and Durrow in the midlands. He may also have established monastic communities at Kells, Swords, Drumcliff, and Glencolumcille. Some of the sites of these monasteries already had druidic associations; all became recognized for their teaching, spirituality, and art. The Books of Durrow and Kells are two of the finest extant examples of illuminated gospels in the Celtic Church, and the high crosses of Durrow, Kells, and Drumcliff still reflect, despite the passage of centuries, vital aspects of Celtic spirituality. It is unclear why Columcille decided to leave such a seemingly successful ministry when he did, sailing for Scotland and settling on Iona. Certain legends say that he left because of a copyright dispute with a different Finnian, the abbot of Moville. The conflict with Finnian supposedly had to do with Columcille's copying a beautiful book of psalms without the abbot's permission, and then refusing to hand over the copy he had made. When the matter was taken to the king, Diarmaid mac Cerbaill, the latter judged in favor of Finnian declaring, according to the story, that "to every cow belongs her calf, to every book, its copy." A battle ensued in 561 between Columcille's tribe and the king's near Drumcliff when he refused to return the book. A synod was then called which resulted in the saint's condemnation. Columcille's soul friend, St. Molaisse (or "Laisren"), abbot of the monastery on Devenish Island, sent him into exile to do penance for his dishonesty and to make reparation for the loss of so many lives. None of this story, however, can be historically verified.

Whatever the reason for Columcille's move, he landed on the shores of Iona in 563 where he founded a religious community, acted as its head, and became a missionary to the Picts in northern Scotland. From the poetry and stories about him which have survived, it seems he never did get over his homesickness for Ireland. His yearning, especially for his beloved cell at Derry, located in an oak grove and surrounded by angels, is expressed in an early poem attributed to him:

> If mine were all of Alba [Scotland]
> From the center to its border,
> I would rather have space for a hut
> In the middle of fair Derry.[13]

Columcille is said to have made at least one journey back to his beloved Ireland to visit his monks and former students before dying on Iona in 597 C.E. at the age of seventy-six.

Adomnan's Life of Columba[14]

Although the Venerable Bede in his *Ecclesiastical History of the English People* (completed in 731 C.E.) never acknowledges the existence of St. Patrick, he specifically mentions Columcille by name and praises him for being "a true monk in life no less than habit." Bede also says that "he left successors distinguished for their abstinence, their love of God, and their observance of the Rule."[15] One of those successors, Adomnan, the ninth abbot of Iona (679–704 C.E.), wrote the earliest Life we have of Columcille, probably in the late 680s, about the same time Muirchu was completing his hagiography on Patrick. Adomnan's writing provides rich descriptions of Columcille's creative personality, his mystical connection with the land and sea, his love of learning, and his great capacity for friendship. It also gives us glimpses of the political, social, and religious life of the Irish and Picts in the sixth and seventh centuries. Richard Sharpe says that this Life "is a source of the first importance for the early history of Ireland and Scotland" and calls it "the most engaging of the Lives of the Celtic saints."[16] As we begin to examine the content of Adomnan's hagiography in order to gain a better understanding of the saint's role as a teacher and soul friend, for the sake of consistency we will use the name "Columba" which his hagiographer preferred rather than that of "Columcille."

Adomnan begins his *Life of Saint Columba* by stating his purpose for writing, that of placing "before my readers' eyes an image of his holy life," thus hoping to inspire them to follow the same path of holiness and wisdom as that taken by the saint. He then proceeds to give a quick overview of Columba's life, listing the biographical data and qualities of the saint he believes most pertinent, including Columba's "study of wisdom." He also refers to Columba as living on Iona for thirty-four years "like a soldier of Christ"—an ideal of Christian holiness connoting strength, commitment, and endurance, that is found in the earliest writings of the church, including the Apostle Paul's, and in the hagiographies with which Adomnan was probably familiar: those of St. Antony of Egypt and St. Martin of Tours.

At this point in his writing, Adomnan openly directs his readers' attention to Columba's spirituality: a daily routine that included study, writing, and prayer. What stands out in this brief description is that Columba's ascetic lifestyle did not produce a somber saint, but a person filled with joy whom others obviously perceived as a friend: "Columba never could spend the space of even one hour without study, or prayer, or writing, or some other holy occupation. So incessantly was he engaged night and day in the unwearied exercise of fasting and watching, that the burden of each of these austere practices would seem beyond the power of all human endurance. And still in all these activities he was beloved by all for a holy joy shown continuously on his face, revealing the joy and gladness with which the Holy Spirit filled his inmost soul."

As in Cogitosus's hagiography of Brigit, the stories which follow Adomnan's preface are not placed in any definite chronological order in the saint's life. Rather, they are grouped according to specific topics or "books." Book I is entitled "Of His Prophetic Revelations," and lists some fifty occasions in which Columba manifested his extraordinary psychic powers of prophecy. Book II, "On His Miraculous Powers," explores, in forty-seven chapters, the amazing miracles linked with Columba's ministry. Book III, "The Apparitions of Angels," shows him constantly, like Patrick, in the company of angels throughout his life and at the time of his death.[17] This book contains stories specifically related to Columba's birth and early years. In order to establish some sense of chronology, we will start with Book III and then move to those stories from the other books which shed light on Columba's personality and ministry.

Columba's Intimacy with God, and a Crisis in His Life

The account of Columba's birth is one of the most vivid and colorful of any Celtic saint's. Adomnan's literary inspiration here is the Bible, especially the scriptural passages related to the angel Gabriel who announces Christ's coming to a startled virgin, Mary (cf. Luke 1:26 ff.), as well as the Old Testament story of Joseph's unusual coat (Gen 37). In echoing these early stories of the angel and the coat which symbolize the specialness of each and God's love for them, Adomnan suggests Columba's uniqueness:

> On a certain night between the conception and birth of Columba, an angel of the Lord appeared to his mother in dreams, bringing to her, as he stood by her, a certain robe of extraordinary beauty, in which the most beautiful colors, as it were, of all the flowers seemed to portray. After a short time he asked for it back, and took it out of her hands. Having raised it and spread it out, he let it fly through the air. She was sad at the loss of it, and said to that angelic man, "Why are you taking this lovely cloak away from me

so soon?" He immediately replied, "Because this mantle is so exceedingly honorable that you cannot retain it very long." When this was said, the woman saw that the cloak was gradually receding from her in its flight. Then she saw that it expanded until its width exceeded the plains, and that in all its measurements it was larger than the mountains and forests. At that she heard the following words: "Woman, do not grieve, for you will bring forth a son to the man whom you married of so beautiful a character that he will be considered by his own people to be one of the prophets of God. Your son has been predestined by God to be the leader of innumerable souls to the country we call heaven."

From the beginning, then, Columba is depicted as destined to be a powerful spiritual leader whose life is especially guided by God. In a following episode Adomnan reinforces this theological statement about Columba's intimacy with God by describing yet another incident in which his hero's leadership is affirmed. In the same story, he makes reference for the first time to a critical period in Columba's adulthood. Although Adomnan does not tell us why Columba had been excommunicated, the cause may in fact be found in the legends mentioned earlier regarding the issue of copyright and the ensuing battle. Whatever the reason, Brendan of Birr's vision affirming Columba's holiness probably couldn't have come at a better time:

After the lapse of many years, when St. Columba had been unjustly excommunicated by a certain synod for some pardonable and very trifling reasons, he came to the same meeting convened against himself. St. Brendan, the founder of the monastery which in the Scotic [Irish] language is called Birra [Birr], saw him approaching in the distance. He quickly arose, and, with head bowed down, reverently kissed him. Some of the elders in that assembly, when they had left the rest, accused Brendan directly: "Why did you not decline to rise in the presence of an excommunicated person, and why did you kiss him?" Brendan replied to them: "If," said he, "you had seen what the Lord has graciously revealed to me this day concerning this chosen one, whom you dishonor, you would never have excommunicated him. For Columba is a person whom God not only does not excommunicate, according to your unjust sentence, but more and more highly esteems…." When he had said this, they stopped bothering him, and…treated him with even greater respect and reverence.

Adomnan does not give us any further information about what must have been a most difficult episode in Columba's life but ends the story of Columba and Finnian with an intriguing statement that seems to link the synod's excommunication of Columba with what Maire Herbert describes as "the main event"[18] in Columba's life: "About that same time Columba, with his twelve disciples and fellow-soldiers, sailed across to

Britain." Considering that there is no particular chronology to the events in Adomnan's hagiography, *and* that he seems to want to avoid any hint of imperfection or wrongdoing on Columba's part, it is difficult to trace the stages of Campbell's "hero journey" in the saint's life. But here, in the mention of Columba's excommunication and move to Iona, we have intimations of the saint's "call to adventure" and his entry into his own "road of trials." Whatever happened that caused accusations to be leveled against the saint, it was surely not a pleasant time for him.[19] His adventure begins in the agony of being perhaps falsely accused, and his road of trials is the exile he embraced when he left his homeland, friends, students, and colleagues for an unknown land.

Considering Columba's great love of friends, it must have been an especially harsh form of suffering, and thus the name "white martyrdom" that was applied to his missionary travels and stay on Iona seems most fitting. Columba's story, however, has its brighter side, for it reveals how sometimes dramatic (and traumatic) decisions made at midlife can usher in not only a new stage of life, but a new phase of leadership and ministry. Such, at least, was true of Columba when the other stories in Adomnan's Life are taken into account.

Columba's Road of Trials

From the first book to the last in Adomnan's storytelling, we find a man who does not allow his trials and difficulties to depress him, but to become occasions for transformation. Still, as in the stories of other heroes and saints, there are many conflicts, challenges, and fearsome adversaries that Columba has to face. Yes, he does have the power to perform the same miracles as Jesus did. Adomnan points this out in the opening lines of Book I when he says that Columba, "by virtue of his prayer, and in the name of our Lord Jesus Christ," healed people of various diseases, expelled "innumerable hosts of malignant spirits" from Iona, raised to life a dead child, and had control over the "surging waves, at times rolling as high as mountains in a great storm." But Columba also faced opposition from the religious leaders of his time, from monsters of the deep, the forces of nature, and perhaps most especially his own dark side, represented by his battle with certain demons. In Adomnan's account, it is clear that Columba—with the help of God and other spiritual resources—meets all these challenges confidently and without fear.

Some of his most difficult adversaries, like those of Patrick, were evidently the pagan druids who, in terms of religious influence, probably had the most to lose, and thus were the most hostile to him. Frequent mention is made of them, primarily when Columba is on his missionary journeys to Scotland. Still, King Brude and his tribe, including his druid advisers, were eventually converted as a result of Columba's persistence. Human foes, however, were not the saint's only worries. In some ways, as the following story about a mysterious water creature demonstrates, they may have been the least of his concerns.

> On another occasion, when the holy man was living
> for some days in the province of the Picts, he was

obliged to cross the river Ness. When he reached the bank of the river, he saw some of the inhabitants burying an unfortunate man, who, according to the account of those who were burying him, was a short time before seized, as he was swimming, and bitten most severely by a monster that lived in the water. His wretched body was taken out with a hook by those who came to his assistance in a boat. Columba, on hearing this, directed one of his companions to swim over and row across the coble that was moored at the farther bank. Lugne Mocumin, hearing the command of the excellent man, obeyed without the least delay, taking off all his clothes, and leaping into the water. But the monster, far from being satiated, was only roused for more prey. Lying at the bottom of the stream, it felt the water disturbed above by the man swimming, and so suddenly rose to the surface. Giving an awful roar, it plunged after him, with its mouth wide open, as the man swam in the middle of the stream. Columba observed this, raised his holy hand—while all the rest, brethren as well as strangers, were stupefied with terror—and, invoking the name of God, formed the saving sign of the cross in the air. He commanded the ferocious monster, saying to it, "You will go no further; do not touch the man; go back with all speed." At the voice of the saint, the monster was terrified, and fled more quickly than if it had been pulled back with ropes....

This story is one of the most fascinating adventure tales that Adomnan tells about the saint. It is the first documentary report of the infamous Loch Ness monster, a mysterious water creature that continues to be the subject of television programs and newspaper accounts. Stories about giant fish or serpents may be inevitable in any collection of Celtic legends since so many streams and lakes were associated with such creatures. That such a well-known monster appears in Adomnan's account, however, speaks highly of the saint's reputation for bravery—and Adomnan's own skill as a hagiographer who wisely knew how to enliven his recollections of the saint.

Other stories in this section of the Life relate Columba's battle with the elements which threatened his own and his men's lives and, like Jesus' calming the waves (cf. Matt 8:23–27), his standing up in the prow of the boat, stretching out his hands to heaven, and praying to the Almighty One, after which "the whole storm of wind and the fury of the sea ceased more quickly than can be told, and a perfect calm instantly ensued." Like Abba Antony in the desert and Cuthbert on Farne Island, Columba must also battle demons who are associated with the color black.[20] "Countless though they were," we are told, they "could not vanquish him, nor was he able, by himself, to drive them from his island until the angels of God came to his aid—as he later told certain persons, few in number." These lines of the story reveal the saint's human vulnerability so that, despite all of his psychological maturity and spiritual power, he still had to call upon "outside" resources to drive the demons away. As will be apparent in other stories about Columba, here in the reference to angels we find one of the saint's primary spiritual resources. Columba overcomes his opponents with the help of a power greater than himself. Also implied in Adomnan's stories of Columba is that, as much as the saint was able to withstand all of these trials and temptations, he learned from them a wisdom which he shared with others.

Columba's Love of Writing and His Divine Intuition

Although there are no specific events in Adomnan's narrative in which one can trace a precise "return" stage in the spiritual journey of Columba, we find it implicitly in the writing, teaching, and spiritual direction he gave while living on Iona. Of all the stories found in Adomnan's account, there are more associated with Columba's life and ministry on Iona than anyplace else. Over a third of Adomnan's stories refer specifically to the last thirty-four years of the saint's life after he had reached that tiny island in 563 C.E. The members of the community which Columba founded on Iona were addressed by him as his *familia*, a chosen group of men who were as close to him as any family might be. This community would have included three types of members: the "seniors" or "elders," "working brothers," and *alumni*, or pupils, a number of whom evidently received their training directly from Columba. Some are mentioned specifically by name, such as Virgnous, "a youth of good disposition," who, on a cold winter night, observed Columba engulfed in a golden light while he prayed, and another by the name of Berchan who is described as "a pupil learning wisdom." In the midst of a very active missionary life, a consistent characterization of Columba is his sitting in his cell writing assiduously or happily immersed in a book. He seems to have had a great love of reading and a deep respect for books, traits that he passed on to his students. Throughout Adomnan's hagiography of the saint, Columba is shown to be a prolific writer and scribe. Although we do not know precisely how many books Columba actually authored,[21] his hagiographer implies that, in the midst of his work as a missionary, confessor, and spiritual guide, Columba wrote a lot. This passion for writing, however, seems to have been frequently interrupted by guests coming to the island. In numerous stories Adomnan emphasizes that, along with his love of books and writing, Columba cared deeply, as a pastoral leader would, for students and colleagues, visitors, and fellow-monks.

Adomnan also frequently alludes to the saint's extraordinary psychic or prophetic powers: his ability to read accurately the signs of the times, and thus to discern astutely the shape of the future. He considers Columba's prophetic powers so important to understanding the saint's life and work that he devotes an entire book in his hagiography to an exposition of them. Those abilities seem to have been with Columba since his birth; they were certainly manifest from his earliest years:

> Among the other miracles which this same man of
> the Lord, while dwelling in mortal flesh, performed
> by the gift of God, was his foretelling the future.
> From his early years, Columba was highly prophetic,
> with an ability to make known to those who were
> present what was happening in other places. Though
> absent in body, he was present in spirit, and could

look on things that were widely apart, as St. Paul said, "He that is joined to the Lord is one spirit." Thus, St. Columba, when a few of the brothers would sometimes inquire into the matter, did not deny that by some divine intuition and through a wonderful expansion of his inner soul he beheld the whole universe drawn together, revealed to his sight as if in one ray of the sun.

This passage about Columba's "divine intuition" is crucial to understanding the saint's mysticism as well as his charism as a teacher and tutor.

On numerous occasions Adomnan relates this divine intuition of Columba's to visions and voices of angels. None of the angels in his account are given a specific name, as in the case of Patrick's Victor, but the intimacy between saint and angels is clear. One story in particular reveals not only Columba's friendship with the angels, but how an inquisitive monk learned from Columba about the unexpected wonders of solitude, as the desert Christians had maintained.

On another occasion, while Columba was living on Iona, he earnestly informed his assembled brethren, "Today I want to go alone to the western plain of this island. Let none of you follow me." They obeyed, and he went out alone, as he desired. But a brother, who was cunning and overly curious, proceeded by another road, and hid himself on the summit of a certain little hill which overlooked the plain. He was anxious to learn Columba's motive for seeking solitude. While the spy on the top of the hill was looking upon the holy man as he stood on a mound in the plain with his arms extended upwards and his eyes raised to heaven in prayer, a wonderful scene presented itself, surely with God's permission. What the observer saw with his own eyes from his place on that neighboring hill was the appearance of holy angels, citizens of the heavenly country, clad in white robes, and flying with wonderful speed to Columba while he prayed. That heavenly host stood near him, and, after a short conversation with the holy man, flew quickly—as if feeling detected—back again to the highest heavens....These great and sweet visits of angels to this holy man took place mostly during the winter nights, when he was watching and praying in lonely places while others slept.

The entire scene is reminiscent of the transfiguration of Jesus, recorded in the ninth chapter of St. Mark's Gospel. On more than a few occasions, Columba is observed in the presence of angels or illuminated by divine light. Each time, like Jesus, the saint warns the monks not to tell anyone.

There are many stories of Columba and angels, but one about a very persistent angel stands out in its stark and evocative imagery. Considering Columba's love of books, this vision is surely one that would have intrigued the saint—although he shows an unwillingness, at least initially, to follow the directive of the angel. This story also alludes to Columba's continuing involvement in the politics of Scotland where two tribal leaders struggled for dominance after the death of Conall, a Pictish king, in 574 C.E.[22]

On another occasion, when Columba was staying on the island of Hinba [near Iona], he saw on a certain night in a mental ecstasy an angel sent to him from heaven. In his hand, the angel held a book of glass, regarding the appointment of kings. When Columba received the book from the hand of the angel, the venerable man followed the angel's command and began to read it. When he was reluctant to appoint Aidan king, as the book directed, because he had a greater affection for Iogenan, his brother, the angel suddenly stretched forth his hand and struck the saint with a scourge. The livid marks from it remained in Columba's side all the days of his life. The angel added these words: "Know for certain," said he," that I am sent to you by God with the book of glass, that in accordance with the words you have read in it, you should inaugurate Aidan as king; but if you refuse to obey this command, I will strike you again." This angel of the Lord appeared for three successive nights, with the same book of glass in his hand and repeated the same commands of the Lord regarding the inauguration of the king. The saint finally obeyed the command of the Lord, sailed across to Iona, and there crowned Aidan, as he had been commanded.

The number three has great significance in the pagan mythology and Christian literature of the Celts. They believed it symbolized added strength or special meaning. In addition to the book and scourge, that the angel appeared three times certainly would have gotten Columba's attention—so that, despite his initial reservations, he finally listened to the angel's command. The story shows that visions and voices should not necessarily be identified with wishful thinking or unconscious projections on the part of the visionary. They often are and can be experienced as having a reality of their own which demands attention *and obedience,* as Columcille learned here, and later mystics, such as Hildegard of Bingen and Joan of Arc, could attest.

As a result of these visions and voices, Columba had knowledge, according to Adomnan, of "many secrets hidden from men since the beginning of the world." Like the twentieth-century Native American shaman, Black Elk,[23] Columba could literally "see" events occurring thousands of miles from his homeland, as well as predict future happenings. When asked the source of his prophetic revelations, Columba responds: "There are some, though very few, who are enabled by divine grace to see most clearly and distinctly the whole compass of the world, and to embrace within their own wondrously enlarged mental capacity the utmost limits of the heavens and the earth at the same moment, as if all were illumined by a single ray of the sun."

As was true of his tutor, Finnian of Clonard, Columba's effectiveness as a teacher was related to these extraordinary intuitive and prophetic powers. Adomnan indicates this in one of his stories about the saint in which we find Columba using his gift of intuition to see beyond a student's present behavior and to foretell his future greatness. This happened, Adomnan tells us, at the time Columba was founding his monastery at Durrow (c. 553 C.E.), when he went to visit St. Ciaran's monastery at Clonmacnoise. As Columcille was being greeted by the community

> a boy attached to the monastery, who was not highly regarded by the senior monks, hid himself as well as he could, and then snuck forward so that he might touch—without being seen—the hem of the saint's cloak without his feeling or knowing it. This, however, did not escape Columba, for he knew with the eyes of his soul what he could not see taking place behind him with the eyes of his body. Stopping suddenly and putting out his hand behind him, he seized the boy by the neck, brought him around, and looked him in the face. The crowd cried out: "Let him go, let him go; why do you touch that unfortunate and naughty child?" But the saint solemnly uttered these prophetic words from his heart: "Let him be, brothers." Then, turning to the boy who at this point was terrified, he said: "My son, open your mouth, and put out your tongue." The boy did as he was told, and in great alarm opened his mouth and put out his tongue. The saint extended his holy hand to him, and after carefully blessing the boy's tongue, prophesied: "Though this youth now appears to you very contemptible and worthless, let no one despise him because of that. For from now on, not only will he not

displease you, but he will give you every satisfaction. From day to day he will progressively advance in goodness and in strength of soul; and from this day, wisdom and prudence will increasingly be a part of him. Great will be his spiritual progress in this community; he also will receive the gift of both sound beliefs and eloquence." This was Ernene, son of Crasen, who was afterwards famous and most highly honored in all the churches of Ireland.

This story, of course, is similar to the one of Jesus and the woman who sought to touch his cloak in order to be healed of her hemorrhaging (cf. Matt 9:20 ff.). The miracle in Adomnan's narrative, however, is not that Ernene was cured immediately of his "naughtiness," but that Columba seemed to know implicitly that affirmation is a bigger inducement to positive growth, whatever age a person may be, than being judged as somehow inferior or incompetent, especially when young. In this case, his compassion for the boy at what may have been a critical juncture (Ernene was, after all, attempting to somehow physically connect with the saint) seems to have made all the difference in the boy's life. Judging from Adomnan's hagiography, Ernene was not the only one to reach out to the saint for encouragement and guidance.

Columba's Teaching and His Death

A distinct pattern that emerges in the second half of Columba's life is that of a wisdom figure who, although living on an island in relative isolation, is constantly sought out by others for advice or guidance—a pattern that can be detected in other Celtic saints' lives. Columba, however, is somehow given the grace—at least in Adomnan's account—never to be perturbed or annoyed by these people who come to him to learn. In fact, the greatest lesson Columba seems to teach them is that of the importance of hospitality—of making others, despite the sometimes quite obvious inconvenience and imposition, feel welcome and at home. The stories in Adomnan's hagiography time and again allude to this pattern and quality. Hospitality seems to have been such a value in Columba's life that on various occasions he reminded his community on Iona that it was more important to be hospitable than to maintain an ascetic diet, an attitude readily affirmed by the traditions of the desert elders. In one of the most famous stories about Columba, we find the saint teaching a younger monk indirectly about the importance of hospitality, as well as of compassion for all of God's creatures, including exhausted cranes.

> At another time, while Columba was living on Iona, he called one of the brothers to him and said: "Three days from now, in the morning, you must sit down and wait on the shore, on the western side of this island, for a crane. A stranger from the northern region of Ireland, it has been driven about by various winds. This crane will come, weary and fatigued, after the ninth hour, and quite exhausted will lie down before you on the beach. Treat that bird tenderly, and take it to some nearby house, where you

can kindly and carefully nurse it and feed it for three days and three nights. When the crane is refreshed after three days of rest, and is no longer willing to stay with us, it will fly back with renewed strength to the pleasant part of Ireland from which it originally came. I entrust this bird to you with special care because it comes from our native land."

The brother obeyed Columba, and on the third day, after the ninth hour, he watched as he had been told for the arrival of the expected guest. As soon as the crane came and alighted on the shore, he gently picked up the weak and hungry bird and carried it to a dwelling that was nearby, where he fed it. On the man's return to the monastery that evening, Columba, without any inquiry, but as if stating a fact, said to him, "God bless you, my son, for your kind attention to this foreign visitor which will not remain here for very long, but will return within three days to its old home." It happened exactly as the saint predicted, for after being nursed carefully for three days, the bird flapped its wings and gently rose to a great height in the sight of its hospitable host. Then, on that calm day, it made its way through the air homewards, flying straight across the sea to Ireland.

By now we have gained a picture of a saint who was a compassionate and very hospitable man with a highly complex personality: a scholar who is frequently found writing or contentedly reading a book; a man of action, subjecting himself to people and to the elements as he journeys from island to island evangelizing, preaching, and above all teaching others about God and ultimate truths; a person with great intuitive and prophetic powers to whom, Adomnan says, "mysteries" were revealed "regarding past or future ages, unknown to the rest of humankind." When Columba died, not only did his monastic brothers mourn deeply his passing but even the elements cried out: "During the three days and nights of his obsequies, there arose a storm of wind without rain which blew so violently that it prevented every one from crossing the Sound. Immediately after the internment of the holy man, the storm stopped at once, the wind ceased, and the whole sea became calm."

Through Adomnan's stories, Columcille's memory lived on at the numerous sites of the monasteries which he had founded, as well as throughout Western Europe. Those stories reveal a spiritual leader with many strengths and talents, a teacher and tutor, as Bede himself says, who taught "by his words and his example."[24] Although eloquent with words (he was, after all, a noted writer, poet, and bard), Columcille frequently seems to have affected his students and community more with his actions than his words, as the desert Christians had often done. This becomes apparent when one considers these vivid stories about him which survived years after his death. What his followers distinctly remembered, according to Adomnan, was what he taught them about prayer and solitude, love and compassion, even about the ministry of consoling those in grief. He had cared for others up to the time when his own dying day approached. They learned not so much by listening to him teach through formal lectures, but rather by living with him and observing him closely day after day. This direct teaching by example through the life he led and the person that he was seems to have been intrinsically linked to his own hospitable nature. A man of considerable gifts as a scholar, scribe, and sage, he did not let his accomplishments make him less accessible, but even more readily available to students, colleagues, and a whole range of visitors who came to Iona for advice and help. In retrospect, we can see that if Patrick was known for his courage and Brigit for her compassion, surely Columcille's outstanding trait was hospitality, reflected in his solicitude for all sorts of people—and even a weary crane.

Hospitality and Soul Friendship Today

In Judeo-Christian tradition, hospitality was and is a traditional value, referred to in numerous stories from the Scriptures and from the Lives of the saints. In the Old Testament, Abraham and Sarah are visited by three strangers who turn out to be manifestations of the divine (cf. Gen 18), a reminder to the Jews of the importance of treating a guest with generosity and kindness. In the New Testament, Jesus constantly refers to this quality which he links directly with the experience of forgiveness. Praising the woman who washes his feet with her tears, while upbraiding the pharisee for failing to provide any such fitting hospitable signs, he says: "You gave me no kiss, but she has been covering my feet with kisses ever since I came in. You did not anoint my head with oil, but she has anointed my feet with ointment. For this reason I tell you that her sins, many as they are, have been forgiven her because she has shown such great love (cf. Luke 7:45–50). Jesus also lists hospitality as among the works of charity by which people ultimately will be judged by God (Matt 25:35 ff.). It is the quality through which we *find* God, as the story of the encounter on the road to Emmaus suggests, when Jesus reveals himself as the Risen Lord to two travelers precisely because they had invited him, a stranger, to stay with them for the night (cf. Luke 24:13–35). All of these stories, and more, were familiar to the Celtic Christians.

Celtic Christians, especially those in Ireland, were known for this quality of hospitality. In fact, the Irish word for *hospitality* is *oigedchaire*, which means "guest-loving." This connection between Christian hospitality and love of guests is explicitly found in an early hagiography of St. Brigit who says, "Every guest is Christ."[25] It also coincides with chapter twenty-three in the *Rule of St. Benedict* in which every guest is to be welcomed as Christ. Not only were students from foreign shores welcomed to Irish monasteries and given a free education, as we've seen, but numerous guest houses were built at Celtic monasteries to shelter visiting clergy and laity alike. To build a guesthouse was considered to be a holy act, as can be discerned in the story of St. Cuthbert who, despite his intense desire to be a hermit, took time out when he moved to the Farne Islands to construct an extra house for visitors.[26]

This quality of hospitality, of course, has tremendous implications for contemporary soul friends, in particular those who act as teachers, tutors, and mentors to others. As we recall from Bede, it was hospitality that initially attracted so many to Ireland to study there in the first place because of the Irish teachers' willingness to make room in their lives—and even their cells—for students with diverse talents and personalities. Today, of course, this sharing of one's cell in most cases cannot be taken literally, unless one is living with students in college dormitories or student apartments, and even there one presupposes a healthy respect for boundaries and some degree of privacy. Rather, the quality of hospitality when it is applied to teaching has more to do with a facilitating role and a fundamental attitude: the *role* of creating an environment which fosters community and facilitates true change, true liberation, which is what all genuine teaching is about; and an *attitude* of respect and gratitude for the wisdom each person brings to any teacher-student relationship, or to any group.

For those who teach in more formal settings, such as in classrooms, workshops, or retreat houses, a facilitating role means providing, like Columcille, a hospitable place where some measure of community can be experienced. Such an experience, of course, can be affected by the size of the class or the number of participants, but even in large numbers a sense of community happens when people start to let down their defenses, set aside their fears, and identify with a larger vision. As Henri Nouwen says in his book *Reaching Out*: "When we look at teaching in terms of hospitality, we can say that the teacher is called upon to create for students a free and fearless space where mental and emotional development can take place."[27] In such a hospitable environment, people are encouraged to disarm themselves, to lay aside their occupations and preoccupations, and to listen with attention and care to the voices speaking in their own center, in their own hearts.

A good teacher, then, attempts to create an environment which is not characterized so much by competition, but by a collaborative stance, one in which students do not perceive their colleagues with suspicion and hostility (i.e., as "strangers" who are determined to outdo them), but as "guests" and fellow seekers who *like themselves* are searching for knowledge that can change their lives, sometimes at their deepest core. A truly effective teacher attempts to establish relationships in which mutual learning can occur by providing a place where students become teachers to each other, and the teacher is perceived, not as a distant, all-knowing "expert," but as a fellow learner who has both competence *and* questions of her or his own.

Teaching well depends upon a fundamental hospitable attitude rooted in the origins of the term *education* itself taken from the Latin word *educo* meaning "to lead forth, to draw out." This attitude presupposes that wisdom already lies within the heart of everyone, and often only awaits discovery. This attitude is grounded in the belief that students come bearing gifts which are often expressed in their stories, their curiosity, even their indifference—an indifference which may be less related to boredom and more to previous suspicions, fears, and hurts. Any hope of transcending roadblocks to learning often depends upon the teacher's ability to let students know that they are accepted and loved for who they are. A good teacher considers all students as guests whose life experiences, questions, and doubts have the potential to make a great deal of difference to everyone, including the teacher. Whether such relationships with students are short-term, lasting only as long as an academic course or workshop, or for a lifetime and beyond, all have the potential to change lives in unexpected ways. The task of the teacher is to help students appreciate the beauty of themselves and of their own gifts, and to be receptive to what their own experiences can teach them.

With this attitude, we can see that all teaching is in varying degrees related to transformation, to the emergence of what the ancients called greatness of soul. It presupposes that every teacher, no matter what topic is being discussed or course being taught, functions to some degree as a spiritual guide who draws out the wisdom that lies within the human heart. As Parker Palmer suggests, "to teach is to create a space in which obedience to truth is practiced;" "to educate is to guide students on an inner journey toward more truthful ways of seeing and being in the world."[28] This obedience to truth, this ability to listen attentively and respond to the stirrings of the heart presupposes that each teacher creates an environment where such knowledge is valued, and a respectful relationship in which the true self can emerge. This true self is, according to Palmer, "the self planted in us by God," and, he adds, the "true self is true friend."[29] If this true self is to emerge and to flourish, the Celts believed, it often needs the nurturing of a friendly teacher or soul friend.

One of the most important gifts a teacher or mentor may give to others is the encouragement to see themselves in a positive light—with potential for leadership in whatever career they choose or vocation which chooses them. Here we need simply recall the powerful story of Sts. Enda and Ciaran who beheld a common vision of a giant tree growing in the middle of Ireland that, as Enda was able to interpret, symbolized both the future greatness of the monastery of Clonmacnoise as well as its founder, Ciaran:

After that Ciaran went to the island of Aran to commune with Enda. Both of them saw the same vision of a great fruitful tree growing beside a stream in the middle of Ireland. This tree protected the entire island, and its fruit crossed the sea that surrounded Ireland, and the birds of the world came to carry off some of that fruit. Ciaran turned to Enda and told him what he had seen, and Enda, in turn, said to him: "The great tree which you saw is you, Ciaran, for you are great in the eyes of God and of men. All of Ireland will be sheltered by the grace that is in you, and many people will be fed by your fasting and prayers. So, go in the name of the God to the center of Ireland, and found your church on the banks of a stream."[30]

Without Enda's prophetic insight *and encouragement,* perhaps neither Ciaran's leadership nor his monastery's would have come to such bounteous fruition.

Another story in this chapter makes the same point: how being a good teacher is being a good host who is able to see and foster the potential competence and leadership of students, no matter what others, or the students themselves, may think. Remember how Columcille, when he saw Ernene (whom others considered worthless), told his fellow monks that the boy would "progressively advance in goodness and strength of soul," and become a monastic leader with the gifts of "both sound beliefs and eloquence." Columcille, according to Adomnan, was able to see this future greatness in the boy through his "divine intuition," a phenomenon described in the hagiography as a special type of knowing "with the eyes of the soul" rather than "the eyes of the body," manifest as "prophetic words from his heart." This innate ability which is more developed in some than in others is often called a "sixth sense," a sense beyond those identified with sight, sound, touch, taste, and smell. Celts would associate this sense with "second sight," the intuitive ability to "see" things that are happening or will happen, although perhaps far removed physically from them. Both Eastern and Western spiritual traditions consider this type of knowing as one of the highest forms of truth, although in the West it has too often been subject to suspicion, if not outright condemnation. For soul friends, however, it can provide another resource for any teaching, mentoring, or guidance that they do.

Intuition, a Special Kind of Knowing

Intuition comes from the Latin word *intueor*, meaning "to look, contemplate, or know from within." Carl Jung describes this ability to assess truth, sometimes in a moment, in a flash, as "a kind of sense perception via the unconscious," a "lucky hunch, different in kind from the slow reasoning of the conscious mind." Intuition gives outlook and insight, gifts particularly strong, he believes, among shamans, prophets, seers, artists, poets, and writers. Artistic expression and mystical experiences are often related to this intuitive perception of reality. As in the case of confessors, teachers, counselors, and other professionals, Jung states that psychotherapists, in particular, have to rely on their intuition if they are to be helpful to any clients.[31] A protégé and colleague of Jung's, Marie-Louise Von

Franz, gets even closer to the meaning of intuition, particularly as expressed in the stories of Columcille, when she defines intuition as "the capacity for intuiting that which is not yet visible, future possibilities or potentialities in the background of a situation." It is "a function by which we conceive possibilities."[32]

While some individuals seem especially gifted from birth with access to this type of knowing, and some races, such as the Celts, seem particularly appreciative of it, intuition can be developed. Frances Vaughan, for one, suggests that the practice of meditation, no matter what specific method is used, can be one of the most direct methods of tuning in to intuition, for it focuses direct attention away from rational, analytical thinking to the nonrational which has insights of its own to provide. She speaks of the need to quiet the mind and to be attentive, without straining, to the silence, as well as being open to the imagery or images that arise. These images can then be reflected upon and, as in the case of dreams, associations made with them to discern their meaning.[33] This meditative approach to life that fosters intuitive perspectives and insights is precisely what many of Columcille's contemporaries remembered most about the saint: his prayer life, his mysticism, his openness to the spiritual realm. Like so many mystics, meditation was for him a bridge to the divine, a meeting of truth and beauty in a radically new way.

Besides prayer and meditation, the stories of Columcille (as well as of other great spiritual leaders in history) show that intuitive insights are frequently revealed when attention is paid to one's voices and visions. Plato portrays Socrates as being attentive throughout his life to "a kind of voice" that first came to him as a child.[34] The desert prophet Elijah is depicted in the Old Testament as hearing God speak in a gentle breeze (1 Kgs 19:11–14). Many of the medieval Christian mystics, including Joan of Arc who was persecuted for following her beloved "voices," are shown to be attentive to this special kind of knowledge. Sometimes in our own lives we hear voices, mysterious inner verbal assertions of what is happening or will occur. Perhaps, because of our own personal formation or the cultural disapproval of such phenomena, we too quickly deny their reality—or the truths they are trying to convey. Jung, however, states that voices are vivid manifestations of intuition, that they show "an intelligence and a clarity superior to the dreamer's actual consciousness. This superiority (in insight or knowledge) is the reason for the absolute authority of the voice." Voices, he says, often have the characteristic of indisputable truth, and can even act as a friend. Although seeming to come from nowhere, he says, "the voice gives me certain contents, exactly as if a friend were informing me of his [or her] ideas." Christians might equate that friend with the Holy Spirit, the friend of the soul, the soul friend. Jung uses similar language, stating that "when visionary pictures are seen or inner voices heard" they are "a true, primordial experience of the spirit."[35]

Visions too have been experienced by many people throughout history, including our own day. Sometimes visions are identified with dramatic experiences of light, such as Columcille's seeing the whole universe revealed "as if in one ray of the sun." Numerous heroes and saints, from Moses in the Old Testament to Jesus in the New, from CuChulainn among the ancient Celts to St. Columcille—all are frequently portrayed, quite literally, in this light: the light of inner illumination or spiritual transfiguration that is reflected outwardly in a luminous face or body, or halo that surrounds the person. Sometimes visionary experiences include both light and voice, as was found in the stories of Jesus on Mount Tabor when he communed not only with God, but with his ancestors (Mark 9), and of the desert father Antony when he saw "the roof being opened…and a certain beam of light descending toward him" from which a voice assured him of divine help.[36] Sometimes visions reveal themselves in specific images. The fourteenth-century English mystic Julian of Norwich saw the universe "…lying in the palm of my hand," "round as a ball," and "no bigger than a hazelnut."[37] Our own visions may have elements of one or all of these. Frequently they may seem like "waking dreams," as if we are taken into another dimension of reality as we look upon or are caught up in something right before our eyes. Jung believes that a vision is a genuine "primordial experience" that is related to intuition itself: "Through our senses we experience the known, but our intuitions point to things that are unknown and hidden, that by their very nature are secret." Like the Late Antique philosopher, Plotinus (ca. 205–270 C.E.),[38] Jung identifies intuition with illumination and vision with an artist's, poet's, or writer's creativity: "It is nothing but a tremendous intuition striving for expression."[39]

Another intriguing aspect of Jung's thought is his association of intuitive knowledge with the "night-side of life." He believed that artists, prophets, and seers especially are nourished by the night. The ancient Celts were a people who loved darkness, and worshipped the moon. They still are people of the night, if one considers their late-night social gatherings that often continue into the early morning hours. This linking of intuitive insights with the night may be why so many of the early Celtic saints are portrayed as going without much sleep, immersing themselves at night, like Cuthbert, in the ocean's waves while praying, or being identified with gold and silver moons as Columcille and Ciaran were in the Life of Finnian of Clonard. This may also account for the Celts' high degree of creativity, mystical awarenesses and, as Jung says, the ability to "catch sight of the figures that people the night-world—spirits, demons, and gods." The Swiss psychotherapist also associates visions and the creativity that flows from them with the feminine: "The creative process has a feminine quality, and the creative work arises from unconscious depths—we might truly say from the realm of the Mothers."[40] Thus the Celts' appreciation of women and the feminine must also have contributed to their intuitive, creative, prophetic sides. Emma Jung says in her own works that while women more naturally are open to the unconscious, intuition, and prophetic gifts, "faculties such as these…do not belong to woman only; there have always been masculine seers or prophets, too, who are such by virtue of a feminine, receptive attitude which makes them responsive to influences from the other side of consciousness….In a creative man, especially, this feminine attitude [of openness and receptivity] plays an important role."[41] It is no wonder that Columcille, as teacher and soul friend, was identified with the crane, a sacred bird for the ancient Celts that represented women.[42]

Teacher, Writer, and Soul Friend

Columcille's feastday is celebrated June 9, a day honoring one of the most talented leaders of the Early Celtic Church, a writer with the soul of a poet and a teacher with wisdom of the heart. If in Roman mythology Aphrodite, goddess of love, is associated with a dove, we can see why Columcille also is linked with that symbol. His was a life of loving that naturally drew others to him, and through him to God, as we know from the numerous references to youths and monastic companions on Iona. Certainly his effectiveness as a teacher and soul friend was due to this love, this care and hospitality. He definitely stands in the ancient tradition of the druids who initially taught him much of what he later integrated with his Christian beliefs. His life, in particular, reminds us that teaching occurs in many ways, most especially through example, and that education itself is not limited only to those who identify themselves professionally as educators; that it is a significant aspect of any mentoring, counseling, advising, spiritual guidance, or therapy that we do.

Every soul friendship depends upon certain qualities, especially that of hospitality, and every *anamchara* needs to rely upon intuition, frequently manifest in voices, visions, and dreams. Learning to trust one's intuition and to use it well is learning to be one's own teacher. Meditation can help a great deal in this ongoing process, as can a lifestyle where room is made daily for quiet and tranquility, even if it means finding it at night or in the early morning hours. Such times can become opportunities for discovering, as Columcille knew, that any effective teaching depends not so much on specific methods as it does upon lis-

172

tening to the heart—the place where intellect, emotion, and spirit converge in the human self.

In the next and final chapter we turn to one other Irish saint, hardly known at all in comparison with the three greats— Patrick, Brigit, and Columcille—yet whose life has much to teach us about soul friendship as we grow older.

CHAPTER 5

Colman of Land Ela
Mentor and Midwife

Two paps has Colman Ela,
A pap of milk, a pap of honey;
His right pap for fair Baithin,
And his other pap for Ultan.

Life of Colman Ela

An amusing story from the *Life of St. Mochuda*, the founder of Lismore monastery who was known for his physical and spiritual beauty, describes the virtues of Mochuda's monks, especially that of obedience: "One day the monks were engaged in labor beside the river which runs through the monastery. One of the senior monks called upon a young monk named Colman to do a certain piece of work. Immediately, as he had not named any particular Colman, twelve monks of the same name rushed into the water. The readiness and exactness of the obedience practiced was displayed in this incident."[1] What was also displayed was the popularity of the name Colman! Not only did numerous monks at Lismore share the name (which means "little dove"), but literally hundreds of saints from the Early Celtic Church with the name *Colman* were and continue to be venerated, primarily in Ireland.[2] Of all these, however, Colman of Land Ela is one of the most important soul friends, considering the stories about him. This Colman lived from about 555 to 611 C.E., dying at the age of fifty-six.[3] He belonged to a family of Meath, but was born in Glenelly in Tyrone. Colman of Land Ela appears in various hagiographies of Irish saints, including the Life of St. Mochuda who is said to have received advice from Colman about where to build his own monastery, as well as a farewell blessing as he set out to do so. The two of them were obviously soul friends who exchanged visits frequently.[4]

Colman was also a contemporary of Columcille's. In fact, as various hagiographies attest, Colman's mother was a sister of Columcille's, thus making Columcille Colman's uncle. In the *Life of Columba* by Adomnan, Colman visits his uncle on Iona where he was delivered from the perils of the voyage by his uncle's prayers. This story describes how one day the saint's companions saw a smile cross Columcille's face, only to be replaced by a look of concern as he called out to his colleagues: "Colman has set sail to come here, and is now in great danger in the surging tides of the whirlpool of Corryvrechan." In another passage, Colman is depicted as already living on Iona for some time, and requesting "fair wind" from Columcille in order to return home. Columcille prays, and Colman lands safely once more back in Ireland.[5] In these references to Colman, including the smile Columcille initially had on his face when he perceived Colman's approach, we can see the fondness each man must have had for the other, with the added understanding that

Columcille, as uncle, must have provided a good deal of mentoring for the younger man.

This theme of mentoring recurs in many of the Lives of the Celtic saints. A topic of some popularity today, mentoring can be defined simply as a relationship of friendship with someone a little more experienced in some aspect of life who is willing to provide the other person with knowledge, skills, guidance, or inspiration. Mentoring relationships, however, cannot be totally equated with formal roles, since they more often evolve in response to the experience or expertise of the mentor, the needs of the other person, and the personalities of both. Still, some of the more common functions include teaching and guiding, or acting as a host, sponsor, counselor, or exemplar. All of these roles, as we've seen, can be associated with soul friendship, including that of acting as a *spiritual* mentor in a relationship often characterized by greater depth, and perhaps more explicitly concerned with vocational decisions and a person's relationship with God. As history frequently shows and the hagiographies of the Celtic saints reveal, being mentored can give one the sensitivity and gratitude for becoming an effective mentor oneself.[6] This seems to have been the case for Colman. What he learned from Columcille, he passed on to friends and monastic companions.

Closely tied in with mentoring, especially spiritual mentoring, is that of being a midwife of souls, what the ancient Greeks called a *mystagogue,* or soul guide, and what contemporary psychologists and psychotherapists associate with *maieutics*, the science and art of attending to the process of giving birth.[7] While midwifery itself has been rightly linked primarily with women helping other women deliver their babies,[8] in the history of spirituality, from the philosophers of the Greeks and the desert Christians to the Celtic soul friends, helping another give birth to his or her own soul includes both genders. Increasingly, even in what must surely rank (alongside another) as one of the oldest professions in humanity's history, midwifery of physical births is being recognized as an innately spiritual process in which both women and men are involved.[9] In his study of many diverse cultures and mythologies, Joseph Campbell equates the person who helps another give birth to the soul with the initiating medicine man or woman of the primitive forest sanctuaries, an elder who frequently appears in myths, fairy tales, and dreams as a wise old man or crone.[10]

As we will see, Colman acted as both mentor and midwife to many people in and outside of his monastery. He also, like so many other Celtic soul friends, brought to birth, through his compassion and creativity, new forms of communal life and spirituality. He did so to such a degree that Oengus the Culdee compares Colman to John, the beloved disciple of Jesus. On Colman's feastday, September 26, in the martyrology that bears Oengus's name, Colman is described as "the great John of Erin's [Ireland's] sons." In an added note, the Irish saint and monastic founder is referred to as "A John was he, like…unto John for wisdom and virginity."[11]

This comparison of St. Colman to St. John "the beloved disciple" of Jesus is most significant, considering the close relationship Jesus had with the younger man, as well as the high regard and devotion Christian Celts had for St. John himself. Perhaps, if any symbol in the Christian tradition epitomizes soul friendship and spiritual mentoring, it is that of Jesus with his disciple John resting his head on his mentor's heart (John 13:21–26). Another image potentially as meaningful is the extraordinary description, as we will see, of the male Colman having two paps with which he fed not only two foster-sons, but his entire community. Since Colman is linked with this evocative imagery, as well as with the beloved disciple, it seems only right to conclude our examination of the soul friend tradition with him.

Although several Irish and Latin hagiographies of St. Colman have survived, we will rely in this chapter upon an Irish Life belonging to the Burgundian Library at Bruxelles. The latter was compiled in 1629 by Friar Michael O'Clery, the chief of the "Four Masters" who, as members of the Franciscan monastery in Donegal, Ireland, transcribed numerous works from the Early Irish Church, among them the Annals of Ireland, as well as hagiographies of the saints.

The Life of St. Colman Ela[12]

Colman's Life is relatively brief compared to other hagiographies. Its text, a combination of prose and poetry, consists of only fifteen pages. There is no personal note by the unknown author whom O'Clery transcribes telling the reader the origins of his work, nor references to the early years of the saint about whom he is writing. Instead, the hagiography begins with a short reference to Colman's ancestors who, interestingly enough, are said to have come from Spain, perhaps, one might conjecture, from the northwestern Celtic province of Galicia:

"Now Colman Ela was of the race of Eremon the son of Miled of Spain, as his genealogy declares." The next sentence proceeds immediately to introduce Cuiniugan, a warrior who, although at first highly antagonistic to Colman, eventually becomes one of his most loving friends. The text then speaks of Colman's coming to the Fir Cell, the tribe which lived on Land Ela where he was to build his monastery and find his place of resurrection: "As to Colman Ela—when he came to Fir Cell, they did not welcome him, and no one was more hostile to him than Cuiniugan."

In terms of Joseph Campbell's monomyth, this seems to be the stage, however briefly described, of Colman's "call to adventure"—his arrival among the Fir Cell. The next stage, "road of trials," begins almost immediately when, in the unfolding adult life of Colman, his hagiographer proceeds to introduce the gripping story of a monster who is troubling the land. This theme of land or kingdom threatened by some sort of monster, dragon, or plague is a frequent one that is found in numerous Arthurian legends, and one that we have already seen in Columcille's hagiography with the Loch Ness Monster. The story in Colman's Life is worth recounting here:

> A trouble had arisen in the land at this time; to wit, there was a pestilent monster in Lough [Lake] Ela, and no man or beast would venture to go near the lake for fear of it. And this was the description of the monster—a small pointed gaping apparition in the shape of a woman. Cuiniugan said to them then: "It would be better for us to set the holy man called Colman Ela to fight the monster, and it would be

better still in our opinion that neither of them should return." Now the king of Fir Cell at that time was Donnchad son of Aed, son of Sathmainide, of the race of Fiacha son of Niall of the nine hostages. "Bring Colman to us," said the king, "that he may preach to us, so that we may know how many among us he can convert."

Colman is brought to them and begins his preaching. To convert the Fir Cell to Christianity, however, he does not rely upon his own skills alone, but seeks help from certain friends, among them the famous Columcille and a Mancan of Liath who brings monastic colleagues with him. These three spiritual leaders meet together and develop a pastoral strategy for converting the king's people: Columcille volunteers to carry Colman's crozier that day; Mancan says that he will sprinkle holy water on the people to make them friendlier to Colman; and Mancan's followers will preach and pray over them, "praising the Creator fervently." This strategy evidently works since, we are told, "it was recreation of mind and heart to the hosts to listen to them. And those who had never thought of God before, turned their thoughts to Him now. And one of the first to offer himself to God and Colman that day was Cuiniugan."

Cuiniugan was not the only one to be moved profoundly by Colman's and his friends' abilities. According to the story, the king and his three sons, Muad, Duinecha, and Aillean were so taken with the saint they promised to give him land on which to settle, as well as to follow him wherever he might go. When Colman hears this, he immediately sets out to confront the monster whose name is Lainn and who has "short bushy hair, unwashed and unkempt, all over its head." Calling upon God for help, Colman, rather than killing the monster himself, seeks the help of the two warriors who believed in him and loved him the most: "And these two, Cuiniugan and Duinecha, went out and beheaded the monster. And they brought the head to Colman. And Colman blessed them both." Colman then promises Cuiniugan that he and his offspring will be with him as his stewards until doomsday, that he will inherit Colman's relics, and that evil will befall Cuiniugan's enemies. To Duinecha, he recites a long poetic verse describing God as "King of the stars, whose protection is never-ending," and promising Duinecha that when he dies "you will be carried to the gentle church" for the funeral rites. The place where the monster was killed, Colman says, will be the place that he inherits:

> This "land" will be the "land" of Colman.
> I am Colman Ela;
> Good also in the sight of the one God
> Are the two who were once against me;
> I myself restrained them in one day.
>
> Cuiniugan answered me gently
> After the sermon which I preached to the king;
> For love of me openly
> He went to slay the monster.

The lesson of this story seems to be that to slay monsters, in whatever form they come, it is not good to go alone, but to seek companions whose love—and sometimes very genuine bravery and determination—can make all the difference.

Land Ela: Swans' Land, and Colman's Paps

Now the hagiographer turns to a description of the founding of the monastery at Land Ela, called Lynally today, located about four miles from Durrow, the site of Columcille's famous monastery. Historians believe this happened about 590 C.E., when Colman would have been about thirty-four years old. Colman is shown proceeding to Land Ela where he builds a "fortified house" and blesses the cemetery in which, we are told, the monster was the first to be buried. Colman's followers also help him build a causeway from Land Ela to a nearby forest, "and swans used to come every hour to sing to them, and relieve their fatigue; so that for this reason the place was called Land Ela (swans' land)." This land, then, was associated not only with a gruesome monster, but also with beautiful singing swans.

As the hagiography proceeds, Columcille, Colman's uncle, enters the picture. Typical of the intimacy between soul friends, he shares with his nephew something that is seriously bothering him: "I think it only right to tell you about a difficulty of mine." Colman, alerted perhaps by Columcille's tone of voice, asks compassionately, "What is this difficulty?" and his uncle responds. He tells Colman about two young brothers named Ultan and Baithin who seem to be from an incestuous family. Although Columcille has baptized them, he acknowledges, "I would rather that they did not live, but that I could permit their destruction without shame to myself, for their father and mother are children of a brother and sister." Columcille seems genuinely perplexed, asking Colman, "What would be your advice to me?" Colman responds immediately, seemingly without a great deal of thought: "Give them to me to nourish and to foster. And let us make a covenant respecting them, for I have two paps such as no saint ever had before, a pap with milk, and a pap with honey, and these I will give to them to suck." The two children were given to Colman, who then recites the following in poetic verse:

> Two paps has Colman Ela,
> A pap of milk, a pap of honey;
> His right pap for fair Baithin,
> And his other pap for Ultan.

Later, following another monster story—this one encountered in Scotland which he and his friend Duinecha kill—Colman returns to mention of his two paps, associating them not only with nurturing the two fosterlings, Ultan and Baithin, but the entire community at Land Ela—if its members are loyal to his monastic rule:

> Every man of the Fir Cell
> Who shall not be steadfastly at my command,
> I entreat the one God truly
> That they may not get the milk of my two breasts.

Then, he seems to equate his wondrous paps with salvation itself:

For these are my own two breasts;
The heavenly city in beauty,
I will not forsake it assuredly
For whatever hardship I may find.

Colman's Fosterlings, and Baithin's Conversion

Much of the rest of O'Clery's hagiography has to do with the two young brothers, Ultan and Baithin, and Colman's relationship with them. This part of the Life of St. Colman may well coincide with Campbell's third stage of the hero's journey: the return home. Surely the initial encounters with monsters had transformed Colman's life, giving him friendships that would last a lifetime, and land for a monastery which he could now use for his community and fosterlings. The Life says that the two youths whom Colman had accepted from Columcille were now studying at Land Ela. Each youth had "special qualities": "Whatever Ultan heard, he remembered; and whatever was done to Baithin, no single word remained with him." The latter description of Baithin's "special" quality, although unclear, strikes the reader as not all that positive an attribute, for it seems to infer that Baithin had a poor memory or lacked attentiveness. For those who have raised adolescent sons, the latter interpretation rings true, and in fact seems to be reinforced when we consider the story about Baithin that follows:

> Colman Ela beat his pupil Baithin, and Baithin went away after the beating, and Colman followed him....Baithin ran away from study, and went to hide himself in the wood above Land Ela. He saw a man

fixing a single wattle [woven twigs], and when a wattle was fixed, he would go to fetch another to fix it in the same way. However slowly this took, the house was gradually built. Baithin saw this, and this is what he said: "If I had done my learning like that, and stuck to it, I believe I would have acquired knowledge."

A second incident reinforces Baithin's original insight:

Then a heavy shower fell. Baithin went to seek shelter under an oak. He saw a drop fall on a certain spot. Baithin made a hole with his heel at the place, and the drop eventually filled the hole; whereupon Baithin said, "If I had done my learning like that, I should have acquired knowledge."

This new awareness of Baithin's, Colman's recalcitrant fosterling, expressed in the lines above, seems to express some type of conversion experience on his part—an interpretation reinforced by what follows. Baithin is quoted as saying:

With drops the pool is filled,
With wattles the round house is made;
The dwelling that is pleasing to God,
Its family increases more and more.

Had I been devoted to my own learning
Near and far,
Though little I might do, I think that
I should have acquired knowledge enough....

> I make a renunciation, during all my time
> I will not forsake my learning;
> Whatever hardship I may find from it,
> I will pursue it from now on.

Baithin then tells Colman directly about his change of heart:

> Baithin himself related this
> to Colman his own tutor,
> He made a strong vow to Colman
> That he would not desert his reading.

> "God himself gave for your instruction, my son,
> To you the noble example,"
> Said gentle Colman, replying to him,
> Full of nobility and true knowledge.

Baithin's new-found commitment to learning—no matter what hardship he might encounter—evidently elicited a change in Colman himself: a movement from initially beating the inattentive student to welcoming him back, like the father in the story of the prodigal son (Luke 15:11–32) with joy and gentleness. Transformation seems to have happened not only in the heart of Baithin, but in Colman's too.

Another Story of Colman's Mentoring, and the Conclusion of His Life

The last story in Colman's hagiography concerns two unnamed youths in his monastic family whom he is mentoring.

Whether or not they were Ultan and Baithin, we do not know, but Colman's decision not to force them to follow the ascetic lifestyle of the monastery says something about his pastoral sensitivities, and his wisdom:

> The two youths grew to be big lads. "Why is it," asked the clerics, "that no task of asceticism is assigned to them, for they are old enough for it?" "I will not assign it," said Colman. "Why?" said they. "For this reason," said Colman. "The future abode of one of them will be in hell, and whatever asceticism he may perform now, he will not perform it at the end of his life, and it is in hell he will go. I will not deprive him of his share of this present world, for there will be no reward for his abstinence. The abode of the other one will be in heaven, and though he performs no asceticism now, he will do so at the last, and will be in heaven."

Colman's message to his fellow monks seems to be quite clear: ultimately it is not asceticism that saves anyone, but the overall quality of life one chooses to live. Those choices are very personal, and only an individual can make them, not any mentor, teacher, or spiritual guide. This is one of the most difficult aspects of any mentoring a person might do: letting go and accepting one's own powerlessness over others' behavior, while still going on loving them, one day at a time, with the hope that they will make the right choices for themselves.

Following this story of the two "big lads," the Irish hagiography of Colman ends abruptly, with O'Clery, the Franciscan, complaining that he had found little of the life of Colman to copy, and even with this sparse amount, "I wrote a great deal of it," he says, "slowly, tediously, wretchedly." Not happy to take all the culpability, O'Clery blames those "who bade me follow the track of the old books till the time of their revision."

Colman's Generativity—and Our Own

St. Colman of Land Ela had a great following in Ireland. Besides that of Oengus's martyrology, he is mentioned in a number of others, including those of Tallaght and Donegal. Nor was Colman's fame confined to Ireland alone. Scotland also had churches built in his honor, and his name is recorded in the *Martyrology of Aberdeen*.[13] Whether he visited any part of Scotland besides Iona or not, it is obvious that he spent most of his life in Ireland, the land of his birth, and that, after confronting monsters, making friends of former antagonists, and welcoming "lost youths," Land Ela was his home, his place of resurrection. This is where he did his mentoring, especially with the two warriors who became his lifelong friends, and the two young brothers whom he adopted as his sons. Intimations of this mentoring appear in the story of how Colman transformed the initially hostile Fir Cell into enthusiastic followers. They also appear in the story of Baithin's intellectual conversion, when we can see how Colman's relationship with him included both challenge or "tough love" (when he kicked Baithin out) *and* gentleness and forgiveness (when he welcomed him back).

In retrospect, perhaps the most outstanding quality that emerges when we consider the mentoring that Colman did is that of generativity, defined by a pioneer in developmental psychology, Erik Erikson, as "primarily the concern for establishing and guiding the next generation." Erikson says that generativity, along with integrity and wisdom, is one of the most important virtues in one's later years. Aging and human maturity depend upon "a sense of comradeship with men and women of distant times and of different pursuits who have created orders and objects and sayings conveying human dignity and love." Erikson especially links generativity with the passing on to succeeding generations this comradeship, this identification with human community, that transcends the ages. Generativity is also, he says, about helping others, especially the young, discover a sense of meaning by which ultimate questions can be faced with some clarity and strength. This quality of generativity, he believes, should not be equated exclusively with individuals, but applies to societal and religious organizations as well. "Generativity itself is a driving power in human organization." Humanity depends upon this very human need to pass on to the next generation the knowledge and wisdom that has been learned from earlier generations.[14]

Like Erikson, Evelyn and Jim Whitehead assert in their writings that to be generative does not necessarily mean that one must be a parent or grandparent. Generativity, as a human instinct and Christian virtue, they say, is not biologically bound. It is, rather, "a willingness to use my power responsibly to serve life that goes beyond myself." According to the Whiteheads, while many of us as parents find that to care for the new life we have brought into the world is a much greater challenge than it was to create it, everyone is called to identify themselves with a larger concern for the world. This concern, felt with special urgency in midlife, to care for and to contribute to the next generation is what generativity is about.[15] It involves both creativity and nurturance, both learning to care and knowing when to let go. "Generativity nurtures life," they say, "not continued dependency." To be generative a person must be strong enough to "let go," gradually releasing into its own autonomy the new life one has created and nurtured.[16] All of these comments, of course, would apply to Colman who, although not a biological father, took on the raising of at least two young boys, "let go" of Baithin so he could learn for himself what he was evidently not learning while staying with Colman and, as was demonstrated in the last story about the unnamed "big lads," was willing both to love and to surrender the results.

When we look back at the lives of the Celtic saints, and Colman's in particular, we can recognize that the final stage found in Campbell's monomyth is ultimately about developing and exercising the virtue of generativity: using what one has learned from one's own road of trials for service to others, to one's own family, community, and wider world. As a spiritual leader or soul friend, it means initiating others into the realm of the sacred, into spirituality as a way of helping them in the so-called "real world." This is certainly what Colman did after his own confrontation with monsters and perceived enemies. As a mentor, he made his life, knowledge, talents, and skills available to the next generation; and, as a spiritual midwife, brought to birth through his own love and creativity a spirituality that nurtured others in profound ways. Considering various aspects of

Colman's generativity, we can begin to see how our own soul friendships need to include both elements.

First, in our mentoring, especially with people younger or perhaps more inexperienced than ourselves, we need to consider the importance of offering both our friendship as well as initiation rituals that can help them through their transitions, and can lead them into new areas of spiritual growth and responsibility. The importance of this was manifest when the druids and druidesses acted as intermediaries of the tribes, initiating younger people into their spiritual heritage. It was also a tradition among the desert elders, both women and men, who acted as confessors and spiritual guides. It is also found in the extraordinary types of work and various roles of Celtic soul friends when as shamans and spiritual guides, pioneers and pastors, teachers and tutors, they opened their cells—and their hearts—to all sorts of pilgrims and seekers of wisdom. We can do the same in our own time, for both young women and young men.

Edith Sullwold, a therapist who has worked with children with serious illnesses, has written that most cultures before our own provided elders who helped adolescents enter into the adult world. "Their teachings were based on collectively recognized and accepted beliefs concerning issues of creation and birth, sexuality, death and its relation to life." Such teachings included "a relation to spirit, or some sense of the Other," while "the mystery of sexuality revealed in adolescence was placed in the context of social and spiritual law." Adolescents today, she says, do not find such collective rituals offered by the elders to support and facilitate their transition into adulthood, and deep, natural instinctive and spiritual changes which give meaning to the passage of our lives are frequently ignored. In an increasingly materialistic culture, Sullwold thinks that the extremely high suicide rate among young people, especially those from fifteen to nineteen years old, may be due to a lack of spiritual sustenance. Sometimes the only recognition our society provides of a major transition is that of allowing young people to get a license to drive a car, or the privilege to drink or vote. Longing for some form of collective support, young people turn to each other for instruction about the issues of life, "but," Sullwold says, "lack of experience and knowledge limit the possibility of true initiation." Concerning young women in particular, while other societies saw all older females, especially grandmothers and aunts, as potential mentors who could offer (besides one's mother) instruction about the essential qualities of womanhood and the responsibility consequent to them, in today's society this is not being provided. Young women often seem cut off from those vital resources, and as a consequence are sometimes uninformed about even basic realities, such as conception, pregnancy, and child care.[17]

Regarding young men, Robert Bly warns of what he calls Western culture's "unprecedented failure of fathering" of young males who, while unconsciously looking for models to emulate and something to fill their spiritual hunger, are instead (through advertising, television, and the Internet) "urged to fill the emptiness with alcohol, sexual conquests, clothes, designer drugs, rudeness, [and] self-pity." "Our society," he writes, "does not offer reliable mentors to help a son establish a link to the adult masculine." Bly warns men specifically of their need to mentor younger men: "It is not women's job to socialize young males.

That is the job of the older men, or from another point of view, it's the job of the entire culture." He also speaks of generativity in terms of reciprocity: "If we take an interest in younger ones by helping them find a mentor, by bringing them along to conferences or other adult activities, by giving attention to young ones not in our family at all, then our own feeling of being an adult will be augmented, and adulthood might again appear to be a desirable state for many young ones." Bly affirms the importance of male mentors in young men's lives, and suggests that when they hold younger men in their hearts, they give to them a blessing: a profound sense of being loved and accepted in a world often experienced as indifferent or outright hostile to them.[18]

Both Sullwold and Bly would most likely endorse such mentoring programs as "Big Sister" or Big Brother" which encourage reliable adults to befriend young people; Jump-Start programs in high schools which help students gain insights into some of the obstacles *within themselves* that limit their academic success; summer camps that with trustworthy staff can introduce younger people not only to a wider world, but sometimes, for the first time, to the awesome world of nature filled, as the ancient and Christian Celts believed, with the presence of God. Individual initiatives and creative programs can make a difference, helping young people tame their own fears, make gentle their dark sides, and face their own monsters of the deep—as both Columcille and Colman did—not alone, but with the experience, expertise, and most of all, guidance of worthy mentors and soul friends. In the long run, such efforts may contribute significantly to the bringing to birth of new hope and new directions in other lives. We might become midwives on their behalf.

Perhaps through some word of encouragement or of challenge, they might come to see themselves in a new light, with a future full of promise, or to take stock of their lives and their relationship with the cosmos. Our acts of generativity, however seemingly insignificant at the time, may indeed be crucial to someone else's development, although we might not discover that until years later. Whether change occurs or not, our generativity is related to a principle enunciated in the *Rule of St. Mochuda*, Colman's soul friend: "As you love your own soul, love the souls of all."[19]

Loving and respecting our own souls means bringing them to birth, attending to our own spiritual growth. This being midwives to our own souls is often linked to our willingness to be creative, to take risks when we are not sure of the outcome. Made in God's image (Gal 3:28) by an unbelievingly creative, imaginative God, *our* essential nature is to be creative. Creativity is the capacity within each of us to bring about change, to in effect change the world. At times our creative attempts may seem—and feel—akin to madness, since they so often begin, as the story of creation (Gen 1–2:4) shows, in chaos and darkness before light appears. Considering the inherent mystical nature of Celts, and especially of the Celtic saints we've studied, it is interesting that Jung says "only the mystics bring creativity into religion," probably due, he says, to their being close to the Holy Spirit with their hearts so intent on union with God.[20]

One source of creativity in our lives and in our work may in fact be what we initially most fear in ourselves or most heartily strive to avoid: our struggles, our supposed weaknesses, our failures. Still, as the poet David Whyte reminds us, "our deepest struggles are in effect our greatest spiritual and creative assets and the doors to whatever creativity we might possess."[21] Often it is the breakdown in our lives that leads to the spiritual breakthrough, as many recovering people can attest. But what is gained in terms of creativity may be the most genuine expression of the creative spirit, the Holy Spirit, for ourselves and for those whose lives we touch. Being creative can also save us from ourselves, our being overwhelmed by self-destructive tendencies, of which Marie Von Franz warns: "One of the most wicked destructive forces, psychologically speaking, is unused creative power....If someone has a creative gift and out of laziness, or for some other reason, doesn't use it, the psychic energy turns to sheer poison. That's why we often diagnose neuroses and psychotic diseases as not-lived higher possibilities."[22] Unused creative energy, she suggests, is worse than lost. Not only do our communities suffer from a gift unused, but we ourselves can become sick when we block expressions of our generativity. In the history of Christian spirituality, this phenomenon is well-documented, for when such medieval mystics as Hildegard of Bingen and such Native American shamans as Black Elk ignored their visions and voices for years, primarily out of fear, they eventually became emotionally and physically sick.

Being creative, being generative, means assuming greater responsibility for the values, beliefs, and spirituality we cherish rather than relying passively upon appointed leaders or outdated ecclesial structures to ensure their vitality. Where leadership is lacking, we need to provide it, and where nothing is being said, we must let our voices be heard. We do this (and also prevent depression and discouragement in ourselves and others) by working not for results but for particular people whom we love. As Thomas Merton wisely wrote in 1966 to James Forest, a young peace activist who was feeling depressed about his work: "Do not depend on the hope of results. When you are doing the sort of work you have taken on...you may have to face the fact that your work will be apparently worthless and even achieve no result at all...As you get used to this idea you start more and more to concentrate not on the results but on the value, the rightness, the truth of the work itself. And there too a great deal has to be gone through, as gradually you struggle less and less for an idea and more and more for specific people....In the end...it is the reality of personal relationships that saves everything."[23] It was certainly this, Colman's great love, that saved the lives of the two young boys whom his uncle wanted put to death. Colman's immediate response of accepting them, without hesitation, had life-changing effects for all of them, especially for Colman himself who must have experienced, as many do, the mysterious paradox of generativity which Jesus himself enunciated: "Give, and there will be gifts for you: a full measure, pressed down, shaken together, and overflowing, will be poured into your lap; because the standard you use will be the standard used for you" (Luke 6:38).

But how can we be truly generative for our friends, our communities, ourselves, and the larger world? What inner resources can we begin to depend upon if we are to become soul friends, mentors, and midwives for others? Here, for guidance, let us turn back to Colman's stories, and in particular to the symbols found within them. In our search for understanding, let us begin with the reference to the landscape and the swans.

The Hermaphrodite

Remember in O'Clery's hagiography of Colman it was said that after the saint settled down, "swans used to come every hour to sing to them, and relieve their fatigue; so that for this reason the place was called Land Ela (swans' land)." Swans appear in numerous myths and legends from many cultures, and are often linked with comforting music. In Greek mythology, they are associated with Apollo, the god of healing and music, oracles, prophecies, and poetry. In Celtic mythology, the four children of Lir, a divinity of the mother-goddess Danu and the father of the sea-god Manannan, are transformed by their jealous stepmother into white swans and sent into exile. What offered them some relief was the gift from their natural mother, it was said, of "making wonderful music." Like the swans of Land Ela, this music brought a great peace and gentleness to the land.[24] Besides music, healing, and gentleness, other symbolic associations with the swan can be found. The French scholar, Gaston Bachelard, equates its long phallic neck with the masculine and its rounded, silky body with the feminine, and thus suggests that the swan's true meaning is that of the hermaphrodite: a bisexual being who has characteristics of both genders, sexually and emotionally.[25] Another scholar, Alain Danielou, suggests that "primordial divinity is essentially bisexual," and that such a figure represents Eros, the spiritual power of connection, as well as of "the creative impulse."[26]

The term itself, *hermaphrodite*, originated in Greek mythology with Hermaphroditos, the son of Hermes (messenger of the gods and healer) and Aphrodite (goddess of love, beauty, fertility, and procreation), who while bathing became united in one body with the nymph Salmacis.[27] This hermaphroditic figure was linked with early visionaries, including the Greek seer Teiresias, who was depicted as an old man with a long beard and female breasts, symbolic, according to Camille Paglia, of the "fullness of emotional knowledge fusing sexes."[28] This fusion of sexes in the myth of the hermaphrodite, however, is definitely not limited to the Greeks, but is popular among many cultures and spiritual traditions. In India, the hermaphrodite was considered a primal force, the light from which life emanates; that is to say, the *lingam*. It is also associated with incarnations of the Mother God.[29] Pre-Columbian Mexicans believed in Quetzalcoatl, the god in whom the laws of the opposites and of the separate sexes were united. In China, Persia, Palestine, and Australia, such a divinity was often linked with spiritual energy and wisdom. Considering Danielou's equating the hermaphrodite with the creative impulse, it is interesting to note that in Egypt certain male leaders known for their creativity are depicted artistically as having feminine characteristics.[30]

Africa too has its appreciation of the hermaphrodite. In the Congo, wooden figures called *Nkisis* are carved with beards, penises, and large breasts. These artistic creations are linked with healing and, in the case of tribal chiefs, with androgyny, paternal and maternal qualities united in one leader.[31] Mircea Eliade believed that the hermaphrodite, in whatever tribe, represents "totality," the "integration of opposites." In his discussion of certain African tribes, he tells of shamans in southern Borneo whom he considers "true hermaphrodites, dressing and behaving like women." He says that their bisexuality arises from the fact "that these priest-shamans are regarded as intermediaries between the two cosmological planes—earth and sky—and also from the fact that they combine in their person the feminine element (earth) and the masculine element (sky).[32] Carl Jung, who studied many of these cultures, also wrote extensively on the image of the hermaphrodite. He posited that "it is a remarkable fact that perhaps the majority of cosmogonic gods are of a bisexual nature." Like Eliade, Jung says that "as civilization develops, the bisexual primordial being turns into a symbol of the unity of personality, a symbol of the self, where the war of opposites finds peace. In this way the primordial being [of the hermaphrodite] becomes the distant goal of man's self-development."[33]

Taking all of the above into account, we can now see more clearly the meaning of the stories of Colman's describing himself as having two paps, one filled with milk, one with honey, with which he fed his adopted sons and entire community. Obviously, besides the subtle imagery of swans, of all the stories of Colman of Land Ela, these paps are the most powerful image of his generativity as a mentor and midwife. Breasts are symbolic of feeding and nourishing, of generativity, linked most often with motherhood. As Campbell says, "the relationship of suckling to mother is one of symbiosis: though two, they constitute a unit."[34] In Colman's hagiography, the storyteller is saying that the saint provided spiritual nourishment that resulted in making both fosterlings and community one with him, Colman, and also one with each other, and one with God. Through his spiritual leadership he became the prime facilitator, the midwife of that spiritual union.

This depiction of Colman's suckling needs to be seen within the historical context of the Middle Ages when the Irish Life was probably first compiled.[35] From our knowledge of that period, Colman's hagiography was definitely not the only one to carry allusions to males nourishing others with their nipples or breasts. The *Life of Saint Malachy* by Bernard of Clairvaux, for example, speaks of the Irish-born Malachy going to see his mentor Bishop Malchus. According to Bernard, the younger man, Malachy, "stayed with him [the bishop] for some years, so that in that lapse of time he might drink deeply from his aged breast, being mindful of the proverb: with the ancient is wisdom."[36] A second hagiography is especially interesting, considering how Colman was compared to the Apostle John. In the introduction to the *Life of Berach*, John, the beloved disciple, is said to have "sucked the fountain of true wisdom from the breast of the Savior."[37] While certainly symbolic, the latter behavior also has highly erotic overtones that may be referring to a practice in the ancient world of men sucking other men's nipples for sexual stimulation and pleasure. This is explicitly alluded to in the *Confession* of St. Patrick when, in his escape from Ireland after years of captivity, he says, regarding the boatmen who at first refused to take him onboard their craft: "Earlier that day I had refused to suck their nipples out of reverence for God."[38]

Aside from this homoerotic side of Celtic males which was documented by ancient classical as well as native Irish writers, depictions of males suckling others (both women and men) are found in numerous medieval mystical writings, all symbolic of spiritual generativity. To name a few: in the thirteenth century, at the time of the canonization investigation of Francis of Assisi,

St. Clare spoke of a dream she had in which she "was climbing a very high stairway [and] when she reached Saint Francis, the saint bared his breast and said to the Lady Clare: 'Come, take and drink.'"[39] In fourteenth-century England, Julian of Norwich refers to the suckling Christ by comparing him to other human mothers who give their children milk.[40] In the sixteenth century, in Spain, the mystic Teresa of Avila describes God and Christ in maternal terms as having breasts.[41]

Women mystics were not the only ones who saw Christ in maternal imagery. The anonymous Monk of Farne Island, England, in the fourteenth century alludes to the androgynous nature of Christ's love, comparing him with "mothers who love their little children tenderly," "who give them the breast," and refers to the Scripture passage, "honey from the rock" (Deut 32:13) as the "sweetness from Christ." The monk also uses the highly erotic language with which many women mystics describe their own relationship with Jesus, quoting Christ as telling him: "All day long I stretch out my hands on the cross towards thee, O man, to embrace thee, I bow down my head to kiss thee when I have embraced thee, I open my side to draw thee into my heart after this kiss, that we may be two in one flesh." As was true of Celtic Christians, the monk's writing reveals a special devotion to John, the beloved disciple, whom he addresses in prayer: "Who could presume to compare you with any other, seeing that you recline trustfully on the bosom of the Only-begotten Son of God, that treasury of all wisdom and knowledge?"[42]

These allusions to breasts and to milk and honey remind us of Colman's paps being filled with milk and honey, powerful symbols, as the mystics recognized, of nourishment. Honey, of course, is associated with the creative activity of bees who themselves were linked in ancient times and the early church with diligence and eloquence. In the teachings of the Greeks, bees symbolized souls,[43] so we can see in the image of honey another expression of soul-making and midwifery. Milk is symbolic in its own right. In Ireland, as in India, cows were considered sacred animals, and the milk of a white cow, in particular, was equated with mystical powers, longevity, and poetic abilities. In a story from St. Ciaran's hagiography, the saint is said to have owned a Dun Cow (a cow of grayish-brown color) that produced milk which could feed a multitude[44]; again, obviously expressive of plenitude and spiritual nutrition.

Whatever filled the breasts of Christ and the saints, whether milk, honey, or as St. Bernard said, wisdom, it is clear that the depiction of suckling from their breasts was prevalent in numerous medieval spiritual, theological, and hagiographical writings as a symbol of spiritual enrichment given to another person by a mentor, elder, or soul friend. The scholar Ellen Ross refers to the presence of breasts on males as "cross-gendering," and explains it, as Julian of Norwich did, in terms of Jesus' motherhood: "Jesus as Mother who feeds the world with his/her body" is "a doubly-gendered Jesus, the literal embodiment of divine mercy reconciled with justice, who functions as the definitive paradigm of God's love for humankind. The double-gendered Jesus who lactates, bleeds, nurtures, heals, and feeds the world with his body becomes the root metaphor for an entire epoch."[45] Linked with Colman Ela, it also becomes a metaphor for ourselves as soul friends.

Considering this, we can see now that references to breasts and suckling in the hagiographical writings of St. Colman probably reflect an emerging awareness in western medieval Christian culture, theology, and spirituality of the need *not* to identify God exclusively with one gender. As evidenced in the writings of the sources quoted above, medieval Christians clearly had less problems with the feminine side of God than many Christians do today. They obviously saw the divine as having both male and female qualities, united in an androgynous, wholistic form. And, of course, if a saint is (as hagiographies portray him or her) an *imitatio Christi*, an imitation of Christ, such hermaphroditic or cross-gendering depictions of the saint reflect medieval Christians' increasing conviction that spiritual leadership—and holiness—is also androgynous.

Androgyny and Spiritual Leadership

The term *androgyny* comes from two Greek words: *andro* (male) and *gyne* (female), and usually refers to the interplay of masculine and feminine energies within the universe and the individual soul. There are numerous allusions to this concept in medieval writings, especially those of the mystics. Bernard of Clairvaux, the soul friend of Malachy,[46] frequently describes Christ *and himself* in androgynous terms. He speaks of Christ's androgyny when he tells his pastoral charges: "Do not let the roughness of our life frighten your tender years. If you feel the stings of temptation…suck not so much the wounds as the breasts of the Crucified. He will be your mother, and you will be his son." Concerning himself, he says in a letter to the parents of a Geoffrey of Peronne: "Do not be sad about your Geoffrey or shed any tears on his account....I will be for him both a mother and a father, both a brother and a sister. I will make the crooked path straight for him and the rough places smooth." In sermons on the Song of Songs, he repeatedly compares references to breasts in the biblical text with prelates, abbots, and spiritual guides' obligations to "mother" the souls in their charge. As Christ's breasts give "such overwhelming joy," Bernard says, so those "who have undertaken the direction of souls" should bring joy and wisdom to others: "Here is a point for the ear of those superiors who wish always to inspire fear in their communities and rarely promote their welfare....Learn that you must be mothers to those in your care, not masters; make an effort to arouse the response of love, not that of fear....Show affection as a mother would, correct like a father. Be gentle, avoid harshness, do not resort to blows, expose your breasts: let your bosoms expand with milk. If you are spiritual, instruct...in a spirit of gentleness...."[47]

Bernard's words remind us of the two sides of Colman's mentoring Baithin: his disciplinary side, in kicking his young charge out, and his gentleness in welcoming him back. In Bernard's own hagiography of Malachy, in which he actually portrays the Irish saint as a midwife helping two women give birth,[48] we come even closer to a type of androgyny that transcends roles which have been defined strictly according to gender. When Bernard speaks of Malachy's paternal and maternal qualities, we find a description that might apply to Colman as well: "He lived as though he were the one father of all. He cuddled them all and he protected them under the shelter of his wings, as a hen gathers her chickens. He did not distinguish sex, age, condition or person; he left no one out, embracing everyone in his merciful heart."[49]

Less than a hundred years after Bernard, St. Francis (1181–1226 C.E.) articulated his own understanding of androgyny when he writes: "We are spouses when the faithful soul is joined to our Lord Jesus Christ by the Holy Spirit. We are brothers to Him when we 'do the will of the Father Who is in heaven' (Matt 12: 50). We are mothers, when we carry Him in our heart and body through divine love and a pure and sincere conscience, and when we give birth to Him through His holy manner of working, which should shine before others as an example."[50]

As soul friends, then, this giving birth to the Savior, to the divine in others and ourselves, is intrinsically related to the integration of masculine and feminine energies within us. Jung says in his writings, "Long before the physiologists demonstrated that by reason of our glandular structure there are both male and female elements in all of us, it was said that 'every man carries a woman within himself.' It is this female element in every male that I have called the 'anima.'"[51] The male element in every female Jung posited as the "animus." Each of us, whatever our gender or sexual orientation, needs to come to name, accept, and integrate these masculine and feminine aspects of ourselves. As Marion Woodman suggests, "Whether we are in homosexual or heterosexual relationships, the two energies, masculine and feminine, are present in both men and women. Their inner complementarity, in its fulfillment, becomes what is called the 'inner marriage,' like the marriage of day and night." She also describes this as "the marriage of the sun and the moon."[52] Both Jung and Woodman consistently speak of the marriage of the masculine and feminine within as an archetypal expression of wholeness. Both also affirm the necessity of such an integration for individuals as well as the wider society.

The ancient Celts worshipped both the sun and the moon, gods and goddesses; they gave proper due to the abilities of both women and men, and did not restrict social and spiritual leadership to one gender alone. Eastern religious beliefs, many of which are so similar to those of the ancient Celts, have long affirmed that all of creation consists of both masculine and feminine constellations or energies which need not be seen as antagonistic to each other, but complementary. The Benedictine monk and protégé of C.S. Lewis, Bede Griffiths, who spent much of his later years in India, wrote of the personal and cultural implications of this: "Every man and woman is both male and female, and in every person the marriage of the male and the female has to take place. When man refuses to recognize the feminine aspect in himself, he despises or exploits woman and exalts reason over intuition, science over art, man over nature, the white races with their dominant reason over the coloured peoples with their intuitive feeling and imagination. This has been the course of Western civilization over the past centuries. Now we are awakening to the place of woman in society, to the meaning of sex and marriage, to the value of art and intuition and to the place of the coloured peoples in the civilization of the world. What has to take place is a 'marriage' of East and West, of the intuitive mind with the scientific reason."[53]

This integration of male and female, reason and intuition, what the Christian Celts called "mind and heart," can be seen in one twentieth-century representative figure from the East, Mohatma Gandhi. Erik Erikson, in his biography of the political and spiritual leader of India, refers to the culture of India and Gandhi himself in ways that recall the devotion of the pagan Celts to their goddesses, especially Ana or Danu, and the classical writers' disgust with Celtic men's homoerotic behavior. Erikson says that in India "the power of the mother goddesses probably has also given India that basic bisexuality which, at least to her British conquerors, appeared contemptible and yet also uncanny and irresistible in every sense of the word." Within this culture, Erikson says, Gandhi "tried to make himself the representative of that bisexuality in a combination of autocratic malehood and enveloping maternalism." Gandhi's identification with both of his natural parents and his internalizing of both types of energies from them, helped him, according to Erikson, "release a new energy capable of awakening corresponding energies in others...almost as though he had provided in his own person a new matrix, had become India herself."[54] St. Colman of Land Ela seems to have done the same for his fosterlings and his community.

The bisexuality that Erikson posits of Gandhi, of course, is not the same as androgyny, although they may overlap. June Singer, analyst and writer, says that "the concerns of the bisexual are mainly *interpersonal*, the androgyne are mainly intrapsychic."[55] In such leaders as Gandhi, this distinction does not hold, but Singer is right to suggest that while bisexuality is about the erotic attraction to both genders, androgyny is the spiritual and psychic task of everyone as they grow older, no matter what their sexual orientation. However, as the study of history as well as recent research have shown, sexual orientation itself is not as simple as some would believe it to be. "Sexual preference," according to one study, "is much less fixed and much more complicated and fascinating than most current thinking holds."[56] Still, androgyny is a fundamental principle, Singer believes, "that has existed for so long that it may be said to be inherent in the nature of the human organism." It is present in everyone, she says, "ready to be tapped as a source of energy." Inner strength and spiritual energy can be discovered in the openness to the opposites within oneself. Inner dualities, however, such as activity-passivity, competition-cooperation, logic-intuition, logos and eros should not be exclusively identified with a certain gender, but constitute inner dynamics everyone shares. "Resolution of our psychic dualities is not in combat between them, but in the active loving of each for the other."[57] In the long run, Singer suggests, a commitment to the inner process of developing our androgyny will result in changed behavior and, I would add, changed mentoring.

Lionell Corbett, another Jungian analyst and teacher, would agree with Singer in a number of ways. Internal "masculine" and "feminine" energies, he writes, should not be totally identified with male and female as culturally defined or conditioned. They represent, he believes, psychological and spiritual principles in their own right. While, because of obvious physical differences of the genders, there may be some association of masculine qualities with those of penetrating, initiating, asserting, and feminine qualities with receiving, harmonizing, and nurturing, we need to beware of equating men with reason and women with emotion or stating, for example, that when a woman is being assertive and logical this is her "masculinity." Perhaps, instead, it is very much a part of her feminine personality. "To equalize the core metaphors," Corbett suggests, "symbolically women may inseminate and men may gestate." Welcoming and integrating the opposites within (in whatever way we might define them) is really about transcending gender stereotypes, and embracing those elements within us that cause tension and harm to others. If we are to be truly generative and creative, if we are to have any sense of integrity about our lives, this slow and painful process has to do with taking responsibility for our own growth rather than blaming our parents, our spouses, our children, other races, other countries, or the other sex for our own misery. Coming to an acceptance and appreciation of what lies within is essentially, as Singer had said and Corbett reiterates, a loving task: "Only through love can these opposites of masculinity and femininity be transcended....In the androgyne masculine and feminine energies are combined but not confused." "As we grow older," Corbett concludes, "we realize our individuality through androgyny."[58] The Celts would agree with him, associating much of this internal process of reconciliation with soul-making, which they linked with aging and preparing for one's own death.

This task of aging, of becoming an elder, of acting as a soul friend, then, is that of accepting, reconciling, integrating those masculine and feminine energies that live within us and, really, in all of creation. Discovering as one ages that there need not be antagonism but rather mutuality between those energies, we can find resources for our work and for our relationships precisely in those parts of us that might seem so foreign and unfamiliar. No matter what our gender, if we have a tendency to always assert ourselves verbally, we might begin to listen more; if we find ourselves always listening patiently, we may need to be more forthcoming about our views. If we have a highly-developed emotional side, it may be time to develop our more rational side; and, if we never acknowledge feelings, it may be important for us to learn to do so. We might take risks instead of standing still—or stand still, instead of always living on the edge. However change begins, and however slowly it seems to come, we will gradually experience a lessening of resentments and hostilities, and the emergence of a greater sense of harmony, balance, and peace. Ours, like that of the saints, is a journey characterized not by spiritual perfection, but spiritual progress. If progress seems slow or minimal, we may need to remind ourselves that the Celtic saints' search for their place of resurrection took many roads and numerous unexpected turns.

Intimately related to all this, of course, is self-knowledge, what Jung describes as "an adventure that carries us unexpectedly far and deep."[59] Resources for this adventure can be found in our dreams, as St. Patrick discovered; in our instinctual side, as St. Brigit's stories imply; in our intuitions, visions, and voices, as Columcille's stories confirm. Having a soul friend ourselves, or a spiritual guide, will of course help us with this ongoing process of reconciliation and integration. Such soul-making, however, often only begins in earnest when our lives become inexplicably immersed in chaos, melancholy, depression, and despair, a condition of soul that Jung calls *nigredo*,[60] a time of darkness alluded to in Dante's *The Divine Comedy* and in St. John of the Cross's *Dark Night of the Soul*. However uncomfortable (and comfortableness is definitely not its trait!), this necessary stage of transformation involves confronting our shadow side—that dark, often addictive side of what has been unacknowledged or repressed on an unconscious level, precisely because we are so afraid of it.[61] Confronting the shadow is about facing our demons, as the desert Christians advised their protégés; it is about confessing from the heart, as Cassian affirmed, so that we might be truly free of the dragons that lie within. It's about facing our monsters, as Columcille and Colman did, engaging them courageously, or forever risking to live an inauthentic life. What contemporary Irish pilgrim guides, Marcus Losack and Michael Rodgers, say about the stories of St. Kevin of Glendalough apply to Colman and each of us as well: "We all fight the monsters of the deep; we all struggle with conflicts and contradictory longings that pull us at times in different directions."[62] Colman's way of dealing with monsters, however, shows something more: how not to confront them alone, but to go to them and defeat them with the support and encouragement of our friends.

In Colman's story, as we recall, the first monster was a female: "a small pointed gaping apparition in the shape of a woman." This figure may reflect Colman's own need to come to terms with his feminine side, his anima, "the intermediary between the conscious personality of a man and the depths of his being, the collective unconscious."[63] It may also reflect his "mother complex," what Robert Johnson calls "the most difficult encounter any man faces," and associates with regression, the desire to evade responsibility, to be taken care of—rather than to care for himself and the world. In words that echo the dramatic encounters Colman had with the first monster, Johnson says: "In

Western mythology, the mother complex is represented by the dragon that every hero has to face and conquer," if he is to become mature.[64] Unless peace is made with that reality *within*, reality *outside ourselves* will be forever conflictual and distorted. The same, of course, applies to every woman and her internal relationship with the masculine. In order to awaken a woman's "creative masculinity," according to Marion Woodman, a similar battle with "mother" must also take place, transforming the unceasing demands of the inner "Devouring Mother" with the "Great Mother" who is capable of great warmth *and* self-assertiveness.[65] What is particularly intriguing about Colman's story is that he chooses not to destroy the monster himself, but after she is dead to bury her at the very location of his monastery—as if he intuitively knew that she held great spiritual power for his monks, and that she would offer fecundity to the land as the swans offered relief to his and his monks' fatigue.

Transcending Stereotypes and Mediating Differences

Colman's stories, with allusions to monsters, swans, and generative breasts, remind us that spiritual leadership in general, and soul friendship in particular, is about integrating our masculine and feminine energies. If we are not committed to this integration of opposites, we will increasingly become one-sided in our ministries and off-center in our work. Likewise our institutions, especially our churches, will become or continue to be exclusionary rather than inclusive; restrictive rather than creative; defensive rather than open to the transforming Spirit of

God. We become involved in this reconciliation process by start-ing with ourselves, but also by relying on our families, friends, and communities to help us with this enterprise. We also may find inspiration, insight, and encouragement for our soul-making by turning to other spiritual traditions which, like that of the Celts, reflect a non-dualistic stance.

One spiritual tradition, similar to the Celts with their *anamchara*, is that of the Native Americans and their *berdache*. According to the recent research of scholars Walter Williams and Will Roscoe, a berdache was someone of either gender who acted as a shaman for numerous tribes in North America, serv-ing in a mediating function between women and men. Both gen-ders of berdache were frequently attributed with spiritual powers, had highly developed intuitive forms of knowledge, and valued visions, dreams, and trance states as sources of informa-tion, direction, ability, and fortune.[66] Evidently like the shamans of Borneo discussed by Eliade, male berdaches engaged in many of the same actions often associated with the female gender, doing "at least some women's work," according to Williams, and mixing together "much of the behavior, dress, and social roles of women and men."[67] This was true of female berdaches as well. Of the 155 tribes that have been documented as having male berdaches, in about a third of these groups "a formal status also existed for females who undertook a man's lifestyle, becoming hunters, warriors, and chiefs." According to Roscoe, "the most visible marker of berdache gender status was some form of cross-dressing, although this occurred much less consistently than is usually assumed." Female berdaches, he says, often "wore men's clothing only when hunting or in battle. Similarly, despite the common description of berdaches as 'doing the work of the opposite sex,' they more often engaged in a combination of men's and women's activities, along with the pursuits unique to their status."[68]

Like the Celts, then, berdaches transcended the strict roles later identified in Western civilization with "masculinity" and "femininity." The tradition of male berdaches helps us see the depiction of Colman nurturing his young as not so unusual—as the tradition of female berdaches who sometimes cross-dressed gives us a new understanding of the desert mother, Pelagia, who after her conversion dressed as a man and was known as Pelagius, and the Celtic shaman and mystic, Joan of Arc, who was so violently and unfairly condemned for her own cross-dressing.[69] Perhaps most of all, though, it is Native Americans' experiences that can show us, according to Williams, how much gender roles in the West are typified by "dichotomies of groups perceived to be mutually exclusive: male and female, black and white, right and wrong, good and evil." Unlike our dominant Western culture, "most American Indian worldviews generally are much more accepting of the ambiguities of life. Acceptance of gender variation in the berdache tradition is typical of many native cultures' approach to life in general." While many berdaches were linked with what we today identify with homosexual, lesbian, or bisexual behavior, they were not denigrated as a result, but valued by family and tribe. As a member of the Crow Nation is quoted as saying, "We don't waste people, the way white society does. Every person has their gift."[70]

Berdaches to an amazing degree are documented as performing some of the same functions as the early Celtic soul friends: acting as leaders in ceremonial events and reconcilers between individuals and tribes; caring for the sick; conducting the singing and dancing rites at funerals. They were also reputed to be very effective teachers of the young, healers through their compassionate service, and frequently in contact with the spirits of their ancestors. Most especially, according to Williams: "The berdache receives respect partly as a result of being a mediator. Somewhere between the status of women and men, berdaches not only mediate between the sexes but between the psychic and the physical—between the spirit and the flesh. Since they mix the characteristics of both men and women, they possess the vision of both. They have double vision, with the ability to see more clearly than a single gender perspective can provide. This is why they are often referred to as 'seer,' one whose eyes can see beyond the blinders that restrict the average person....They utilize their strength to be of special benefit to others, in particular to their own family."[71]

What the berdache tradition recommends to us is the development of natural gifts and erotic energies in service to families and tribes. And whatever our sexual orientation, it presupposes that we begin to develop that interior reconciliation between our masculine and feminine sides. In practice, it may mean moving beyond gender stereotypes in new ministries of creativity and service. This approach of interior integration is rooted in a healthy and inclusive spirituality, one that values feminine and masculine elements and energies. It presupposes that our communities and churches welcome both genders as active participants and spiritual leaders—a model, I would suggest, that is already found in the "double monasteries" of the

Early Celtic Church where collaboration between lay and ordained, male and female leaders frequently occurred, and where being ordained in itself did not preclude having a family. Uniting in ourselves both masculine and feminine energies, we might, in our ministries, as Bernard of Clairvaux advocates, be "both a mother and a father, both a brother and a sister" to others, making "crooked paths straight and rough places smooth." Then the words which Bernard applied to his soul-friend, Malachy, may apply to us as well: "He left no one out, embracing everyone in his merciful heart."

The Heart and Its Perception

As mentioned, St. Colman of Land Ela's feastday is September 26, a date that celebrates the life and soul friendship of a holy man who suckled two foster-sons with his amazing paps. Whether one translates the term "paps" as referring to either nipples or breasts, they seem a fitting symbol of what constitutes the nurturing aspect of all soul friendships, no matter the gender, as well as the mentoring and midwifery that each of us is called to do. That Colman is said to have fostered two young boys is significant. Two was the number associated, like the swan, with the hermaphrodite, a person who combines aspects of both genders. The number two also figures prominently in Greek, Roman, and Celtic culture: Hermes, the Greek god and father of Hermaphroditos, although not married, had two sons; the city of Rome is said to have been founded by Remus and Romulus, two orphans suckled by a she-wolf[72]; while the Romano-Celtic goddess of fertility, Dea Nutrix, is shown in statues of her suckling twin babes.[73] This, along with the two paps with which the celibate Colman suckled two boys, reveals that generativity is not limited to procreation, but to the transforming power of one's love, that boundless energy which, when truly free, overflows all the ideological vessels that our society and churches construct to contain it. In all of his stories, in terms of levels of meaning, Colman stands as a fitting symbol of the creative union of opposites, a union that must take place in each of us, male or female, if we are to reach maturity and become effective elders for our families, communities, and tribes. Colman's acting as a healer and reconciler (or as Jung says, "a subduer of conflicts") reveals what we all are capable of doing when we commit ourselves to our own process of reconciliation within.

Paps or breasts, of course, are close to the heart, and the heart is what connects mentors and friends to one another. To be a mentor and midwife of the soul, to be a soul friend, is based upon a communion of the heart, an intimate connection that begins, for the Christian, with Jesus, *the* companion of one's soul. Colman evidently had this relationship with Christ, since he was compared, as we saw, with John the beloved disciple, and was called "the great John of Erin's sons." Colman of Land Ela must have frequently laid his head on Christ's heart, reclining, as the Monk of Farne Island said, "trustfully on the bosom of the Only-begotten Son of God, that treasury of all wisdom and knowledge." Praying and listening attentively to Christ is what all Christian soul friends must do; to the Christ who is, from a Jungian perspective, both the living symbol of the Self and of androgynous energies each of us can assimilate and express.

This is what John, the beloved disciple, was known to do, and what the Monk of Farne, Colman, and so many other mystics, practiced. They understood that essential to all inner work is this attentive listening to the heart, that deepest part of ourselves, expressed in feelings and intuitions, dreams and visions, imagination, yearnings, and tears.

Conclusion

Stronger than a hundred is the counsel of the heart.

Medieval Welsh Poem

T his book has been about the soul friend, as reflected in the stories of the Celtic saints. These stories have shown us the various dimensions of soul friendship, and roles of leadership that can be associated with it—whether one sees oneself as a spiritual guide or shaman, pioneer or pastor, teacher or tutor, mentor or midwife, or a combination of all of these. To know these tales is to be initiated into a vital spiritual tradition, for all storytelling is an initiatory process, passing on from one generation to another ancient truths. Stories initiate us into the sacred memory of a tribe or people, and link us directly with the wisdom of the elders. They also give us an identity. They are the glue that holds a family, tribe, nation, and planet together. To know and identify with the stories of the *anamchara* makes us capable of incorporating that spiritual heritage into our self-understanding, relationships, work, and daily life.

Looking back upon those stories, we are conscious of certain important aspects of that special relationship between friends. First of all, as the popular saying of St. Brigit reminds us, everyone needs a soul friend, since "anybody without a soul friend is like a body without a head." All of us need at least one soul friend to help discern the sacredness of the life we have been given to live, and to help celebrate and remember the sacred journey each of us is on. The ancient saying of St. Brigit acknowledges this human need and sacred trust. To have such a person in our lives or to be such a person for others is to experience great joy and felicity. As Aelred of Rievaulx, a twelfth-century Northumbrian monastic writer of Celtic blood, states in his classic, *Spiritual Friendship*: "What happiness, what security, what joy to have someone to whom you dare to speak on terms of equality as to another self; one to whom you can unblushingly make known what progress you have made in the spiritual life; one to whom you can entrust all the secrets of your heart and before whom you can place all your plans."[1] Such a person or persons is cause for gratitude for, as Thomas Merton has acknowledged: "Merely reading books and following the written instructions of past masters is no substitute for direct contact with a living teacher."[2]

A second awareness is that soul friendship, while it can embody many leadership roles and be identified in numerous ways, is always rooted in the heart. This heart-work draws upon inner strengths and resources that the stories of Patrick, Brigit, Columcille, and Colman express, and that every soul friend needs to develop and incorporate into their lives: the virtues of courage, compassion, hospitality, and generativity; the resources of dreams, instincts, intuitions, and masculine/feminine energies. All of these are associated with the heart, and its inherent wisdom. Our contemporary culture is discovering the reality of the heart—beyond its romantic connotations. In the field of psychology, the heart has been described as "the seat of imagination," and imagination as "the authentic voice of the heart."[3] This is a valuable insight if we relate it to our own prayer life, as Ignatius of Loyola recommends,[4] or to any mentoring that we do, especially helping others discern their calling, their vocation, their "dream." While Carl Jung thought that the professions of psychotherapy and counseling are specifically rooted in our hearts, every form of soul friendship is as well. Quoting the medieval physician, Paracelsus, Jung says that "where there is no love, there is no art," and "the practice of this art [of healing therapy] lies in the heart; if your heart is false, the physician within you will be false."[5] Early Celtic Christians held a similar belief, stating that the best spiritual guide or soul friend is the person who is "competent to answer for his [or her] own soul first."[6] Those insights, of course, are not altogether new to the great world religions or to our Judeo-Christian heritage.

In the history of Judeo-Christian spirituality, the heart stands as a key symbol of our spiritual center, containing a depth that is often linked with our psyche or soul. From the heart flows the emotional, intellectual, volitional, and moral aspects of our personalities and deeper selves. As such, the heart possesses, if we but acknowledge it, wisdom far more real and insightful than reason alone can provide. The word heart (*lebab* in Hebrew and *cardia* in Greek) occurs more than a thousand times in the Scriptures; most of these references are not describing the physical organ of the heart, but the heart as the root or source of these faculties. Augustine himself saw the heart as containing an unfathomable depth in which a person's truth resides, a truth and a depth that only God can fill. Not only did the Celtic Christians affirm this, but also the great leaders and spiritual writers of the Reformation, including Martin Luther, George Herbert, George Fox, John and Charles Wesley, and John Bunyan. The latter, in his *Pilgrim's Progress*, speaks of "the dusty Parlor of the heart" in need of constant sweeping, and describes the life of holiness in terms Celts especially would appreciate: "heart-holiness, family-holiness, conversation-holiness."[7]

Jesus was aware of the tradition of the heart found in his own Jewish spiritual heritage, a tradition that believed wisdom, discernment, and knowledge are seated in the heart (cf. Exod 28:3, Deut 8:5, 1 Kgs 3:12). He encouraged people to pay attention to where their hearts lead them, "for wherever your treasure is, that is where your heart will be too" (Luke 12:34). He consistently called for repentance, a change of heart (Matt 4:17). In continuity with his message and ministry, the practice of the Celtic soul friend shows that this *metanoia* often depends upon three things: the genuine desire to change one's life, the presence of a loving person in whom one can confide, and the sharing of one's story with this person. *Metanoia* also has much to do with centering our hearts in God as we speak honestly, without deception, from out of our own centers. According to the Celts who had such a great appreciation of triads, every soul friendship is made up of more than two persons. It naturally includes three: a third holy presence, God, the ultimate soul friend, who unites the other two. Giving over of one's heart, exploring with someone else what the Irish poet Patrick Kavanagh refers to as the "secret room in the heart,"[8] is what characterizes soul friend relationships.

When two people speak truthfully and, at times, courageously, transformation begins, and can become an ongoing reality. "In the end," as Francis de Sales reminds us, "only the language of the heart can ever reach another heart."[9]

A third awareness regarding soul friendship also concerns the heart: learning to see and listen with it. James Hillman links mentoring and spiritual guidance with having a "perceptive eye," that is, having the ability to see something essential in the other. This "eye," he says, is "the eye of the heart. Something moves in the heart, opening it to perceiving the image in the heart of the other": the image of potential greatness, of calling, of vocation which the mentor or guide, with his or her perceptive eye, can then help foster in the life of the protégé. The stories of the Celtic saints and soul friends are filled with examples of what Hillman calls these "perceptual relationships." This eye of the heart is essential to any soul friendship today. Such relationships can impart a blessing with their sight, insight, and inspiration. As Hillman says about these friendships, they are like "two acorns on the same branch, echoing similar ideals"; what bliss there is in finding, he says, "a corresponding soul who singles us out! How long we move about, desperate to discover someone who can really see us, tell us who we are."[10]

Besides James Hillman, a number of early Irish writers were fond of the expression "to see with the eyes of the heart," while the opening lines of St. Benedict's Rule, written in the sixth century, imply that the heart has an ear with which any novice or neophyte should learn to listen attentively.[11] The Celtic saints both *saw* and *heard* with the heart, paying attention to what their physical eyes saw and their experiences taught them, but also to what their feelings, intuitions, and instincts were telling them to do. They knew that this attentiveness to the inner world gave them the ability to hear the voice of the Holy Spirit in their hearts, speaking to them possibly of works yet to be created, of spiritual adventures yet to be undertaken, of contributions to family, kin, and tribe yet to be made. In many ways, prayer for soul friends is the discipline of beginning to listen, truly listen with the eyes and ears of God. In the heart, we discover our identity and vocation. In the heart can also be found God's peace, or *quies*, a Latin word expressing both sanity and serenity. In the heart we find a window to our souls. By praying daily, by paying attention to the heart, we begin to acquire a wisdom of the heart that transcends intellectual knowledge alone.

All the Celtic soul friends were teachers of prayer, and spiritual leaders leading souls to God. Out of prayer, miracles of transformation, and healing, forgiveness happen; in prayer we learn and discern the right direction of our lives, and what God, neighbor, and our deepest selves are calling us to do. In prayer, we learn to listen to the heartbeat of God, as did John the beloved disciple. When it comes to prayer, those of us who learn from the Celtic spiritual tradition will appreciate praying outdoors, observing closely the landscape, the movement of the moon at night across an open sky, the sun rays reflected in the falling snow. We might develop a daily routine in which we rise early, perhaps at dawn as the first streaks light the horizon, to welcome the day. We might prefer to jog or walk the same route, being attentive to the changes related to the seasons that remind us of the changes in our own lives—the pattern of birth, maturation, aging, death, renewal. Whatever time of day or night, this prayerful attention to our natural surroundings, whether in forest, desert, city, or town, helps us discover—or recover—a sense of wonder, a depth of feeling named "joy" that transcends the conflicts and sorrows that we carry.

Praying in a Celtic way is also related to our families, to our ancestors, and to the stories we tell about them. This prayer of *anamnesis*, of remembering with gratitude, has a long and rich history, beginning with Jesus' own Jewish heritage, and reflected in the Eucharist. Through remembering the past and the telling of stories about our elders and ancestors, we learn something more about our own identities, and the recognition of our own need for being generative. Like other peoples, such as the ancient Romans, Native Americans, Chinese, and Japanese, we might construct a family prayer-shrine in a part of the house where pictures of our ancestors are placed and a candle lit to honor their ongoing presence with us. Children learn from this example of respect, and this practice of remembering both living and dead. They learn about the pattern to which T.S. Eliot refers in his poetry: how "the communication of the dead is tongued with fire," and "as we grow older, the World becomes stranger, the pattern more complicated of dead and living."[12] By watching us light the fire at the prayer-shrine, our children learn about the importance of remembering, and of handing over to God the needs and petitions that lie within our hearts.

Praying in the Celtic tradition presupposes that we can pray anywhere or any time for, as the early Celts knew from the writings of the desert father, John Cassian, prayer is simply the opening of our hearts and lives to God. Still, as they recognized, we each need to find a place of solitude, a *dysert*, perhaps a "cell" or room of our own for reflection, journaling, recalling the dreams that have come to us at night or in the early morning hours. We also realize, from the early Celts' example, the value of carving out from our hectic schedules times of retreat at least once a year, perhaps by spending a few days at a retreat house or a place where the natural landscape speaks to us of the majesty of God. Some of us too, if possible, undertake pilgrimages to the lands of our ancestors where we experience, often in unexpected ways, the healing, forgiving, and guiding powers of God, as Celtic pilgrims did before us.

Finally, soul friendship is about sharing stories, the stories of our lives. Martin Foy, my great-great-grandfather, affirmed that everyone has a story to tell, one that upon reflection may reveal what he discovered in the telling of his: the experience (as the Israelites had on their journey to the Promised Land) of being led by some mysterious force, a higher power, a holy spirit, perhaps, like St. Patrick an angelic guide. In order to discover this, it is important to tell our stories not only as my ancestor did his, when our hearts are overflowing, but perhaps most especially when they are cold and our lives seem hopelessly "stuck," empty, without meaning. Whenever we do so, for whatever reason we do so, we often begin to experience a new direction in our lives, a new vitality or energy, a new strength. A medieval Welsh poem reminds us, "stronger than a hundred is the counsel of the heart."[13] Stories are key to the acquisition of this strength, for they often reveal, as Jung has written about healing therapy, the "heights and depths of human suffering." The telling of a person's "secret story," Jung says, is crucial to transformation, and healing therapy only really starts "after the investigation of that wholly personal story. It is the patient's secret, the rock against which he is shattered. If I know his secret story, I have a key to the treatment….The crucial thing is the story. For it alone shows the human background and the human suffering…."[14]

The desert and Celtic Christians knew this truth centuries before Jung recommended the practice to psychiatrists, psychologists, and pastoral counselors. They knew from experience what other ancient spiritual traditions affirmed as a sound psychological and theological principle: "If you are looking for a healer's cure, you must lay bare the wound." Or as Homer says in the *Iliad*, "Speak out, don't hide it in your heart."[15] This fundamental idea is one that John Cassian wrote about: how important it is for everyone to speak directly from the heart to another person, a form of self-disclosure that often begins with some form of inventory or general examination of one's life. "All the corners of our heart," he writes, "must therefore be examined thoroughly," for only then will we manage "to destroy the lairs of the wild beasts within us and the hiding places of the venomous serpents."[16] Any such close scrutiny of ourselves, of course, requires courage, an inner strength that comes from the Latin word *cor*, meaning heart. Many times we are afraid to peer into our hearts, to face the truth about ourselves. Often a soul friend can help us with the task that Abba Poemen recommended: "Teach your mouth to say that which you have in your heart."[17] Inviting people to tell their stories is to help them discover common roots, experience a healing of their pasts, and transform weakness into strength, despair into hope, isolation into community.

The desert and Celtic Christians and Jung were not the only ones to affirm this practice of uniting story with heart.

Chief Joseph of the Nez Perce Indians of Oregon, in the nineteenth century, advised his followers and the white men who considered them enemies: "I believe much trouble would be saved if we opened our hearts more."[18] Storytelling that arises from the heart is a sacred act, a holy art, and in the context of soul friendship becomes a significant form of spiritual mentoring. Being a soul friend is making room in our lives and hearts for the sharing of others' stories.

This hospitable receptivity involves three simple movements. The first occurs when we make ourselves available in an unhurried manner, welcoming the other person in a warm, supportive way that will allow him or her to feel comfortable in telling us their story. This presupposes a great deal of patience in not forcing the other to disclose too quickly when he or she may not yet be prepared to do so. For whatever reason (sometimes fear, sometimes denial or shame), it might take years before a person is ready for full disclosure. However, when that moment finally comes, it may well be due largely to the hospitality, acceptance, and patience of the soul friend. As the desert father Abba Zeno gently said to the young monk who (because of his great shame) repeatedly put off telling the older man of his sexual desires, "It is you who must say what is the matter with you." Only then did the young man make his revelation:

> Covered with shame, I made known to him my passion, and he said to me: "Am I not a man too? Do you want me to tell you what I know? That you have been coming here for three years with these thoughts and you have not let them out." I prostrated myself,

begged him and said, "For the Lord's sake, have pity on me." He said to me, "Go, do not neglect your prayer, and do not speak ill of anyone." I returned to my cell, and did not neglect my prayer; and by the grace of Christ and by the prayers of the old man, I was bothered no longer by that passion.[19]

The second movement is listening attentively to the story being told and holding it gently for awhile. As Augustine makes clear in his writings, the meaning of confession is to testify, to witness, "to speak out what the heart holds true."[20] During this time of listening to and holding the story, the soul friend seeks to discern and guide what the other is attempting to articulate. In this context, a soul friend frequently acts like a mirror, reflecting the acceptance, mercy, and love of God, which in turn (precisely because of that loving acceptance) invites the other to look into his or her own heart or, as Augustine would express it, into his or her own face. The purpose of disclosing one's heart is to learn *diacrisis*: the discernment of spirits, the naming of our sometimes proud, vain, illusory, or obsessive drives.[21] Being a soul friend is about helping others name, claim, and tame their dark sides so that they may experience healing, greater freedom, and spiritual growth. Whatever soul-sicknesses we might identify, coming to an awareness of their destructive power can be a turning point: like finally seeing for the first time, when for years we have been blinded, either by the darkness of our ignorance and willfulness, or the bright light of our illusions. Being a soul friend is being someone who provides clarity and manifests God's acceptance in the flesh, so that another person can perhaps experience the joy of being forgiven. Whether the soul friend functions in a more formal professional role or in a more personal relationship, such an experience of acceptance and forgiveness can be, according to Paul Tillich, the greatest experience anyone can have: "the fundamental experience in any encounter with God."[22]

The third movement connected with storytelling is that of affirming the other person's disclosure through our words or gestures of support, and then returning the story to the teller with the understanding that only he or she can live it out. As expressed in the Tamastslikt Cultural Center of the Nez Perce Indians in Pendleton, Oregon, not only does every person have a story to tell (as my ancestor believed), but *every person is a story*. To embrace our life with all its conflicts and richness, and our personality with all its gifts *and limitations* is to become aware of our life as an evolving story. A soul friend is someone who listens reverently to the living story that presents himself or herself, while allowing that person to acknowledge his or her own pain. Such a receptive openness can often make it possible for the other to discern what that pain might be and asking him or her to learn from it. While suffering often can cause people to retreat or isolate themselves, or to despair, the soul friend is there to help them carry their burden for awhile, as Brigit recommended to her nuns. Everyone needs some relief at times from the pain of living—even Christ allowed Simon to take up his cross when it had become so unbearable. Being heard by a friend, as well as hearing oneself speak, often is enough to make it possible to return to our daily lives with renewed energy and hope, accepting that our life, our story, really is a gift—not just a burden or cross that we must bear. Sometimes the most helpful role of a soul friend is to recognize the invisible load that another person carries, and thus make it possible for him or her to carry it.

An important aspect of this carrying is related to the experience of *being heard* by a compassionate, nonjudgmental friend. Most people are not looking for a perfect soul friend who has his or her life "together." Rather, soul friendships often develop precisely because we perceive the other to be human like ourselves, struggling as we are to make sense out of life, and to find some degree of inner peace and harmony. No human soul friend is perfect, nor should we expect ourselves to be. Despite the portrayal in their hagiographies, not even the saints were without faults and human limitations. As we recall from the stories, St. Patrick was at times impatient and depressed, and lost his temper and cursed his enemies. Brigit, despite all the miracles Cogitosus describes, seems to have been a bit dense about practical matters, dropping bacon on the floor as she cooks and not finding it until a month later, as well as wrecking her chariot when she was so caught up in prayer. Columcille's own intense devotion to study, seated for long hours at his desk while others did the manual labor, probably caused difficulty for his community at times. What makes Patrick, Brigit, and Columcille so appealing is not so much their fantastic powers, but their struggle with their own very fallible humanity, as well as their love of others and their ultimate reliance upon God.

This perception that the soul friend is struggling too creates bonds of mutuality and reciprocity which invite greater disclosure on the other's part. Without mutuality, there will be no sense of connection between people, nor any substantive self-revelation. Even when one is acting professionally as a confessor, counselor, or spiritual director, in roles that require discernment about how open one should be about one's own life,[23] the other person must experience at least an *attitude* of mutuality in which he or she is fully accepted and respected as an equal. Sometimes even the smallest acknowledgement, such as "I understand," can give the other person reassurance that he or she is not alone. As Jung says about the dynamics of healing therapy that I would see as applying to soul friendship, one must never hide behind a "smoke-screen of fatherly and professional authority"; rather, the effective helper, he says, needs to at some point "emerge from his [or her] anonymity and give an account of himself [or herself]." Only when one is perceived as a "friend and fellow-sufferer" will the other person have the confidence to disclose what is really going on.[24]

Being perceived as a fellow-sufferer and friend, of course, is not foreign to Christianity and its founder. Aside from the ancient Celts and the desert Christians, the original source of soul friendship is Jesus himself whose words, recorded by his beloved Disciple John, "I call you friends" (John 15:15), encourage us to follow his example: "Love one another, as I have loved you" (John 15:12–17). In terms of our Christian identity, ultimately what the stories of the Celtic saints reveal is how they did precisely what Jesus did, and what he asks of each of us to do: to live graciously and gratefully; to live compassionately by loving one another; to center our lives daily in the Holy One. For Christians, stories and storytelling are not at all a new phenomenon, for our roots go back to the story of a Storyteller, a man who because of his healing power and the significance of his words became identified as "the Word," who is "life" (1 John 1:1). When we share our stories, as he did his, and reflect upon them, when we together seek to discern the traces of God's love, we begin to discover that our stories, like his, are full of laughter and tears, anguish and surrender, death and new life. We also begin to see that the new God of acceptance and forgiveness discovered in the stories we share is the same God of old, the God of our ancestors who "lives among" us and "will make his home" among us, whose name is God-with-us, who "will wipe away all tears" (Rev 21:1–4).

Notes

Introduction

1. Robin Flower, *The Irish Tradition* (Oxford University Press, 1947), p. 106.

2. For information on the Celtic soul friend tradition and its influence on the evolution of the sacrament of penance in the West, see O. D. Watkins, *A History of Penance,* Vols. I & II (London: Longmans, Green and Co., 1920), especially Vol. II on the "Keltic System," pp. 756 ff., and James Dallen, *The Reconciling Community: The Rite of Penance* (New York: Pueblo Publishing Co., 1986), pp. 103–118. An ironic part of that history is that the church in Rome, preferring the public forms of penitence and reconciliation that had developed in early Christian history, initially opposed this form of spiritual guidance; that is, until 1215 at the Fourth Lateran Council when participation *with a priest* in these encounters was made obligatory. Then, later, at the Council of Trent in the 1500s, these encounters were legally defined as one of the seven great sacraments of the Roman Catholic Church: the sacrament of reconciliation, popularly referred to as "confession" before Vatican II.

3. Whitley Stokes, ed., *The Martyrology of Oengus the Culdee* (London: Henry Bradshaw Society, 1905), p. 65.

4. See Kathleen Hughes, *The Early Celtic Idea of History and the Modern Historian* (Cambridge: Cambridge University Press, 1977), p. 3.

5. See Chapter 6, Clarissa Pinkola Estes, "Story as Medicine," pp. 77–92, in Charles and Ann Simpkinson, eds., *Sacred Stories: A Celebration of the Power of Story to Transform and Heal* (Harper-SanFrancisco, 1993).

6. See James Hillman, *The Soul's Code: In Search of Character and Calling* (New York: Random House, 1996), pp. 31–32.

7. See Marcus Borg, *Meeting Jesus Again for the First Time* (HarperSanFrancisco, 1995), especially Chapter 6, "Images of Jesus and Images of the Christian Life," pp. 119–137.

Chapter 1

1. See Robert O'Driscoll, ed., *The Celtic Consciousness* (New York: George Braziller, 1981), pp. xii, 11, 333 ff.

2. See Peter Berresford Ellis, *The Celtic Empire* (Durham, N.C.: Carolina Academic Press, 1990), pp. 9–22.

3. See Peter Cherici, *Celtic Sexuality: Power, Paradigms and Passion* (Hampton, Conn.: Tyrone Press, 1994), especially pp. 138–144.

4. See C. H. Oldfather, trans., *Diodorus Siculus: The Library of History*, Books IV.59–VIII, Vol. III (Cambridge, Mass.: Loeb Classical Library, Harvard University Press, 1939), pp. 179–181.

5. For a full description of Caesar's views of the Celts, including the druids, see S. A. Handford, trans., *Caesar: The Conquest of Gaul* (Baltimore, Md.: Penguin Classics, 1951), Chapter 1, "Customs and Institutions of the Gauls and Germans," pp. 29–35.

6. See John T. McNeill, *Celtic Penitentials and Their Influence on Continental Christianity* (Paris: Librairie Ancienne Honore Champion, 1923), pp. 90 ff. He shows that while the patristic writers, such as John Cassian, Pachomius, and Basil (with which all of whose works the Christian Irish were familiar), refer to the practice and value of confession which they learned from the desert monks, there is no specific reference in those writings to penances being assigned the penitent. That seems to be uniquely an Irish contribution, derived from the druids.

7. O'Donovan, O'Mahony, Hancock, trans., *Senchus Mor* (Dublin: The Commissioners for Publishing the Ancient Laws and Institutes of Ireland, 1865), p. 31.

Notes

8. See Felim O Briain, "Saga Themes in Irish Hagiography," in *Feilsgribhinn Torna,* Seamus Pender, ed. (Cork: 1947), p. 36.

9. See Proinsias MacCana, "Celtic Religion and Mythology," in Sabatino Moscati, et al., eds., *The Celts* (New York: Rizzoli, 1991), p. 597. One of the best compilations of early Welsh literature is found in Jeffrey Gantz, trans., *The Mabinogion* (New York: Penguin Press, 1976).

10. See Cecile O'Rahilly, ed., *Tain Bo Cualnge* (Dublin: Dublin Institute for Advanced Studies, 1984), p. 272, for an example of at least one monastic scribe's disapproval of the content of the text of this famous Irish epic.

11. See John McNeill, *Celtic Penitentials and Their Influence on Continental Christianity,* p. 100.

12. See Kathleen Hughes, "Introduction to a History of Medieval Ireland," pp. 1–33, and VIII, "The Church and the World in Early Christian Ireland," p.110, in David Dumville, ed., *Kathleen Hughes: Church and Society in Ireland,* A.D. *400–1200* (London: Variorum Reprints, 1987).

13. For an excellent interpretation of these early legends as well as compositions of beautiful art, see Jim Fitzpatrick, *The Book of Conquests* (Limpsfield, England: Dragon's World Ltd, 1978), and *The Silver Arm* (Limpsfield, England: Dragon's World Ltd., 1981). All the quotations from the Mythological Cycle are taken from Fitzpatrick's books, unless otherwise noted, although no page number is cited since Fitzpatrick's books do not have numbered pages. Amy Oakley, writing in *Enchanted Brittany* (New York: The Century Co., 1930), refers on pp. 87, 98, and 103 to the Breton soul and its being characterized by an appreciation of beauty, romance, death and, of course, the sea.

14. See Marie-Louise Sjoestedt, in *Gods and Heroes of the Celts* (Berkeley, Calif.: Turtle Island Foundation, 1982), p. 8, where she says, "It is chiefly in Ireland that Celtic paganism survived long enough to be committed to writing." Although medieval Welsh writers

made a significant contribution to Celtic mythology, the content of their stories, with their references to King Arthur, his knights and royal court, as well as to the presence of Norsemen in Ireland and Britain, is definitely a later development than the Irish stories. Concerning the development of Welsh sagas, see Miranda Green, *Celtic Myths: the Legendary Past* (British Museum Press, 1993), p. 11.

15. See Jeffrey Gantz, *The Mabinogion*, pp. 71, 79.

16. Elizabeth Gray, ed., *Cath Maige Tuired* (Naas, Ireland: Irish Texts Society, 1982), p. 59.

17. Ibid., p. 61.

18. See W. Y. Evans Wentz, *The Fairy-Faith in Celtic Countries* (Gerrards Cross, England: Colin Smythe Humanities Press, 1977), for a full account of fairy-folk and mystical awarenesses throughout Celtic lands.

19. See Cecile O'Rahilly, ed., *Tain Bo Cualnge,* p. ix, for the mid-seventh century dating. According to Miranda Green in *Celtic Myths: The Legendary Past,* pp. 10 and 21, the *Tain* was probably first composed in the eighth century C.E., but the earliest surviving manuscript of the *Tain* is found in the *Book of the Dun Cow*, compiled in the twelfth century at the monastery of Clonmacnoise.

20. Cecile O'Rahilly, ed., *Tain Bo Cualnge*, pp. 202, 152.

21. Ibid., p. 201.

22. See Whitley Stokes, "Life of Brigit," *Lives of Saints from the Book of Lismore* (Oxford: Oxford at the Clarendon Press, 1890), pp. 187–188.

23. Cecile O'Rahilly, ed., *Tain Bo Cualnge*, p.171.

24. Ibid., pp. 203–204.

25. See Carl Jung, *The Archetypes and the Collective Unconscious* (Princeton University Press, 1975), pp. 86–87. Jung associates this trait, among others, with a man who has a close relationship with his mother.

26. See Cecile O'Rahilly, ed., *Tain Bo Cualnge,* pp, 227, 220–223, 231–233 for above quotations.

27. Quoted in Christiane Eluere, *The Celts: Conquerors of Ancient Europe* (New York: Harry Abrams Inc., Publishers, n.d.), pp. 141–142.

28. Athenaeus is quoted in Simon James, *The World of the Celts* (London: Thames and Hudson, 1993), p. 53.

29. It may also reflect something of the conflict within oneself between good and evil. George Simms, in *Exploring the Book of Kells* (Dublin: O'Brien Press, 1989), p. 25, describes a similar scene in the Book of Kells as that found on the high cross. In the Book of Kells, two men, pulling each other's beards, form a capital N, and introduce the words, "No man can serve two masters. He will either hate the one and love the other or hold to the one and despise the other."

30. See A. W. Haddan and W. Stubbs, eds., *Councils and Ecclesiastical Documents Relating to Great Britain and Ireland* (Oxford: Clarendon Press, 1873), Vol. II, pt. 1, pp. 292–293.

31. See the fascinating stories about Brigit, Ita, and Samthann in Edward Sellner, *Wisdom of the Celtic Saints* (Notre Dame, Ind.: Ave Maria Press, 1993), pp. 70–75, 150–155, 194–199.

32. Unfortunately, only about a hundred Latin Lives and fifty written in Irish survive. For an excellent introduction to the subject and history of Celtic hagiographies, see Kathleen Hughes, *Early Christian Ireland* (Ithaca, N.Y.: Cornell University Press, 1972), pp. 219–247; Richard Sharpe, *Medieval Irish Saints' Lives* (Oxford: Clarendon Press, 1991); and John Carey, Maire Herbert, and Padraig O Riain, eds., *Saints and Scholars: Studies in Irish Hagiography* (Dublin: Four Courts Press, 2001). Besides my own collection, found in *Wisdom of the Celtic Saints,* which contains selections from primary sources and original translations of two female saints, Ita and Samthann, other collections of Celtic hagiographies can be found in such sources as Gilbert H. Doble, *The Saints of Cornwall* (Oxford: Holywell Press, 1970); Charles Plummer, ed., *Lives of the Irish Saints,* Vols. I and II (London: Oxford University Press, 1922); and Whitley

Stokes, trans., *Lives of Saints from the Book of Lismore,* (Oxford: Oxford at the Clarendon Press, 1890).

33. See Thomas Taylor, trans., *The Life of St. Samson of Dol* (London: SPCK, 1925).

34. See Dana Carleton Munro, ed., *Life of St. Columban by the Monk Jonas* (Felinfach, Ireland: Llanerch Publishers, 1993).

35. See Peter O'Dwyer, *Celi De: Spiritual Reform in Ireland, 750–900* (Dublin: Editions Tailliura, 1981), pp. 16 ff., and William Reeves, *The Culdees of the British Islands* (Dublin: M. H. Gill, 1864), pp. 4–5, 66.

36. See Lisa Bitel, "Women's monastic enclosures in early Ireland: a study of female spirituality and male monastic mentalities," *Journal of Medieval History,* 12 (1986), p. 25, where she says: "We do not know whether any of the hagiographers, poets, and scholars who recorded the corpus of Irish literature and learning were women, since no woman ever left her name on a document. But on the Continent many manuscripts attributed to men have been shown to be the products of women's hands; perhaps this will be the case in Ireland as well." For reference to Kildare's scriptorium, see Kathleen Hughes, *Early Christian Ireland*, p. 227.

37. See Charles Plummer, *Irish Litanies* (The Henry Bradshaw Society, 1925), p. 93.

38. William Reeves, "Adamnan's Life of Saint Columba," *Historians of Scotland* (Edmonston and Douglas, 1874), p. 34.

39. Robert Meyer, trans., *Bernard of Clairvaux's Life and Death of Saint Malachy the Irishman* (Kalamazoo, Mich.: Cistercian Publications, 1978), p. 11.

40. See, for example, Reeves, "Adamnan's Life of Saint Columba," p. 35.

41. See Alan Orr Anderson and Marjorie O. Anderson, eds., trans., *Adomnan's Life of Columba* (Oxford: Clarendon Press, 1991), p. lvii.

42. Quoted in Alison G. Elliott, *Roads to Paradise* (London: Brown University Press, 1987), p. 84.

Notes

43. Benedicta Ward, trans., *The Sayings of the Desert Fathers* (London: Mowbrays, 1975), p. 191.

44. A. Veilleux, *Pachomian Koinonia,* Vol. III (Kalamazoo, Mich.: Cistercian Publications, 1982), p. 107.

45. Colm Luibheid, trans., *John Cassian: Conferences* (New York/Mahwah, N.J.: Paulist Press, 1985), pp. 57–58.

46. Ibid., pp. 68–70.

47. See Edward Sellner, "What Alcoholics Anonymous Can Teach Us About Reconciliation," *Worship*, Vol. 64, no. 4, July, 1990, pp. 331–348, for a discussion of Alcoholics Anonymous's history and practice connected with Steps Four and Five.

48. See Nora Chadwick, *The Age of the Saints in the Early Celtic Church,* (London: Oxford University Press, 1961), pp. 103 ff. and 149.

49. See Cassian's Conference 16, Chapter III, in P. Schaff and H. Wace, eds., *A Select Library of Nicene and Post-Nicene Fathers of the Christian Church,* Vol. XI (Grand Rapids, Mich.: Wm. B. Eerdmans, n.d.), p. 451.

50. According to recent findings by archaeologists, there was an extensive trade between the East and the coasts of Ireland, Wales, Scotland, and England in those days, and mention is made in a litany from the *Book of Leinster* of seven monks from Egypt who died while visiting Ireland and were buried there. See C. A. R. Radford, "Imported Pottery at Tintagel, Cornwall," *Dark Age Britain* (London, 1956), pp. 59 ff., and C. Thomas, "Imported Pottery in Dark Age Western Britain," *Medieval Archaeology*, 1959, pp. 89 ff. Regarding the monks from Egypt, see Charles Plummer,"Seven Monks of Egypt in Disert Uilaig," *Irish Litanies*, pp. 65, 118.

51. See "Irish Pilgrims in Jerusalem and Rome," in Peter Harbison, *Pilgrimage in Ireland* (Syracuse, N.Y.: Sycracuse University Press, 1991), pp. 29–31. For an account of a seventh-century bishop's journey to the Holy Land, see the narrative by the Celtic monk on Iona, Adamnan, in *De Locis Sanctis,* edited by Denis Meehan (Dublin Institute for Advanced Studies, 1983).

52. In Ireland alone, this scene is commemorated in at least fifteen illustrations on the high crosses. See Eamonn O'Carragain, "The Meeting of Saint Paul and Saint Anthony: Visual and Literary Uses of a Eucharistic Motif," *Keimelia: Studies in Medieval Archaeology and History in Memory of Tom Delaney*, edited by Patrick Wallace and Gearoid Mac Nichaill (Galway: University Press, 1988), pp. 1–58.

53. In the Introduction of the *Life of Brendan* (found in C. Plummer's *Lives of the Irish Saints,* Vol, II, p. 44), for example, the Irish voyager is said to have been like "faithful Abraham, a pre-eminently prophetic psalmist like David…, a distinguished sage like Solomon…, a lawgiver to hundreds like Moses…."

54. See Felim O Briain, "Miracles in the lives of the Irish Saints," *Irish Ecclesiastical Record*, No. 66, 1945: 331–42, and "Saga Themes in Irish Hagiography," in *Feilsgribhinn Torna*, ed. Seamus Pender (Cork: 1947): 25–40.

Chapter 2

1. March 17 originally was associated in Rome with the pagan feast of Liber Pater, the Italian god of wine, fertility, and young men's sexuality. On this day, in a more formal family ritual, Roman boys who had reached puberty would put on the toga of manhood, while in the streets, following this domestic ceremony, a giant phallus was paraded through the fields and into towns and cities, accompanied by the singing of crude songs. See Augustine, *City of God*, Book 7: 21.

2. This, at least, is the approximate date of his birth and the "traditional" date of his death. For a succinct summation of scholarly views concerning when and where he was born and died, see John Walsh and Thomas Bradley, *A History of the Irish Church, 400–700* A.D. (Dublin: Columba Press, 1991), pp. 13–21.

3. See Noel Dermot O'Donoghue, *Patrick of Ireland: Aristocracy of Soul* (Wilmington, Del.: Michael Glazier, Inc., 1987).

4. Joseph Duffy, *Patrick in His Own Words* (Dublin: Veritas Publications, 1975), pp. 12, 17, 22.

Notes

5. See, for example, Maire de Paor, *Patrick: the Pilgrim Apostle of Ireland* (Dublin: Veritas, 1998), pp. 90–91.

6. From "Notes on Fiacc's Hymn," Whitley Stokes, ed., *The Tripartite Life of St. Patrick*, Vol. II (1887), p. 425.

7. See Mircea Eliade, *Shamanism: Archaic Techniques of Ecstasy* (Princeton: Princeton University Press, 1964), especially the first three chapters.

8. Quoted in Liam de Paor, *Ireland and Early Europe* (Dublin: Four Courts Press, 1997), p. 71.

9. According to Richard Sharpe—*Medieval Irish Saints' Lives* (Oxford: Clarendon Press, 1991), p. 13—there is now general agreement that another hagiographer, Tirechan, wrote before Muirchu, but Muirchu's is the first relatively "complete" hagiography as such.

10. All of the quotations from Muirchu's Life of St. Patrick that follow rely upon the text found in Ludwig Bieler, *The Patrician Texts in the Book of Armagh* (Dublin: Dublin Institute for Advanced Studies, 1979), pp. 62–123, and A. B. E. Hood, *St. Patrick: His Writings and Muirchu's Life* (London: Phillimore & Co., 1978), pp. 81–98.

11. See Joseph Campbell, *The Hero with a Thousand Faces* (Princeton, N.J.: Princeton University Press, 1973), for his description of these stages. I have summarized and interpreted them in terms of ministry and leadership. Although he devotes a brief section of his book to "The Hero as Saint" (pp. 354–356), Campbell does not explore the subject in depth.

12. Germanus is an historical figure whose feastday is celebrated July 31. There is some controversy whether Patrick ever visited Germanus, but Ludwig Bieler, in *St. Patrick and the Coming of Christianity* (Dublin: Gill and Son, 1967), p. 27, states that there is "a genuine link of St. Patrick with Auxerre and St. Germanus."

13. Considering both the account of another hagiographer, Tirechan, and Muirchu's own descriptions, there evidently was a strong folk tradition that Patrick had druid-mentors. See Bieler, *The Patrician Texts in the Book of Armagh*, pp. 125 and 63.

14. See, for example, the battle between the sun-god Lugh and one-eyed Balor, in Frank Delaney, *Legends of the Celts* (New York: Sterling Publishing, 1991), pp. 7 ff.

15. See Thomas Merton, *The Wisdom of the Desert* (New York: A New Directions Book, 1960), p. 50.

16. As Jesus is in the Gospels, Patrick is frequently compared to Moses. See Bieler, *The Patrician Texts in the Book of Armagh*, p. 165.

17. The Rule states that even a priest who has sinned "is entitled to nothing on the part of the church...unless he does penance at the will of an abbot or a pious soul friend." For the entire Rule, see J. G. O'Keefe, "The Rule of Patrick," in *Eriu*, Vol. 1, 1904: 216–224.

18. Quoted in Joan Halifax, *Shamanic Voices* (New York: E. P. Dutton, 1979), p. 6.

19. See Joseph Duffy, *Patrick in His Own Words*, p. 18.

20. Both his love of nature and the onslaught of dreams are evident in Patrick's *Confessio*. For twentieth-century manifestations of the same, see Bede Griffith, *The Golden String* (Springfield, Ill.: Templegate, 1954), and John Neihardt, *Black Elk Speaks* (Lincoln: University of Nebraska Press, 1979). Joan Halifax, in her *Shamanic Voices*, p. 9, relates how unexpected dreams, not initially understood by the shaman, frequently inaugurate his or her vocation.

21. Henri Nouwen, *The Wounded Healer* (Garden City, N.Y.: Doubleday, 1972), especially pp. 90–96.

22. For an excellent discussion on the roles and responsibilities of the Greek philosophers, see I. Hadot, "The Spiritual Guide," in A. H. Armstrong, ed., *Classical Mediterranean Spirituality* (New York: Crossroads, 1986), pp. 436–459.

23. Regarding Alcoholics Anonymous's Fourth and Fifth Steps, see Edward Sellner, *Step Five: Telling My Story* (Center City, Minn.: Hazelden Foundation, 1992).

24. Patrick's *Confessio*, chapter 3, in J. Duffy, *Patrick in His Own Words*, p. 25.

25. See Peter Brown, *The Making of Late Antiquity* (Cambridge, Mass.: Harvard University Press, 1978), p. 69, where he says that "the theme of the invisible companion is one of the most poignant and carefully elaborated strands in Late Antique religiosity."

26. See Mary Watkins, *Invisible Guests* (Hillsdale, N.J.: The Analytic Press, 1986).

27. See Carl Jung, *Memories, Dreams, Reflections* (New York: Vintage Books, 1961), pp. 181 ff.

28. John Henry Newman writes of a fever which almost killed him on his way back from a pilgrimage to Italy in the spring of 1833. He associated that experience of being saved with an emerging conviction that he had some special "work to do in England." See his *Apologia Pro Vita Sua* (New York: Image Books, 1989), pp. 150–152.

29. See, for example, May Sarton, *Plant Dreaming Deep* (New York: W. W. Norton & Co., 1968), p. 35, and *The House by the Sea* (New York: W. W. Norton & Co., 1981), p. 8.

30. See Noel Dermot O'Donoghue, *Patrick of Ireland,* pp. 22–23.

31. A good selection of these prayers before sleeping is found in Alexander Carmichael, *Carmina Gadelica: Hymns and Incantations Collected in the Highlands and Islands of Scotland in the Last Century* (Edinburgh: Floris Books, 1992), pp. 295–308.

32. See Paul Tournier, *A Listening Ear: Reflections on Christian Caring* (Minneapolis, Minn.: Augsburg, 1987).

33. See Carl Jung, "The Problem of the Attitude-Type," *Two Essays on Analytical Psychology, Collected Works,* Vol. 7, par. 78.

34. See Ludwig Bieler, "X: The Celtic Hagiographer," in Richard Sharpe, ed., *Ireland and the Culture of Early Medieval Europe* (London: Variorum Reprints, 1987), p. 250.

35. See Whitley Stokes, ed., *The Tripartite Life of Patrick* (London, 1887), p. 253.

36. Joseph Duffy, *Patrick in His Own Words,* p. 17.

Chapter 3

1. See Bertram Colgrave and R. A. B. Mynors, eds., *Bede's Ecclesiastical History of the English People* (Oxford: Oxford University Press, 1969), p. 411.

2. See "The Bohairic Life of Pachomius," in Armand Veilleux, trans., *Pachomian Koinonia*, Vol. I (Kalamazoo, Mich.: Cistercian Publications, 1980), p. 46.

3. See Mary Pollard, *In Search of St. Brigid, Foundress of Kildare* (Co. Kildare, 1988), p. 20.

4. See "Ultan's Hymn," quoted in Whitley Stokes, trans., "Life of Brigit," in *Lives of Saints from the Book of Lismore* (Oxford: Clarendon Press, 1890), p. 199.

5. Similarities between Brigit and Hildegard can be easily discerned in Hildegard's own hagiography which portrays her, like Brigit, as someone who cared for the marginalized, went on preaching tours, spoke of God in terms of the natural world, and was a healer. See Mary Palmquist, ed., *The Life of the Holy Hildegard* (Collegeville, Minn.: Liturgical Press, 1995).

6. See Gerald of Wales, *The History and Topography of Ireland* (New York: Penguin Books, 1982), pp. 81–82, and Dom Louis Gougaud, Gaelic Pioneers of Christianity (Dublin: M. H. Gill and Son, Ltd., 1923), p. 109. Besides Kildare, two other sites in Ireland, Cashel (associated with St. Patrick) and Durrow (associated with Columcille), were said to have kept a perpetual fire going.

7. See Rita Minehan, *Rekindling the Flame* (Newbridge, Ireland: Solas Bhride Community, 1999), p. 14. The entire book provides an excellent guide for pilgrims to Kildare.

8. See James Kenney, *The Sources for the Early History of Ireland: Ecclesiastical* (Dublin: Irish University Press, 1920), p. 358.

9. See Liam de Paor, *Ireland and Early Europe* (Dublin: Four Courts Press, 1997), p. 71, and Peter Berresford Ellis, *Celtic Women* (London: Constable, 1995), p. 146.

Notes

10. See Marie Louise Sjoestedt, *Gods and Heroes of the Celts* (Berkeley, Calif.: Turtle Island Foundation, 1982), p. 60.

11. Selections from Brigit's hagiography by Cogitosus, found in J. P. Migne, *Patrologia Latina*, LXXII, cols. 777–790, are from the English translation by George Rochefort and Edward Sellner.

12. See footnotes in Bertram Colgrave and R. A. B. Mynors, eds., *Bede's Ecclesiastical History of the English People*, pp. 237, 356, 420.

13. See Kim McCone, *Pagan Past and Christian Present in Early Irish Literature* (Naas, Ireland: An Sagart, 1991), p. 181.

14. See Daithi O hOgain, *The Hero in Irish Folk History* (New York: St. Martin's Press, 1985), p. 19.

15. Bernard Peebles, trans., "Life of Saint Martin, Bishop and Confessor," in *The Fathers of the Church*, Vol. 7 (Washington, D.C.: Catholic University of America Press, 1949), pp. 106–108.

16. See Daithi O hOgain, *Myth, Legend, and Romance* (New York: Prentice Hall Press, 1991), p. 26. The fox appears in many native stories, and in Japan is even considered a shape-shifting deity, Inari. See Karen Smyers, *The Fox and the Jewel* (Honolulu: University of Hawaii Press, 1999).

17. See Father Gregory Telepneff, *The Egyptian Desert in the Irish Bogs* (Etna, Calif.: Center for Traditionalist Orthodox Studies, 1998), p. 60.

18. See Sean Connolly, "Vita Prima Sanctae Brigitae: Background and Historical Value," *Journal of the Royal Society of Antiquaries of Ireland*, Vol. 119, 1989, especially pp. 14–16.

19. Ibid., #54, p. 28.

20. See Alcoholics Anonymous, *Alcoholics Anonymous* (New York: A. A. World Services, 1952) and Alcoholics Anonymous, *Twelve Steps and Twelve Traditions* (New York: A. A. World Services, 1952), especially chapters on Step Twelve. For information on sponsorship see Edward Sellner, *Guidance on Our Journey: Sponsorship and Ongoing Recovery* (Center City, Minn.: Hazelden, 1984).

21. Whitley Stokes, trans., "Life of Brigit," *Lives of Saints from the Book of Lismore* (Oxford: Oxford at the Clarendon Press, 1890), pp. 187–188.

22. See Charles Plummer, *Lives of the Irish Saints,* Vol. II, p. 100, for the story about one of the earliest and most generative of the Irish saints, Ciaran of Saighir, and how his monastery was built with the help of a wild boar, wolf, badger, and fox "as if they were monks themselves." Matthew Fox, in his book, *A Spirituality Named Compassion* (Minneapolis, Minn.: Winston Press, 1979), pp. 165–168, explores how animals can act as spiritual directors, as does Don Holt in *Praying With Katie: God, My Cat, and Me* (Kansas City, Mo.: Andrew McMeel, 2001).

23. See Edward Armstrong, *Saint Francis: Nature Mystic* (Berkeley, Calif.: University of California Press, 1973), for his thorough discussion of the derivation of the nature stories in the Franciscan Legend.

24. See Joseph Campbell, *Primitive Mythology* (New York: Penguin Books, 1987), pp. 34–49.

25. Ibid., *The Hero With a Thousand Faces* (Princeton, N.J.: Princeton University Press, 1973), p. 390.

26. See Mircea Eliade, *Shamanism* (Princeton, N.J.: Princeton University Press, 1974), pp. 88–99.

27. See Erich Neumann, *The Great Mother: An Analysis of the Archetype* (Princeton, N.J.: Princeton University Press, 1974), pp. 268–280.

28. See Miranda Green, *The Gods of the Celts* (Gloucester: Alan Sutton, 1986), pp. 179–181.

29. See Bruno Bettelheim, *The Uses of Enchantment* (New York: Alfred A. Knopf, 1976), pp. 75–76, 145, and 160–164.

30. See Carl Jung, "Dream Symbols of the Individuation Process," in Joseph Campbell, ed, *Spiritual Disciplines: Papers from the Eranos Yearbooks* (Princeton, N.J.: Princeton University Press, 1960), pp. 381–385.

31. Carl Jung, *Two Essays on Analytical Psychology* (Princeton, N.J.: Princeton University Press, 1972), p. 26–28. For a discussion of

the differences between Freud and Jung as they relate to Eros, see June Singer, *Boundaries of the Soul* (Garden City, N.Y.: Doubleday, 1972), pp. 180–181.

32. Carl Jung, ed., *Man and His Symbols* (Garden City, N.Y.: Doubleday and Co., 1964), p. 207.

33. Daniel Day Williams, in his *The Minister and the Care of Souls* (New York: Harper & Row, 1977), p. 43, defines pastoral care simply as "service to persons in the spirit of Christ."

34. J. E. Cirlot, *A Dictionary of Symbols* (New York: Philosophical Library, 1971), p. 84.

35. See Charles Jaeckle and William Clebsch, *Pastoral Care in Historical Perspective* (New York: Jason Aronson, 1975), p. 9, where they define a pastor as "a representative person who confesses Christian faith and brings Christian meanings to bear upon human problems." St. Brigit, along with the other Celtic saints, was certainly such a representative figure.

36. See in its entirety the classic by John T. McNeill, *A History of the Cure of Souls* (New York: Harper & Row, 1977).

37. For an excellent example of women writing about the sacredness of the body and how it can be "one's primary spiritual director," see Mary Ann Finch, "Befriending the Body," *The Way*, January 1989, Vol. 29, No. 1:60–67. Regarding men's writings, see Robert Bly, *Iron John: A Book About Men* (Reading, Mass.: Addison-Wesley Publishing Co., 1990), pp. 222 ff., in which he advocates that men "keep track of the wild animals inside us," along with "the healing energy stored in waterfalls, trees, clay, horses, dogs, porcupines, llamas, otters...."

38. See, for example, Carlos Castaneda, *Journey to Ixtlan* (New York: Simon and Schuster, 1972), and *Tales of Power* (New York: Simon and Schuster, 1974), especially pp. 88–97.

39. Dom Louis Gougaud entitles his entire book *Gaelic Pioneers of Christianity* (Dublin: M. H. Gill and Son, 1923); his reference to the saints as guides to souls is found on p. 148.

40. See Thomas Merton, *The Springs of Contemplation* (New York: Farrar, Straus, Giroux, 1992), p. 136.

Chapter 4

1. See J. M. Flood, *Ireland: Its Saints and Scholars* (Dublin: The Talbot Press, n.d.), pp. 85–87.

2. Two excellent sources on education in the Celtic Church are Fergal McGrath, *Education in Ancient and Medieval Ireland* (Blackrock, Ireland: Skellig Press Ltd., 1979), and John Healy, *Ireland's Ancient Schools and Scholars* (New York: Benziger Brothers, 1890).

3. Quoted in Peter O Dwyer, *Celi De: Spiritual Reform in Ireland 750–900* (Dublin: Editions Tailliura, 1981), p. 8.

4. See Bertram Colgrave and R. A. B. Mynors, eds., *Bede's Ecclesiastical History of the English People* (Oxford: Oxford at the Clarendon Press, 1969), p. 313.

5. Quoted by Ludwig Bieler, in Richard Sharpe, ed., *Ireland and the Culture of Early Medieval Europe* (London: Variorum Reprints, 1987), p. 217.

6. Gerald of Wales, *The History and Topography of Ireland* (New York: Penguin Books, 1985), p. 84.

7. Colgrave and Mynors, eds., Bede's *Ecclesiastical History of the English People,* p. 227.

8. See the "Irish Life of Colum Cille" in Maire Herbert, *Iona, Kells, and Derry* (Oxford: Clarendon Press, 1988), p. 259.

9. See "A Poem in Praise of Colum Cille" in Thomas Kinsella, ed., *The New Oxford Book of Irish Verse* (Oxford: Oxford University Press, 1986), pp. 3–9.

10. Reference to Christ as "my Druid" appears in a poem attributed to Columba, quoted in William Skene, *Celtic Scotland: A History of Ancient Alban,* Vol. II (Edinburgh: David Douglas, 1877), p. 114. See Shirley Toulson, *Celtic Journeys: Scotland and the North of England* (London: Hutchinson & Co., 1985), p. 63 ff., for a description of Iona.

Notes

11. John Walsh and Thomas Bradley, *A History of the Irish Church, 400–700 A.D.* (Blackrock, Ireland: Columba Press, 1991), p. 75.

12. "Life of Columcille" in Whitley Stokes, trans., *Lives of Saints from the Book of Lismore* (Oxford: Oxford at the Clarendon Press, 1890), p. 174.

13. Ibid., p. 175.

14. Selections which are quoted in this chapter are from *The Life of St. Columba, Founder of Hy; written by Adamnan,* ed. William Reeves (Dublin: the Irish Archaeological and Celtic Society; Edinburgh: the Bannatine Club, 1857).

15. See Colgrave and Mynors, *Bede's Ecclesiastical History of the English People,* Book III, Chapter 4, pp. 221–225.

16. See the Introduction in Richard Sharpe, trans., *Life of St. Columba* (New York: Penguin Books, 1995), pp. 1–99.

17. This third book seems to have been based entirely upon an earlier hagiography by Cummene, abbot of Iona from 657–669 C.E., whose work had been assisted by an uncle, Segene, another abbot who had compiled testimonies by Columba's contemporaries shortly after the saint's death. See Maire Herbert, *Iona, Kells, and Derry,* pp. 18–25, for a full discussion of this.

18. Ibid., p. 202.

19. See Columban biographer Ian Finlay, *Columba* (London: Victor Gollancz, Ltd., 1979), p. 89, where he develops a very plausible argument that the time preceding Columba's move to Iona was a "major crisis" in the saint's life.

20. Unfortunately, the demonic is frequently associated in Christian hagiographies with the color black, as is found in the *Life of Antony* by Athanasius. Even in the *Book of Kells*, a picture of the temptation of Christ depicts the tempter as a black man. Black men, however, were evidently not only recipients of prejudice from certain desert monks (see the story of Father Moses, a black Ethiopian monk at Scetis in Egypt, in Benedicta Ward, *The Sayings of the Desert Fathers* [London: Mowbrays, 1975], p. 117), but a source of great fascination

for many in late antiquity, considering the large number of wall deco-rations and other Hellenic forms of art which have survived, picturing black males as hypersexual, with huge penises and prominent erec-tions. See John Clarke, *Looking at Lovemaking: Constructions of Sexuality in Roman Art 100 B.C.–A.D. 250* (Berkeley, Calif.: University of California Press, 1998), pp. 119–142. What is clear is the inherent prejudice in early Christianity against blacks in general when the color white was equated with goodness, and black with evil. For an excellent article on the subject, see Peter Frost, "Attitudes toward Blacks in the Early Christian Era," *The Second Century,* 8, 1991: 1–11.

21. See Michael Richter, *Medieval Ireland* (New York: St. Martin's Press, 1988), pp. 55–56, where he states that the manuscripts Columcille wrote "were held in high esteem in Ireland" after the saint's death, and "not even the elements could affect them." The only docu-ment still preserved that may have been written by him is a psalter, called *Cathach* (Book of Battles), which is now in the Royal Irish Academy in Dublin.

22. William Skene, *Celtic Scotland*, Vol. II, pp. 121 ff.

23. John Neihardt, *Black Elk Speaks* (New York: Pocket Books, 1973), pp. 191 ff., where Black Elk describes how, while in Paris, he traveled in a vision across the ocean to his parents' village in the Black Hills of South Dakota.

24. See Colgrave and Mynors, *Bede's Ecclesiastical History of the English People,* p. 221–225.

25. Sean Connolly, "Vita Prima Sanctae Brigitae: Background and Historical Value," *Journal of the Royal Society of Antiquaries of Ireland,* Vol. 119, 1989: #16, p. 17. A similar statement can be found in the Life of St. Cronan when he tells a certain novice in his monastery, "In the guest is received Christ." See Diarmuid O Laoghaire, *Irish Spirituality* (Dublin: M. H. Gill & Son, Ltd., 1956), p. 16.

26. See D. H. Farmer, ed., "Life of Cuthbert," in *The Age of Bede* (New York: Penguin Books, 1983), pp. 65–68.

Notes

27. Henri Nouwen, *Reaching Out* (Garden City, N.Y.: Doubleday, 1975), pp. 54–60.

28. Parker Palmer, *To Know as We Are Known: A Spirituality of Education* (San Francisco: Harper & Row, 1983), p. 69, and *The Courage to Teach* (San Francisco: Jossey-Bass Publishers, 1998), p. 6.

29. Ibid., *Let Your Life Speak: Listening to the Voice of Vocation* (San Francisco: Jossey-Bass Publishers, 2000), pp. 68–69.

30. See Edward Sellner, *Wisdom of the Celtic Saints* (Notre Dame, Ind.: Ave Maria Press, 1993), pp. 84–85.

31. See Carl Jung, *The Archetypes and the Collective Unconscious* (Princeton, N.J.: Princeton University Press, 1975), pp. 282, 303; and *The Practice of Psychotherapy* (Princeton, N.J.: Princeton University Press, 1970), pp. 34, 281; and *The Structure and Dynamics of the Psyche* (Princeton, N.J.: Princeton University Press, 1969), pp. 141, 314–315.

32. Marie Von Franz, *Jung's Typology* (New York: Spring Publications, 1971), pp. 30 ff.

33. As in much of life, Vaughan also recommends that people always check out the accuracy of intuitive perceptions with the help of others, especially a spiritual guide, since such knowledge is particularly prone to wishful thinking, neurotic anxiety, or projection; that is, seeing connections where there are none because of our ego desires or, in some instances, our paranoia. See Frances Vaughan, *Awakening Intuition* (New York: Doubleday, 1979), in its entirety for a comprehensive and practical view of the topic.

34. See Erich Segal, *The Dialogues of Plato* (New York: Bantam Books, 1986), p. 17 for mention of this voice. Socrates is also frequently portrayed in meditation; see pp. 236 and 283.

35. Carl Jung, *Psychology and Religion: West and East* (Princeton, N.J.: Princeton University Press, 1973), pp. 38 ff., and 346.

36. See Robert Gregg, trans., *Athanasius: The Life of Antony and the Letter to Marcellinus* (New York/Ramsey, N.J.: Paulist Press, 1980), p. 39.

37. See Edmund Colledge and James Walsh, trans., *Julian of Norwich: Showings* (New York/Ramsey, N.J.: Paulist Press, 1978), pp. 130–131.

38. A neoplatonist philosopher and mystic, Plotinus indirectly influenced Christian thought, especially that of St. Augustine, Pseudo-Dionysius, and the theologians and mystics of the Middle Ages. See D. J. O'Meara, *Plotinus: An Introduction to the Enneads* (Oxford, 1993), and Margaret Miles, *Plotinus: on Body and Beauty* (Oxford: Blackwell Publishers, 1999).

39. See Carl Jung, *The Spirit in Man, Art, and Literature* (Princeton, N.J.: Princeton University Press, 1966), pp. 94 ff.

40. Ibid., pp. 95 ff.

41. Emma Jung, *Animus and Anima* (Dallas, Tex.: Spring Publications, 1985), pp. 53 ff.

42. See Miranda Green, *Symbol and Image in Celtic Religious Art* (London: Routledge,1989), pp. 142, 183. Ian Finlay, *Columba,* pp. 24 and 154, says that Columcille was called "the crane-cleric."

Chapter 5

1. Rev. P. Power, ed., *Life of St. Declan of Ardmore and Life of St. Mochuda of Lismore* (London: Irish Texts Society, 1914), p. 121.

2. Peg Coghlan, in *Irish Saints* (Cork, Ireland: Mercier Press, 1999), p. 5, says that "at least 350 Colmans" are listed in the martyrologies of Irish saints.

3. His death is recorded in the Annals of Tigernach, compiled at the monastery of Clonmacnoise. See Charles Plummer, *Vitae Sanctorum Hiberniae,* Vol. I (Oxford: Oxford at Clarendon Press, 1910), p. lvi.

4. See Rev. P. Power, ed., *Life of St. Declan of Ardmore and Life of St. Mochuda of Lismore*, p. 91.

5. See Richard Sharpe, trans., *Life of St. Columba* (London: Penguin Books, 1995), pp. 118, 165–166.

Notes

6. For more discussion on mentoring and its roles, see Edward Sellner, *Mentoring: the Ministry of Spiritual Kinship* (Cambridge, Mass.: Cowley, 2002).

7. See Jan Stein and Murray Stein, "Psychotherapy, Initiation and the Midlife Transition," p. 298, in Louise Carus Mahdi, Steven Foster, and Meredith Little, *Betwixt & Between: Patterns of Masculine and Feminine Initiation* (La Salle, Ill.: Open Court, 1987).

8. See Farah Shroff, ed., *The New Midwifery* (Toronto: Women's Press, 1997), for a brief history of midwifery.

9. As is clear from the title of Ina May Gashin's book, *Spiritual Midwifery* (Summertown, Tenn.: The Book Publishing Co., 1990), midwifery includes attentiveness to both the physical and spiritual aspects of birthing. She also speaks of the inclusion of males in the process of giving birth.

10. See Joseph Campbell, *The Hero with a Thousand Faces* (Princeton, N.J.: Princeton University Press, 1973), p. 9.

11. See Whitley Stokes, ed., *The Martyrology of Oengue the Culdee* (London, 1905), pp. 196, 213.

12. All of the following quotations are taken from Charles Plummer, trans., "Life of Colman Ela," in *Lives of the Irish Saints,* Vol. II (Oxford: Oxford at the Clarendon Press, 1922), pp. 162–176. I have modernized some of the words and phrases for greater understanding.

13. Rev. John Canon O'Hanlon, *Lives of the Irish Saints,* vol. IX (Dublin: James Duffy and Sons, n.d.), p. 606.

14. See Erik Erikson, *Identity: Youth and Crisis* (New York: W. W. Norton & Co., 1968), pp. 138–141.

15. See Evelyn and James Whitehead, *Seasons of Strength: New Visions of Adult Christian Maturity* (Garden City, N.Y.: Image Books, 1986), pp. 141–143.

16. Ibid. *Marrying Well* (Garden City, N.Y.: Doubleday, 1986), pp. 236–241.

17. See Edith Sullwold, "The Ritual-Maker Within at Adolescence," in Louise Mahdi, Steven Foster, and Meredith Little,

eds., *Betwixt & Between: Patterns of Masculine and Feminine Initiation*, pp. 11–131.

18. See Robert Bly, *Iron John: A Book About Men* (Reading, Mass.: Addison-Wesley, 1990), p. 97, and *The Sibling Society* (New York: Vintage Books, 1996), pp. 129–130, 181, 236; also, with Marion Woodman, *The Maiden King* (New York: Henry Holt and Co., 1998), pp. 22–23.

19. Rev. P. Power, ed., *Life of St. Declan of Ardmore and Life of St. Mochuda of Lismore*, p. xxxi.

20. Carl Jung, *Mysterium Conjunctionis* (Princeton University Press, 1989), p. 375.

21. See David Whyte, *The Heart Aroused* (New York: Doubleday, 1994), p. 64.

22. Quoted in Susan Shaughnessy, *Walking on Aligators* (HarperSanFrancisco, 1993), p. 201.

23. Quoted in William Shannon, *Silent Lamp: the Thomas Merton Story* (New York: Crossroad, 1992), p. 246.

24. See T. W. Rolleston, *The Illustrated Guide to Celtic Mythology* (London: Studio Editions, 1993), pp. 38–39.

25. See J. E. Cirlot, *A Dictionary of Symbols* (New York: Philosophical Library, 1983), p. 322; 145–147.

26. Alain Danielou, *The Phallus: Sacred Symbol of Male Creative Power* (Rochester, Vt.: Inner Traditions, 1995), p. 88.

27. See Simon Hornblower and Antony Spawforth, eds., *The Oxford Classical Dictionary* (Oxford University Press, 1998), pp. 689–690, 120.

28. Camille Paglia, *Sexual Personae* (New York: Vintage Books, 1990), p. 45.

29. See Andrew Harvey, *Hidden Journey*, p. 172.

30. Hemiunu, for example, who directed the building of the Great Pyramid, is portrayed as having large breasts, while the fourteenth-century B.C.E. pharaoh Akhenaten has a narrow waist and broad hips. See The Metropolitan Museum of Art, *Egyptian Art in the Age of*

the Pyramids (New York: Harry Abrams Inc., 1999), pp. 229–231, and Paul Johnson, *The Civilization of Ancient Egypt* (HarperCollins, 1999), p. 87.

31. See Evan Maurer and Niangi Batulukisi, *Spirits Embodied: Art of the Congo* (Minneapolis, Minn.: The Minneapolis Institute of Arts, 1999), pp. 63, 70, 73, 109, 113, for photographs and descriptions of these beautifully striking figures. Kongo peoples have much in common with the ancient Celts in their being matrilineal, animists, and worshippers of their ancestors.

32. Mircea Eliade, *Shamanism: Archaic Techniques of Ecstasy* (Princeton University Press, 1974), p. 352.

33. Carl Jung, *The Archetypes and the Collective Unconscious* (Princeton University Press, 1975), pp. 173–175.

34. Joseph Campbell, *The Masks of God: Primitive Mythology* (New York: Penguin Books, 1987), p. 67.

35. See James Kenney, *The Sources for the Early History of Ireland: Ecclesiastical* (Dublin: Irish University Press, 1929), pp. 399–400, where he says that the Irish text "may be a compilation, made in the later middle ages, of legends in prose and verse current among the Fir Cell...."

36. Robert Meyer, trans., *The Life and Death of Saint Malachy the Irishman* (Kalamazoo, Mich.: Cistercian Publications, 1978), pp. 24–25.

37. Ibid., *Lives of the Irish Saints,* Vol. II, p. 22.

38. See Joseph Duffy, *Patrick in His Own Words* (Dublin: Veritas, 1975), p. 19 and J. B. Bury, in *The Life of St. Patrick and His Place in History* (New York: Book of the Month Club, 1999), p. 293, says that this suckling that Patrick was asked to do was a symbolic act of adoption. I would disagree. Bury's interpretation which was first published in 1905 typifies the tendency among early twentieth-century scholars, such as Nora Chadwick, Ludwig Bieler, and Charles Plummer to avoid or deny the sexual implications of many of the passages found in the hagiographies and penitentials.

39. Quoted in Ingrid Peterson, *Clare of Assisi* (Quincy, Ill.: Franciscan Press, 1993), p. 186.

40. Edmund Colledge and James Walsh, trans., *Julian of Norwich: Showings* (New York: Paulist Press, 1978), p. 298.

41. Kieran Kavanaugh and Otilio Rodriguez, *Teresa of Avila: the Interior Castle* (New York: Paulist Press, 1979), pp. 179–180.

42. See Dom Hugh Farmer, ed., *The Monk of Farne* (London: Darton, Longman and Todd, 1961), pp. 64, 69, 149–150.

43. See J. E. Cirlot, *A Dictionary of Symbols*, pp. 23–24.

44. Whitley Stokes, trans., *Lives of the Saints from the Book of Lismore* (Oxford: Clarendon Press, 1890), pp. 267–268.

45. See Ellen Ross, *The Grief of God* (New York: Oxford University Press, 1997), pp. 11, 135.

46. Bernard so loved Malachy that when the Irish prelate died, Bernard buried him in his own habit and wore Malachy's for the rest of his life. Bernard also had himself buried next to Malachy before the high altar of Clairvaux. See Peg Coughlan, *Irish Saints*, p. 66, and John Watt, *The Church in Medieval Ireland* (Dublin: Gill and Macmillan, 1972), p. 23.

47. Quoted in Caroline Walker Bynum, *Jesus as Mother* (Berkeley, Calif.: University of California Press, 1984), pp. 115–118.

48. Robert Meyer, trans., *The Life and Death of Saint Malachy the Irishman*, p. 62.

49. Ibid., p. 109.

50. See Regis Armstrong, and Ignatius Brady, *Francis and Clare: the Complete Works* (New York: Paulist, 1982), p. 63.

51. Carl Jung, *Man and His Symbols* (Garden City, N.Y.: Doubleday & Co., 1964), p. 31.

52. See Robert Bly and Marion Woodman, *The Maiden King*, pp. 116–122.

53. See Bede Griffiths, *Marriage of East and West* (Springfield, Ill.: Templegate, 1982), p. 165.

54. See Erik Erikson, *Gandhi's Truth* (New York: W. W. Norton & Co., 1969), pp. 44, 157.

55. June Singer, *Androgyny: Toward a New Theory of Sexuality* (New York: Doubleday, 1976), p. 34.

56. See Martin Weinberg, Colin Williams, and Douglas Pryor, *Dual Attraction: Understanding Bisexuality* (New York: Oxford University Press, 1994), p. 8.

57. See June Singer, *Androgyny: Toward a New Theory of Sexuality*, pp. 35–36.

58. See Lionel Corbett, "Transformation of the Image of God Leading to Self-Initiation into Old Age," in Louise Carus Mahdi, Steven Foster, and Meredith Little, *Betwixt & Between: Patterns of Masculine and Feminine Initiation*, pp. 378–381.

59. Carl Jung, *Mysterium Conjunctionis,* p. 520.

60. Ibid., p. 497.

61. For an exploration of the shadow, see Connie Zweig and J. Abrams, eds. *Meeting the Shadow: the Hidden Power of the Dark Side of Human Nature* (New York: G. P. Putnam's Sons, 1991), and Robert Johnson, *Owning Your Own Shadow* (HarperSanFrancisco, 1993).

62. Michael Rodgers and Marcus Losack, *Glendalough: A Celtic Pilgrimage* (Dublin: Columba Press, 1996), p. 28.

63. Robert Johnson, *Ecstasy: Understanding the Psychology of Joy* (HarperSanFrancisco, 1987), p. 36.

64. Ibid., *Lying with the Heavenly Woman: Understanding and Integrating the Feminine Archetypes in Men's Lives* (HarperSan-Francisco, 1994), especially pp. 17–19.

65. See Marion Woodman, "From Concrete to Consciousness: the Emergence of the Feminine," in Louise Carus Mahdi, Steven Foster, and Meredith Little, *Betwixt & Between: Patterns of Masculine and Feminine Initiation*, pp. 202–222.

66. Will Roscoe, *Changing Ones: Third and Fourth Genders in Native North America* (London: Macmillan Press Ltd., 1998), p. 6.

67. See Walter Williams, *The Spirit and the Flesh: Sexual Diversity in American Indian Culture* (Boston: Beacon Press, 1986), p. 21.

68. Will Roscoe, *Changing Ones: Third and Fourth Genders in Native North America*, pp. 6–8.

69. For the story of Pelagia, the beautiful actress of Antioch, see "Pelagia: Beauty Riding By," in Benedicta Ward, *Harlots of the Desert* (London: Mowbrays, 1987), pp. 57–75. A major accusation against Joan of Arc at her trial was her cross-dressing; see William Trask, trans., *Joan of Arc in Her Own Words* (New York: Turtle Point Press, 1996).

70. See Walter Williams, *The Spirit and the Flesh: Sexual Diversity in American Indian Culture*, pp. 3, 57.

71. Ibid., pp. 36, 41–43.

72. See Kathyrn Welch, *The Romans* (New York: Rizzoli, 1997), pp. 34–35.

73. See Miranda Green, *Dictionary of Celtic Myth and Legend* (London: Thames and Hudson, 1992), p. 99.

Conclusion

1. Aelred of Rievaulx, *Spiritual Friendship* (Kalamazoo, Mich.: Cistercian Publications, 1977), p. 72.

2. Thomas Merton, *Contemplation in a World of Action* (New York: Image Books, 1973), p. 299.

3. James Hillman, *Thought of the Heart* (Dallas, Tex.: Spring, 1981), p. 2.

4. Ignatius of Loyola was one who highly valued the use of the imagination for prayer. See Louis Puhl, trans., *The Spiritual Exercises of St. Ignatius* (Chicago, Ill.: Loyola University Press, 1951).

5. Carl Jung, *The Spirit in Man, Art, and Literature* (Princeton University Press, 1966), pp. 29–30.

Notes

6. Peter O'Dwyer, *Celi De: Spiritual Reform in Ireland, 750–900* (Dublin: Editions Tailliura, 1981), p. 180.

7. John Bunyan, *Pilgrim's Progress* (Baltimore, Md.: Penguin, 1974), pp. 61, 119.

8. See Patrick Kavanagh, *Tarry Flynn* (Penguin Books, 1978), p. 178.

9. Quoted in Cheslyn Jones, et al., *The Study of Spirituality* (New York: Oxford University Press, 1986), p. 480.

10. James Hillman, *The Soul's Code: In Search of Character and Calling* (New York: Random House, 1996), pp. 120–121, 163 ff.

11. Anthony Meisel and M. L. del Mastro, trans., *The Rule of St. Benedict* (Garden City, N.Y.: Image Books, 1975), p. 43.

12. T. S. Eliot, *Four Quartets* (New York: Harcourt Brace Jovanovich, 1943), pp. 31, 51.

13. Kenneth Jackson, *Studies in Early Celtic Nature Poetry* (Cambridge: Cambridge University Press, 1935), p. 57.

14. Carl Jung, *Memories, Dreams, Reflections* (New York: Vintage Books, 1961), pp. 117, 124.

15. Quoted in Boethius's *Consolation of Philosophy*, Book I, found in H. F. Stewart, E. K. Rand, and S. J. Tester, trans., *Boethius: Tractates, De Consolatione Philosophiae* (Cambridge, Mass.: Harvard University Press, 1918), pp. 145, 147.

16. See Edgar Gibson, trans., "The Institutes of John Cassian," in P. Schaff and H. Wace, eds., *Nicene and Post-Nicene Fathers of the Christian Church*, Vol. XI (Grand Rapids, Mich.: Wm. B. Eerdmans, 1986), p. 234, and Colm Luibheid, trans., *John Cassian: Conferences* (New York: Paulist Press, 1985), pp. 57–58.

17. Benedicta Ward, trans., *The Sayings of the Desert Fathers* (London: Mowbrays, 1975), p. 95.

18. See Kent Nerburn, *The Wisdom of the Great Chiefs* (San Rafael, Calif.: New World Library, 1994), p. 19.

19. Quoted in Columba Stewart, "Radical honesty about the self: the practice of the desert fathers," *Sobornost*, 12, 1990, pp. 31–32.

20. Quoted in Garry Wills, *Saint Augustine* (New York: Penguin Putnam, Inc., 1999), p. xvi.

21. Thomas Merton, *Contemplation in a World of Action*, p. 299.

22. Paul Tillich, *The New Being* (New York: Charles Scribner's Sons, 1955), p. 13, and *The Courage to Be* (New York: Charles Scribner's Sons, 1952), p. 165.

23. See Gerald May, *Care of Mind, Care of Spirit* (New York: Harper & Row, 1982), pp. 8–9, for a discussion of the limits on mutual self-disclosure in professional relationships. Also see Spiritual Directors International, *Guidelines for Ethical Conduct* (San Francisco, Calif.: SDI, 2000), for expectations and responsibilities of spiritual directors. The ministry of spiritual direction as it is increasingly being practiced today attempts to balance the wisdom of the ancients with the "professionalism" of contemporary psychology. While there is some controversy over this, the importance of boundaries and confidentiality, as well as the need for regular supervision, usually in peer groups with colleagues, is increasingly seen as essential aspects of this vocation.

24. See Carl Jung, *The Practice of Psychotherapy* (Princeton, N.J.: Princeton University Press, 1966), pp. 8–9, and *Memories, Dreams, Reflections*, p. 133.